THE BERNESE ALPS

About the Author

Kev Reynolds is a freelance author, photojournalist and lecturer whose first title for Cicerone Press (*Walks & Climbs in the Pyrenees*) was published in 1978, and has been in print ever since. He has produced many books on the Alps, a series of trekkers' guides to Nepal and, nearer to home, several guides on walking in southern England. He also contributes regular features for the outdoor press, writes and illustrates brochures for tourist authorities, and occasionally leads walking or trekking holidays in various high mountain regions. The first honorary member of the British Association of European Mountain Leaders (BAEML), and a member of the Alpine Club, Austrian Alpine Club and Outdoor Writers' Guild, Kev's enthusiasm for the countryside in general, and mountains in particular, remains undiminished after a lifetime's activity. When not trekking or climbing in one of the world's great mountain ranges, Kev lives among what he calls 'the Kentish Alps', and during the winter months regularly travels throughout Britain to share that enthusiasm through his lectures. Check him out on **www.kevreynolds.co.uk**.

Cicerone titles by the same author:

100 Hut Walks in the Alps
Alpine Points of View
Walking in the Alps
Walks in the Engadine –
Switzerland
Walking in the Valais
The Jura (with R Brian Evans)
Ticino – Switzerland
Central Switzerland
Alpine Pass Route
Chamonix to Zermatt – the Walker's
Haute Route
Tour of Mont Blanc
Tour of the Vanoise
Écrins National Park

Walks & Climbs in the Pyrenees
The Pyrenees
The Wealdway & The Vanguard
Way
Walking in Kent Vols I & II
Walking in Sussex
The South Downs Way
The North Downs Way
The Cotswold Way
Annapurna – a Trekker's Guide
Everest – a Trekker's Guide
Langtang, with Gosainkund &
Helambu – a Trekker's Guide
Kangchenjunga – a Trekker's Guide
Manaslu – a Trekker's guide

THE BERNESE ALPS

by
Kev Reynolds

2 POLICE SQUARE, MILNTHORPE, CUMBRIA LA7 7PY
www.cicerone.co.uk

© Kev Reynolds 1992, 1997, 2005
ISBN 1 85284 451 5
First published 1992
2nd Edition (revised) 1997
3rd Edition 2005
A catalogue record for this book is available from the British Library.

Advice to Readers

Readers are advised that while every effort is taken by the author to ensure the accuracy of this guidebook, changes can occur which may affect the contents. It is advisable to check locally on transport, accommodation, shops, and so on, but even rights of way can be altered. The publisher would welcome notes of any such changes.

Mountain walking can be a dangerous activity, carrying a risk of personal injury or death. It should be undertaken only by those with a full understanding of the risks and with the training and/or experience to evaluate them. Whilst every care and effort has been taken in the preparation of this book, the user should be aware that conditions can be highly variable and can change quickly, thus materially affecting the seriousness of a mountain walk.

Therefore, except for any liability which cannot be excluded by law, neither Cicerone nor the author accept liability for damage of any nature (including damage to property, personal injury or death) arising directly or indirectly from the information in this book.

Front cover: The Gasterntal above Kandersteg in the Kandertal region of the Bernese Alps

CONTENTS

Map Key

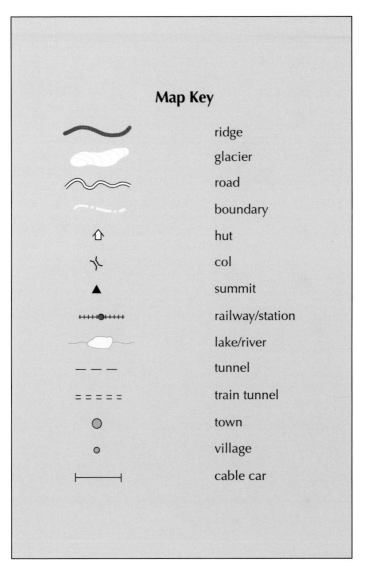

	ridge
	glacier
	road
	boundary
	hut
	col
	summit
	railway/station
	lake/river
	tunnel
	train tunnel
	town
	village
	cable car

THE BERNESE ALPS

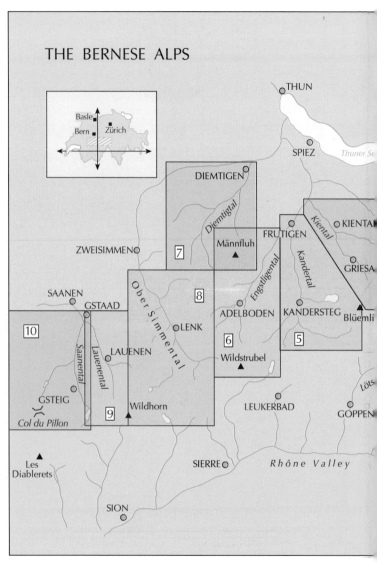

Basle
Bern Zürich

THUN

SPIEZ

Thuner Se

DIEMTIGEN

Diemtigtal

FRUTIGEN

Kiental

KIENTA

ZWEISIMMEN

Männfluh

7

ADELBODEN

Engstligental

Kandertal

GRIESA

8

SAANEN

GSTAAD

Ober Simmental

LENK

6

KANDERSTEG

Blüemli

5

10

Saanental

Lauenental

LAUENEN

Wildstrubel

GSTEIG

9

Wildhorn

LEUKERBAD

Löts

GOPPEN

Col du Pillon

Les
Diablerets

SIERRE

Rhône Valley

SION

8

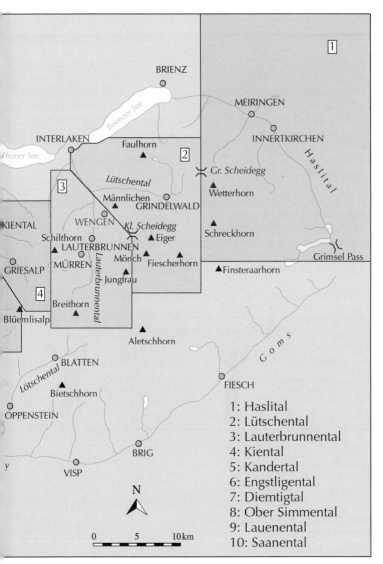

BRIENZ

MEIRINGEN

INNERTKIRCHEN

Brienzer See

INTERLAKEN

Faulhorn ▲

Thuner See

Haslital

2

Gr. Scheidegg ✕

Lütschental

Wetterhorn ▲

3

Männlichen ○

GRINDELWALD

KIENTAL

WENGEN ○

Kl. Scheidegg ✕

Schilthorn ○

Eiger ▲

Schreckhorn ▲

LAUTERBRUNNEN ▲

Lauterbrunnental

Mönch ▲

Fiescherhorn ▲

MÜRREN ▲

GRIESALP ○

Jungfrau ▲

▲Finsteraarhorn

Grimsel Pass

4

Breithorn ▲

Blüemlisalp ▲

Aletschhorn ▲

G o m s

BLATTEN ○

Lötschental

Bietschhorn ▲

FIESCH ○

OPPENSTEIN ○

y

BRIG ○

VISP ○

N

0   5   10km

1: Haslital
2: Lütschental
3: Lauterbrunnental
4: Kiental
5: Kandertal
6: Engstligental
7: Diemtigtal
8: Ober Simmental
9: Lauenental
10: Saanental

9

MOUNTAIN SAFETY

Every mountain walk contains an element of danger, and those described in this guidebook are no exception. All who walk or climb in the mountains should recognise this and take responsibility for themselves and their companions along the way. The author and publisher have tried to make the information contained herein as accurate as possible before the guide went to press, but they cannot accept responsibility for any loss, injury or inconvenience sustained by persons using this book.

International Distress Signal
(*To be used in emergency only*)
Six blasts on a whistle (or flashes with a torch after dark) spaced evenly for one minute, followed by a minute's pause. Repeat until located by a rescuer. The response is three signals per minute followed by a minute's pause.

The following signals are used to communicate with a rescue helicopter.

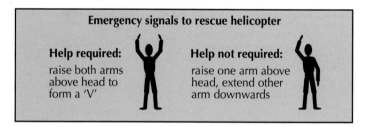

Emergency signals to rescue helicopter

Help required:
raise both arms above head to form a 'V'

Help not required:
raise one arm above head, extend other arm downwards

Note: Mountain rescue can be very expensive – be adequately insured (see Appendix A).

Emergency telephone number: ☎ 117 (police)

Swiss Air Search & Rescue (REGA): ☎ 1414
Weather report: ☎ 162 (German)

PREFACE TO THE THIRD EDITION

Since the second edition of this guide-book was published, I've spent many more weeks in the Bernese Alps on research for various writing projects, leading walking groups, researching new routes and devising multi-day treks that celebrate the scenic delights of the region. It's been a joy to relive a number of those new walks in these pages, as well as revisit most of those described in earlier editions, for every day among the mountains was uplifting, and left me eager to share some of the magic through this updated guide. Much of the original text has been rewritten, many more illustrations have been included, fresh maps drawn, and the layout redesigned for this edition by the Cicerone team, with whom it is always a pleasure to work.

This book benefits from the correspondence of other walkers who suggested the inclusion of routes they discovered for themselves, drew my attention to changes to some of the routes included in previous editions, or made recommendations in respect of accommodation, transport, maps and other information. Their input is much appreciated, and I am especially grateful to Nicolas Chagnon, David Hasell, Kenneth Penny and David Slater for taking the trouble to write. My thanks also to Russell Palmer, Roland Minder and Nick Robb at the Switzerland Travel Centre in London; to the staff of tourist offices throughout the district; and to Troy Haines of Alpinehikers, and Marc Jones and Diane Sifis whose enthusiasm for the Lauterbrunnen/Mürren region was both infectious and informative. Kofi Brunnen at Pension Suppenalp in the Blumental above Mürren, and Herr and Frau König at Hotel-Garni Alpina in Lenk were wonderfully generous with their hospitality, while those with whom I've shared a number of walks included in this guide added much by their company; in particular Roland Hiss, David and Jenny Ingram, David Stafford, Alan and Morna Whitlock, my daughters Claudia and Ilsa, and my wife, without whose love, support and encouragement this book would not have been written.

Finally, all the information contained in this guide is given in good faith and routes described offered in the hope that readers will gain as much enjoyment from walking in the Bernese Alps as I have during the long weeks of research. However, one should be aware that changes do occur from time to time, not only to resort facilities, accommodation, roads, and public transport, but to the landscape too; sometimes through natural causes

– rockfall, avalanche, landslip or flooding – but also by the hand of man. It may be that you will discover paths that have been rerouted, or mountain features altered to such an extent that some of the descriptions are no longer valid. Should this be the case, I first of all sincerely hope that such changes do nothing to spoil your holiday, and secondly, would appreciate a note giving details in order that I can check them out for future editions of this guide. A postcard sent to me c/o Cicerone Press Ltd, 2 Police Square, Milnthorpe, Cumbria LA7 7PY would be greatly received.

Kev Reynolds

INTRODUCTION

With the classic trio of Eiger, Mönch and Jungfrau as their most potent symbol, the Bernese Alps are among the best-known mountains in all of Europe. Rising out of lush green meadows they tower above chalets bright with geraniums and petunias; a stark contrast of snow, ice and rock against a kaleidoscope of flower, shrub and pasture; an awesome backdrop to an Alpine wonderland.

Flanking the north slope of the Rhône Valley the chain of the Bernese Alps is aligned roughly east to west, stretching from the Grimsel Pass above the Haslital in the east, to the Col du Pillon below Les Diablerets in the west, thus forming the longest continuous range of mountains in the Alps that does not comprise part of the continental divide. Their more familiar title, the Bernese Oberland, refers to the northern side of the range only; the highlands of canton Bern, but of the Bernese Alps proper, among their numerous summits almost 40 reach above 3600m, while the huge glacial basin on the south side of the Jungfrau gives birth to the Grosser Aletschgletscher, the largest icefield not only in Switzerland, but of all the Alpine regions. Elsewhere lofty

Neatly shaved meadows at Mürren in the Lauterbrunnental

waterfalls cascade into gorge-like valleys carved from the mountains by glaciers long since departed, and lakes fill the lower valleys like small inland seas, while more modest tarns lie trapped here and there in hillside scoops to throw the mountains on their heads as a mirror-like bonus to those who wander their trails.

Perhaps it is no surprise that the most visually diverse and dramatic part of the range has been declared a UNESCO World Natural Heritage site – the first in the Alps. The Jungfrau-Aletsch-Bietschhorn site covers an area of 540sq km (208 sq miles), and a number of its footpaths are included in this guide.

But the whole of the Bernese Alps region is a paradise for walkers. Footpaths – thousands of kilometres of them – lead enticingly through the valleys, over hillsides and across high passes. Waymarked with the thoroughness and efficiency for which Switzerland is noted they offer sufficient scope and variety to satisfy the dreams of most mountain walkers for a decade or more of holidays, while the resorts of Grindelwald, Wengen, Lauterbrunnen, Mürren, Kandersteg and Adelboden – to name but a few – have their own unique atmosphere and appeal. They are, of course, among the most popular in all Switzerland.

The heart of the Bernese Alps is an arctic wasteland. In a huge basin behind the walls of rock that glower over Grindelwald's pastures there lies a vast tract of snowfield and glacier jelled into a mass of permanent winter, like some displaced polar ice-cap. It's a monochrome landscape of stark, yet resounding beauty; a wonderland of white from which stiletto peaks and abrupt massifs emerge as islands of stone in a great ice sea.

Glaciers hang suspended on north-facing slopes too, but by comparison these are just modest streams, the last remaining vestige of those tremendous icefields that once carved and fretted some of the loveliest valleys in all of Europe.

But by far the greater part of the Bernese Alps is covered with flower-rich grasslands; meadows and pastures steeply tilted below broad crests from which you gaze with a sense of wonder at a backdrop of towering mountains, at their snowy crowns with blue-tinged glaciers snaking between them. This visual contrast is one of its major attractions, and the reward for those who take to the footpaths; the winding highways that explore an alpine wonderland.

THE BERNESE ALPS

Every corner of the range has its own touch of magic. There are the rock climbers' slabs of the Engelhörner above Rosenlaui, and the multi-summited Wetterhorn which peers down on Grindelwald and stands as a cornerstone, not only of the Bernese Alps, but of mountaineering history. Grindelwald boasts so much of appeal; its glaciers, its tremendous scope for

A short walk from Schynige Platte reveals an ever-changing panorama. The Jungfrau invariably dominates (Route 9)

walkers, climbers and skiers, its magnetic views and, of course, the Eiger. But in truth the Eiger is only one of many great peaks here. More attractive still are the Schreckhorn, Finsteraarhorn and the Fiescherhorn, seen to great effect from some of the walks outlined within these pages.

The Jungfraujoch railway is one of the engineering marvels of Switzerland and is accessible from either Grindelwald, Wengen or Lauterbrunnen. But since this volume is primarily intended for walkers, the railway lies outside the scope of this book. Wengen, of course, is not. Set on a natural shelf high above the Lauterbrunnen Valley, it has an exquisite outlook – especially to the Jungfrau, one of the loveliest mountains to be seen anywhere. Among the more

popular outings from this resort is the walk to the Wengernalp, from whose safe and gentle pastures one may gaze on avalanches that pour from the Jungfrau almost every day in summer.

Lauterbrunnen lies in its own deeply-cut trench, an amazing place of huge walls and feathery cascades. At the head of its valley, in a more open level of grassland, is the little hamlet of Stechelberg which makes a superb base for a walking holiday, for it has numerous possibilities for exploratory outings to mountain huts, to 'lost' tarns, seemingly barren screes and hidden hillside terraces.

On its own hillside terrace on the west side of the Lauterbrunnen Valley, Mürren has a deserved reputation for its stunning mountain vista. Perhaps better-known these days as a skiing centre, it is no less lovely in summer when a splay of footpaths lead to scenes of enchantment. A little lower than Mürren, but a near-neighbour, Gimmelwald shares those scenes, and shares too a cableway to the Schilthorn, whose summit restaurant is known as Piz Gloria since a James Bond movie was shot there.

To the west of Gimmelwald the high pass of the Sefinenfurke, approached in the shadow of the Gspaltenhorn, will take adventurous walkers over the mountains to the charming little hamlet of Griesalp at the head of the Kiental. This is a gentle pastoral valley whose unfussed charm contrasts the blockbuster tourism of Grindelwald or Lauterbrunnen. With the sub-valley of Spiggengrund nearby it gives plenty of scope for walkers who prefer to wander in solitude.

From the Kiental one peers up at the big snowy mass of the Blüemlisalp whose several 3500m summits overlook the ice-cap of the Petersgrat to the south, and the deep fjord-like bowl that contains the Öeschinensee to the northwest. This lake is pictured on so many calendars, chocolate boxes and jigsaw puzzles that it's a familiar sight to many long before they actually see it for themselves, and is probably the most visited mountain feature around Kandersteg. Kandersteg draws walkers and climbers alike with its wide choice of outings. There's so much to explore nearby, including the superb Gasterntal, a peaceful valley whose walls are streaked with

waterfalls, and whose meadows are so rich in flowers that it's sometimes difficult to find the grass.

Running parallel to the Kandertal (the valley of Kandersteg) is the Engstligental, with Adelboden in its upper reaches. The village is set on the hillside, not in the valley bed, looking south to the Wildstrubel, a mountain that Adelboden shares with its neighbour to the west, Lenk.

Lenk's valley is the Simmental, one of the most important in the Bernese Alps by virtue of its ease of communications with country to the west over a brace of passes. But Lenk lies near its head in a tranquil landscape, untroubled by through-traffic, unbothered by big mountains. It's a neat village set in a shallow plain, with a fine western wall of pastureland pitted with limestone hollows, and with easy walkers' passes that lead across the hills to the Lauenental, which has the Wildhorn at its head.

By comparison with Lauenen, Lenk is a bustling metropolis. For Lauenen is a secretive place that nevertheless deserves to be on the list of all who delight in mountain walking. It has much to commend it; not least a day's circuit that takes you to a green tarn, a nature reserve, a superb waterfall and a mountain hut in an idyllic setting. There are other outings of value, too, of course, one of which takes you over another gentle pass among woods and meadows, and down to Gsteig, last of the villages tucked under the mountains on the northern side of the chain. Above Gsteig rises the big massif of Les Diablerets which marks the last of canton Bern and the first of canton Vaud. All to the west is French-speaking territory; some fine mountains and charming valleys which long-distance walkers tackling the Alpine Pass Route explore on their way to Montreux. But for the purposes of this guidebook, Col du Pillon which marks the canton border, is the limit of the region under review.

On the south side of the chain, the Bernese Alps slope down to the Rhône Valley. Yet the border of canton Bern follows the crest of the main ridge. All to the south falls into canton Valais (Wallis to German-speaking Swiss), the region that is treated to its own guidebook in the same series: *Walking in the Valais*.

THE MOUNTAINS

In the public eye mountaineering in the Bernese Alps has been focussed on the Eiger through an avalanche of publicity matched only, perhaps, by that afforded the Matterhorn. The Eiger's north wall has been the scene of many epic dramas played out in full view of the telescopes of Kleine Scheidegg, but elsewhere along the chain there are other peaks, other faces, other ridges that offer sport of considerable charm yet without notoriety, and whose features make a colourful background for walkers wandering the magnificent network of footpaths nearby.

Meiringen is not a mountaineering centre as such, but it has some fine mountains almost on its doorstep – most of which are known only to climbers. On the approach to the Grosse Scheidegg, by which

The easy path linking Kleine Scheidegg and Männlichen is one of the busiest in the Bernese Alps. The Wetterhorn is clearly seen across Grindelwald's basin.

From the Schedelsgrättli, a fine view east shows big Oberland peaks beyond the Üschenental (Route 82)

Grindelwald may be reached, the slabs of the Engelhörner group are laced with routes, while to the south of these shrinking glaciers hang from such peaks as the Wellhorn, Wetterhorn and the Hangendgletscherhorn; the last mentioned also looms over the little-known Urbachtal that flows out to Innertkirchen.

Grindelwald, with Alpiglen and Kleine Scheidegg on its western slope, has long been the historical base for major climbs on the Eiger. But also accessible from Grindelwald are several mountain huts that lie on the approach to big mountains too far from any village base; huts that make ideal destinations for walkers, lying as they do amid wildly romantic surroundings. The Schreckhorn Hut springs instantly to mind. The walk to it leads alongside glaciers, scrambles up rocks that wall an icefall, and gives the most

incredible views of the Fiescherhörner, Agassizhorn and Finsteraarhorn (highest summit in the Bernese Alps at 4274m), not to mention a curious peep at the 'back' of the Eiger.

Another hut approach that reveals the inner sanctum of the mountain world, is that which goes from Stechelberg to the Rottal Hut on the southwest flanks of the Jungfrau. Here you virtually rub noses with the Gletscherhorn and Ebnefluh, and have a privileged view of the Breithorn seen in profile. All around mountains rise in an upthrust of rock and ice – the fabled Lauterbrunnen Wall so assiduously explored in the 1930s by the great Münich-based climber, Willo Welzenbach.

Next to the Breithorn stands the Tschingelhorn, with the saddle of Wetterlücke between them. On the far side of the Tschingelhorn nestles the

Mutthorn Hut, almost entirely sur-rounded by ice. With several fine peaks made accessible from it, this hut proves popular with mountaineers in summer and is also visited on one of the walks described here, prior to a crossing of the Petersgrat with descent into the Lötschental in full view of the Gletscherstafel Wall, and the Bietschorn, one of the most difficult mountains hereabouts.

After Grindelwald, Kandersteg is the most important mountaineering centre of the chain. Again, several huts are accessible from the village, and climbs may be had on the various Blüemlisalp peaks as well as on the Balmhorn and Altels which rise to the south at the entrance to the Gasterntal.

Of the easier high summits of the Bernese Alps, both Wildstrubel and Wildhorn should be mentioned. The Wildstrubel has as one of its major fea-tures the large snow-filled basin of the Plaine Morte, from which several tops rise. Climbed from either Kandersteg, Adelboden or Lenk, the Wildstrubel itself consists of a number of summits which barely rise above its south-eastern glacier.

West of the Wildhorn massif comes Les Diablerets, a great lump of mountain at 3210m, with summer ski-ing on its glaciers and across whose main summit runs the invisible bound-ary separating canton Bern from canton Vaud. Les Diablerets dominates a large area and is seen to great effect from the softer, more luxurious hill-sides to the north, where tarns gleam in the sunshine, insects seethe among flower-strewn meadows and birds warble in the forests. Walkers' country, this is, with views of lofty mountain peaks. Far away in the west a glimpse is to be had of the Dents du Midi and the distant snows of Mont Blanc. Big mountains all.

These are indeed big mountains with snow and ice-caked summits, but this book is concerned not with climb-ing mountains, not with reaching summits, but with wandering in their shadow; spending days of delight exploring valleys, ambling over hill-sides clattering with cowbells and crossing remote passes in order to gain fresh valley systems. The Bernese Alps are not short of prospects.

GETTING THERE

By Air

While details in this section were correct at the time of writing, readers should be aware that information in regard to air travel is particularly vulnerable to change. Apart from complex fare structures, schedules are often rearranged at short notice, new routes introduced and abandoned, while the growth of cut-price, no-frills carriers often results in fledgling air-lines being formed, merged, taken over or collapsing with alarming frequency. The best advice, therefore, is to check the current situation with either your local travel agent, the Switzerland Travel Centre (address in Appendix A), or by browsing the Internet.

Gentle countryside above Adelboden, on the way to the Hahnenmoos Pass on Route 87

British Airways: www.britishairways.com currently operates out of London Heathrow, Gatwick, and Manchester.
EasyJet: www.easyjet.com flights from London Gatwick, Stansted, Luton and Liverpool.
SWISS International Airlines: www.swiss.com has 42 daily scheduled departures from London Heathrow and City, Birmingham, and Manchester.
Aer Lingus: www.aerlingus.com flies a regular service between Dublin and Zürich.

Online booking agents

www.cheapflights.com – simply feed your requirements into the search engine and await the response.
www.skyscanners.net – an easy-to-use interface.
www.ebookers.com – accommodation and transport to numerous destinations.

Note: Flight tickets can also be arranged through the Switzerland Travel Centre in London (☎ freephone 00800 100 200 30, stc@stlondon.com)

Swiss airports to consider are either Basle, Geneva or Zürich, with regular scheduled flights from the UK being operated by major carriers throughout the year. British Airways, EasyJet and SWISS currently dominate the market from a choice of airports; Aer Lingus also flies a regular service from Dublin.

Both Geneva and Zürich airports are fully integrated into the Swiss rail network, being just an escalator ride from a mainline station, while a bus service links Basle airport with the town's main railway station.

Fly-Rail baggage transfers: Passengers with pre-booked accommodation can take advantage of a unique 'fly rail baggage' scheme which enables 'nothing to declare' baggage checked-in at the departure airport to be transported directly to the railway station of the chosen resort. There's no waiting at the arrival airport's carousel, or hustling your baggage from plane to train. The system is straightforward and convenient, and also works on the homeward journey. However, the scheme is not applicable for EasyJet flights, or for British Airways passengers with 'E' tickets.

Travel by Train

With a combination of Eurostar from London's Waterloo station to Paris via the Channel Tunnel, and TGV to Lausanne, high-speed rail travel provides a viable (but possibly more expensive) alternative for those who prefer not to fly. Currently Eurostar operates at least 14 trains per day for the 3-hours-plus journey between Waterloo and the Gare du Nord in Paris. There you transfer to the Gare de Lyon for TGV departure to Lausanne; a journey of around 4½hrs. Change at Lausanne for Bern for onward trains to your choice of final destination.

For up-to-date rail information, contact Rail Europe (☎ 08705 848 848 www.raileurope.com). Note that the Switzerland Travel Centre can take reservations for Eurostar, TGV, and Swiss rail travel (☎ freephone 00800 100 200 30).

Under 26? Consider purchasing a *Billet International de Jeunesse* (BIJ), which enables discounts of up to 50% to be made on international rail journeys. Contact Rail Europe, 179 Piccadilly, London W1 (for telephone and email details see above).

Internet train times: To work out your rail journey through Switzerland in advance, log on to www.rail.ch, feed in details of the journey's start, destination and date of travel, and you will receive all the information you require, including platform numbers where a change of train is needed, plus connecting bus services where appropriate.

Travel by Road

Should you prefer to drive to Switzerland, note that a *vignette* (sticker) must be purchased and displayed on your vehicle when travelling within the country. This is, in effect, a motorway tax, the current cost of which is CHF40. Valid for multiple entries during the licensed period shown on the sticker, the vignette can be bought at the Swiss border of entry, or in advance from the Switzerland Travel Centre (see Appendix A).

The minimum age for driving in Switzerland is 18, and motorists are advised to obtain a Green Card from their insurers to receive the same insurance protection as in the UK.

Major road passes into the Bernese Alps region are the Susten (open June–November), Grimsel (open June–October), Col du Pillon and the Jaun Pass both of which are open throughout the year. Roads are well-maintained, and an increasing number of tunnels are being created to avoid some of the higher passes. The interlinking motorway system is good, and journey times can be surprisingly low considering the complex topography; but expect delays at peak times. The motorway speed limit is 120kph (75mph); in built-up areas it's 50kph (31mph), and 80kph (50mph) on other roads unless signed to the contrary.

PUBLIC TRANSPORT IN THE BERNESE ALPS

Switzerland's public transport system is second to none, being fully integrated, efficient and punctual, and of great value to the walker. Railways serve many parts of the region. From

Gondolas, chairlifts and cablecars enable walkers to access high paths without effort

either Thun or Interlaken, trains run along the south side of the Thunersee and the north shore of the Brienzer See.

Trains go to Meiringen and Innertkirchen in the Haslital; to Grindelwald and Lauterbrunnen, and from both these places to Kleine Scheidegg, before tunnelling through the Eiger to emerge on the Jungfraujoch as the highest railway in Europe. Wengen is also reached on the Lauterbrunnen–Kleine Scheidegg line, while on the other side of Lauterbrunnen's valley, Mürren is fed by funicular with a change of trains being made at Grütschalp. Downvalley another funicular climbs steeply from Wilderswil to Schynige Platte for the start of one of the finest walks in the Alps.

Railways also serve Kandersteg via Spiez, then continue through the Lötschberg Tunnel to the Rhône Valley and other parts of the country. Also travelling via Spiez a railway runs the length of the Simmental, serving such places as Oey in the mouth of the Diemtigtal, Zweisimmen and Lenk. Going beyond Zweisimmen on a separate line trains also run to Gstaad, which has rail access with Montreux through the scenic Pays d'Enhaut.

Yellow postbuses are seen almost everywhere there is a motorable road. The region covered by this guide is admirably served, with practically every village having a bus route to it – if not a postbus, then a vehicle owned by a private company licensed by the postal service. In village centres the

main collecting point will be outside the post office (PTT). In outlying areas railway stations will also have a post-bus stop, and there are certain strategic points in some valleys without habitation where passengers may be picked up on request. Look for the PTT *Haltestelle* sign.

In addition to the network of rail and postbus services, numerous resort villages have cablecars, chairlifts, gondolas etc that the walker can use to his advantage. Where these occur brief details are given in the text.

Various incentives are available that encourage the use of either railways or the postbus services. Purchased in advance from the Switzerland Travel Centre, these are summarised below:

Swiss Pass: This entitles the holder to unlimited travel by postbus, rail or lake ferry for periods of 4, 8, 15 and 22 days, or a month. Discounts are also given on most forms of mountain transport.

Swiss Youth Pass: Advantages are the same as for holders of the Swiss Pass, but young people under 26 can obtain the Swiss Youth Pass at a 25% discount.

Swiss Flexi Pass: Similar to the above, except that validity ranges from 3, 4, 5, 6, or 8 days.

Swiss Half-Fare Card: Valid for one month, the card allows unlimited purchase of train, bus, boat and some cablecar tickets at half price.

Swiss Transfer Ticket: The STT is useful for visitors planning to stay for a

The Wilderswil-Schynige Platte funicular gives access to one of the finest walks in the Alps (Route 9)

period of one month, and gives one free round-trip to any destination in the country. This can start at any Swiss airport or border, but each leg of the journey must be completed on the same day. Holders of the Swiss Transfer Ticket can also claim discounts on most mountain lift systems.

Swiss Card: An extended version of the Swiss Transfer Ticket, the Swiss Card gives the holder a 50% discount on all further train, bus or boat journeys.

Swiss Travel System Family Card: Children under 16 years of age travel free if accompanied by at least one parent in possession of a Swiss Card, Swiss Pass or Flexi Pass. Non-family members between 6–16 years receive a 50% discount. The Family Card is available free of charge from the Switzerland Travel Centre in London.

Regional Pass Berner Oberland: Covering all rail journeys, lake ferries and most bus services, the Regional Pass gives free travel on several mountain lifts and funiculars, and reductions of 25–50% on others. The Pass is available for periods of either 7 or 15 days.

ACCOMMODATION

There should be no difficulty in finding suitable accommodation anywhere in the region covered by this book. There are campsites, youth hostels, mountain huts and moderately-priced pensions; a growing number of *matratzenlagers* that attract individuals as well as groups, and extremely grand hotels for those without wallet restrictions. There are also hundreds of intermediate hotels and *gasthofs* and, in a number of resorts, chalets or apartments available for short-term rent. Package holidays provide another option

Official campsites

Campsites exist in many valleys. Some offer rather basic facilities, while others have not only first-class toilet and washing blocks, but also provide laundry and drying rooms. Lists of camping and caravan sites are produced annually by the Touring Club of Switzerland (**www.tcs.ch**), and the Swiss Camping Association (**www.campingswiss.ch**). Another website that lists campsites throughout the country is **www. campingnet.ch**. Please note that off-site camping is prohibited in Switzerland.

Youth Hostels

Several youth hostels (SJH) in the Bernese Alps provide reasonably priced accommodation. Affiliated to Hostelling International, they are primarily open to all young people holding a valid membership card. Small dormitories and family rooms are generally available. For a current list of hostels in Switzerland, visit **www.youthhostel.ch** or contact the Schweizer Jugendherbergen, Schaffhauserstr. 14, Postfach, CH–8042 Zürich.

Matratzenlagers

Modestly-priced dormitory accommodation is provided in a number of hotels, mountain inns, restaurants, cablecar stations and farms throughout the region. Variously known as *matratzenlager*, *massenlager* or *touristenlager*, standards vary considerably. Some have traditional two-tier bunk beds, others consist of large communal

The tiny Weber Hut is visited on the Schynige Platte to First walk (Route 9)

sleeping quarters with a long line of mattresses (sheet sleeping bags recommended). Almost all have decent washroom facilities including showers. Meals are also provided. Tourist offices can usually provide a list of such places.

Mountain Huts

Huts belonging to the SAC (Swiss Alpine Club) are primarily intended as an overnight base for climbers preparing for the ascent of a neighbouring peak, although a number mentioned within this guide are also used by walkers and trekkers. Most are located in spectacular surroundings far from habitation and give a memorable experience for both the first-time and frequent user. Mixed-sex dormitories are the norm (take your own sheet sleeping bag), and in a few, washing facilities are rather primitive. Where a guardian (hut keeper, or warden) is in residence during the summer months, meals and refreshments are usually available. Some huts can be very busy in the high season, and especially at weekends. Should it be your intention to spend a night in one, you're advised to telephone ahead to make a reservation. Outline details are given throughout the guide, but for more information, log onto the hut's website, where one exists, and contact details are given.

Since several routes in this guide visit huts, a note on hut etiquette may be useful for first-time users. On arrival remove your boots and change into a pair of special hut shoes (clogs or rubber slippers) which you'll find on racks

in the boot room or porch. Locate the guardian to book sleeping space for the night, and any meals required. Meal times are usually fixed, but a choice of menu is not always available. Tea, coffee, soft drinks, beer and wine are usually on sale. As soon as you're able, go to your dormitory, make your bed and keep a torch handy as the room may be unlit overnight. Payment is usually made in cash the night before departure.

Should you plan to spend several nights in huts during your holiday, it would be worth buying a reciprocal rights card from the British Mountaineering Council (BMC); 177–179 Burton Road, Manchester M20 2BB (**www.thebmc.co.uk**) to obtain a discount on overnight fees – but not meals. Membership of other Alpine Clubs also enables you to claim discounted overnight fees.

Holiday Apartments

Giving a degree of freedom and flexibility, self-catering apartments are an option worth considering by families or groups of friends planning to stay in one centre. The majority of resort villages mentioned in this guide have apartments or chalets to rent, usually for a one week minimum.

Hotels and Mountain Inns

A large number and variety of hotels exist throughout the Bernese Alps, ranging from small family-run establishments to large 4-star buildings that are part of an international hotel chain.

In addition, mountain inns and pensions that may not be star-rated, are located in some of the villages as well as more remote outlying districts. A few mountain restaurants also offer good value overnight accommodation in bedrooms or dormitories.

Package Holidays
Holiday packages that provide both accommodation and travel, can offer a useful service at a competitive price for walkers looking for a base in a specific resort. Visit your local travel agent and check the brochures of companies such as Crystal, Inghams, Kuoni, Thomson etc.

Mountains make their own weather. This is an old adage that is certainly true of the Bernese Alps. Since the range more or less faces north and is the first of the main mountain areas to collect the weather patterns flooding in across northwest Europe and the low Swiss plains, it attracts a worse record (so far as rain and low cloud are concerned) than most other Alpine regions.

Summer thunderstorms are to be expected when precipitation will almost certainly be in the form of rain below 2000m, and possibly snow above that level – the Jungfraujoch, for example, records an annual precipitation in excess of 4000mm (158 inches). However, when the Fohn winds blow there will be clear skies for several days at a time (these may occur two or three times a month during the summer), but this is usually succeeded by more rain. Despite its generally poor reputation, however, my own experience of wandering among the Bernese Alps over several decades, has been much more positive, for I've enjoyed more good weather than bad, and a reasonable amount that could be considered indifferent. Hardly a day has occurred when the weather was so foul it was impossible to go walking, so do not allow the possibility of a few days of rain dissuade you from visiting these wonderful mountains. If you go prepared for the worst and hope for the best, you'll not be disappointed.

Average monthly temperatures and precipitation figures (in mm) for

	Jan	Feb	Mar	Apr	May	Jun	Jul	Aug	Sept	Oct	Nov	Dec
min °C	-5	-3	-1	3	8	10	11	11	8	4	-2	-5
max °C	0	4	9	13	18	20	21	20	17	11	5	0
precipitation	56	49	62	77	97	120	118	114	96	71	68	65

Walkers relax below the Grosse Chrinne in a quiet
corner away from Grindelwald's crowds

Bern, lying north of the Bernese Alps at an altitude of 510m (1673ft) are given in the box on p.27.

The Swiss meteorological service, MeteoSwiss, publishes a 4-day forecast which provides a general view of weather trends. The broadcast daily weather report is, of course, more helpful, and a local weather bulletin is usually posted in the window of tourist offices and mountain guides' buereaux. For an internet report in English, visit **www.meteoswiss. ch/en** – this gives a daily forecast as well as a five-day prediction. Current weather conditions throughout Switzerland can be checked on **www.MySwitzerland.com**.

NOTES FOR WALKERS

The majority of walks described in this guide have been chosen with a particular viewpoint, lake, alp hamlet, hut or pass as the destination, while the principal objective is to enjoy a day's exercise among some of the most uplifting scenery in all the Alps. There's something here to meet the needs of every walker, at every level of experience and ambition. But in order to gain the most from an active walking holiday in the Bernese Alps, one needs to be in reasonably good physical condition on arrival.

These mountains are high, and although this is not a climbing guide, walks to a few 'minor' summits are included. Yet even without summits, many of the routes described venture

to vantage points at elevations of well over 2000m (half as high again as the summit of Britain's highest mountain), and some of the trails are both steep and exposed. Of course, there are many walks of a more modest nature, but which also enjoy stunning views. Just avoid being over-ambitious for the first few days of the holiday, until you're acclimatised and better able to appreciate the Alpine scale of the landscape.

Walks have been graded into three numerical categories, with the highest grade reserved for the more challenging routes. This grading system is purely subjective, but is included as a rough guide of what to expect. Moderate walks (Grade 1) should appeal to active members of the family who want reasonably short walks without too many steep sections. The majority of routes are graded 2 or 3, largely as a result of the challenging nature of the district. A full definition of these grades is given at the end of this Introduction.

Throughout the region footpaths are signed with typical Swiss efficiency

SAFETY CHECK LIST

- Before setting out on a mountain walk check the weather forecast (see above) and be aware that Alpine areas are subject to rapidly changing conditions. When on a long walk watch for signs of a deterioration in the weather, and be prepared for the worst by having suitable clothing.

- Study route details beforehand, noting any particular difficulties and the amount of time needed to complete the route. Make sure you can be back safely before nightfall.

- On a full-day's walk carry food (and emergency rations such as chocolate or dried fruit), and at least one litre of liquid per person to avoid dehydration.

- Leave details of your planned route and expected time of return, with a responsible person.

- Be vigilant when crossing wet rocks, scree, snow patches and mountain streams. Should a section of your path be safeguarded with fixed rope or chains, check that they have not worked loose before relying on them.

- Do not stray onto glaciers unless you have experienced companions and the necessary equipment (and know-how) to deal with crevasse rescue. Keep away from icefalls and hanging glaciers.

- Avoid dislodging stones onto others who might be below you.

- Never be reluctant to turn back in the face of deteriorating weather, or if the route appears to be hazardous. In the event of being unable to reach your planned destination, try to send a message.

- Carry map and compass (and GPS if you have one), and know how to use them.

- Always carry some first aid equipment, as well as a whistle and a torch for emergencies. The emergency telephone number for rescue is 117 – try not to use it!

- Make a note of the International Distress Signal printed at the front of this guide: six blasts on a whistle (and flashes with a torch after dark) spaced evenly for one minute, followed by a minute's pause; then repeat until an answer is received and your position located. The response is three signals followed by a minute's pause.

- Be insured against accidents (rescue and subsequent medical treatment), for although mountain rescue is highly organised and efficient in Switzerland, it can be extremely expensive for the casualty. (See Appendix A for a list of specialist insurers.)

- Finally, please help keep the mountains and valleys litter-free.

Most paths are well maintained, waymarked and signed at junctions with typical Swiss efficiency. Footpath signs generally conform to a national standard, are painted yellow, and bear the names of major landmark destinations such as a pass, lake, hut or village or, indeed, sometimes a name that does not appear on the map, but which refers to a specific trail junction. Estimated times are given in hours (Std:*stunden*) and minutes (min), while a white plate on some of the signs announces the name and altitude of the immediate locality. Rarely do paths in this book stray onto unpathed territory, but where they do, occasional cairns and/or waymarks act as your guide. In such places it is essential to remain vigilant to avoid becoming lost – especially in poor visibility. If in doubt about the continuing route, return to the last point where you were certain of your whereabouts, and try again. By regular consultation with the map during your walk, it should be possible to keep abreast of your position and anticipate junctions or a change of direction before you reach them.

Waymarks are either painted yellow (the *Wanderweg*) for easy, mostly valley walks; white-red-white for the higher, more demanding *Bergweg* trails; while a third type of waymark which indicates an *Alpenweg* is coloured blue and white. These are reserved for difficult routes which may involve sections of scrambling, via ferrata (fixed rope, metal rungs or ladders), or glacier crossings. Only the most experienced of mountain walkers should attempt these.

For safety's sake do not walk alone on remote trails, on moraine-bank paths or glaciers. If you prefer to walk in a group but have not made prior arrangements to join an organised walking holiday, the staff at several tourist offices in the region arrange day walks in the company of a qualified leader. These take place throughout the summer months and are sometimes free of charge to guests staying in the organising resort. Enquire at the local tourist office for specific details.

SUGGESTED EQUIPMENT LIST

Experienced mountain walkers will no doubt have their preferences, but the following list is offered as a guide to newcomers to the Alps. Obviously some items will not be needed if you envisage tackling only low valley walks.

Clothing

- Walking boots – must be comfortable, a good fit, have ankle support and plenty of grip in the soles
- Trainers or similar for wear in hotels and villages
- Wind- and water-proof jacket and overtrousers
- Warm hat and sunhat
- Gloves
- Fleece or sweater
- Shirts – 2 or 3 for a fortnight's holiday

- Warm trousers or slacks (not jeans which can be very cold when wet and take ages to dry)
- Shorts (optional)
- Socks
- Underwear

Miscellaneous
- Rucksack – with waterproof liner and/or cover
- Sheet sleeping bag (for those who intend to sleep in huts or *matratzenlagers*)
- Bivvy bag – in case of emergencies
- Collapsible umbrella – excellent rain protection; especially useful for spectacle wearers
- Trekking pole(s) – highly recommended
- Headtorch plus spare bulb and battery

A walker on the Regenboldshorn, a short diversion from the Pommernpass on Route 92

- Water bottle – minimum 1 litre capacity
- Sunglasses, suncream/sunblock and lip salve
- First aid kit
- Map and compass (and GPS if available)
- Whistle
- Watch
- Guidebook
- Penknife
- Camera and films (unless digital)
- Altimeter
- Binoculars

RECOMMENDED MAPS

The series of maps published by the Swiss national survey – Landeskarte der Schweiz (LS) – are works of art. Open any sheet and a picture of the country immediately leaps from the paper, for by shading, contours and colouring, the line of ridge and rock face, the flow of glacier and stream, the curve of an amphitheatre, the narrow cut of a glen, the expanse of a lake or forest on a hillside all announce themselves clearly. They are a source of inspiration for study at home, and a real pleasure to use in the mountains. Check the LS catalogue on **www.swisstopo.ch/en/**.

The yellow/orange-covered *Wanderkarte* series at 1:50,000 carry the letter 'T' with their personal identification number; these have major walking routes outlined in red, mountain huts circled, and postbus stops also shown. Although the 1:25,000

Snowpeaks on the Lauterbrunnental's headwall are clearly seen from the path to the Rottal Hut (Route 43)

series shows greater detail, the 1:50,000 scale should be perfectly adequate for most walkers' needs here, while the commercial publisher Kümmerly + Frey publishes a 'holiday map' at 1:120,000 (*Berner Oberland*) which gives a good overview of the region and could be useful for planning purposes.

Map suppliers are listed in Appendix A, but note that some tourist authorities produce their own *Wanderkarten* that show local walking routes, and these are on sale at tourist information offices. Specific sheets are mentioned in the valley details within the guide.

USING THE GUIDE

The layout of this guide follows an east–west convention, beginning with the Haslital and working west from valley to valley as far as Col du Pillon below Les Diablerets. Each valley system is treated as a separate unit, or chapter, for which a locator map is provided. These locator maps are designed to show the general alignment of the district, with major features identified; they do not indicate either the location or route of walks described in the text. For that you will need to consult the topographical map recommended for that area.

Within each valley chapter details are given in regard to the various villages or resorts, their access, facilities, tourist information, huts etc, and a number of walks of various grades are then described. At the head of each walk a note is given as to the general location of that route, to make it easier for the reader to find it on the map. All the walks are listed in an index at the back of the book, detailing the grade and length of time each route should take. An explanation of the grading system is found below.

Distances and heights are quoted throughout in kilometres and metres. Details are taken directly from the map where possible, but in attempting to measure the actual distance of each walk, it has been necessary to make an estimation, for with countless zig-zags on many of the routes, it's impossible to be precise.

Times quoted for each walk are approximations only, and **refer to actual walking time and make no allowances for rest stops, consulation with the map or photographic interruptions** – such stops can add considerably to the overall time you are out (add 25–50% to times quoted), so bear this in mind when planning your day's itinerary. Although such times are given as a planning aid they are, of course, entirely subjective, and each walker will have his or her own pace which may or may not coincide with those quoted here. By comparing your times with those given in this guide, you should be able to compensate accordingly.

Abbreviations have been used sparingly, but some have of necessity been adopted. Although most should be fairly obvious, the following list gives clarification.

APR	Alpine Pass Route
CHF	The Swiss Franc (Confederation Helvetia Franc)
hrs	hours
km	kilometres
LS	Landeskarte der Schweiz (Swiss national survey maps)
m	metres
mins	minutes
PTT	Post Office (Post, Telephone & Telegraph)
SAC	Swiss Alpine Club
TGV	Trains à Grande Vitesse

GRADING OF WALKS

Walks described in this guide have been chosen with the express intention of helping you make the most out of a holiday in the Bernese Alps of Switzerland. Since it is hoped that walkers of all degrees of commitment and experience will find something useful here, a grading system has been used to direct readers to the standard of outing best suited to their individual requirements. As mentioned above, the walks have been graded into three categories, but since the grading of walks is not an exact science, each category will cover a fairly wide spectrum. Inevitably there will be anomolies that may be disputed, but they are offered in good faith and as a rough guide only.

Grade 1: Suitable for family outings. Most cover short distances, or are routed along gently-graded paths with little altitude gain.

Grade 2: These involve moderate walking, mostly on clear footpaths

Below the Schilthorn the Grauseeli tarn adds colour to a bowl of scree (Route 57)

with a reasonable amount of height gain. Walkers should be adequately shod and equipped.

Grade 3: More strenuous routes on sometimes rough or unclear paths. These may involve scrambling or the use of ladders, fixed ropes etc. A 'head for heights' is called for as many paths are exposed in places. On some Grade 3 routes there will be passes to cross, a summit to reach, or involve glacier travel (individual sections will be marked in the text). In short, true Alpine walking. As there will be steep ascents and descents, and fairly long distances involved, walkers attempting Grade 3 routes need to be physically fit and well-equipped.

INFORMATION AT A GLANCE

Currency:
The Swiss franc (CHF): 100 centimes/rappen:CHF1. Although Switzerland is not in the Euro zone, some hotels and retail outlets accept payment by Euro. Change will be given in Swiss francs. Major credit cards are accepted almost everywhere (not in mountain huts). Cash machines (ATMs) are common at banks in most resorts.

Formalities:
Visas are not required by holders of a valid UK passport, or other EU nationals. Visitors from other countries should enquire at their local Swiss Embassy.

Health precautions:
At the time of writing no vaccinations are required by visitors entering Switzerland, unless they've been in an infected area within 14 days of arrival. There are no endemic contagious diseases here, but be aware of the powerful sunlight, and use a broad spectrum suncream (factor 20+) as protection against potentially harmful UV rays that can cause sunburn and lead to skin cancer. Note too that Switzerland, along with much of Central Europe, harbours the Ixodes tick, whose bite causes TBE (tick-borne encephalitis). Risk is seasonal, from March to September, and those who take part in outdoor activities may be vulnerable. An injection of TBE immunoglobulin gives short-term protection; ask your GP for advice. Any medical treatment in Switzerland must be paid for. In the event of hospitalisation or visit to a doctor a deposit must be paid, or proof of health insurance shown. Make sure you have adequate insurance cover that includes personal accident, sickness and rescue. (See Appendix A for a list of specialist insurers.)

International dialling code:
When phoning *to* Switzerland from the UK use 0041. To phone the UK *from* Switzerland, the code is 0044, after which the initial 0 of the area code is ignored. Cashless call boxes are operated by a phonecard (Taxcard) on sale at post offices, newsagents and railway stations for CHF5, CHF10 and CHF20. Many call boxes also accept payment by credit card.

Language spoken:	In the Bernese Alps, German (or *Schwyzerdütsch*) is the regional language, although English is widely understood throughout the area covered by this guide.
Tourist information:	Switzerland Travel Centre Ltd, 1st Floor, 30 Bedford Street, London WC2E 9ED (☎ freephone 00800 100 200 30 **stc@stlondon.com www.switzerlandtravelcentre.co.uk**) Destinationen Berner Oberland, c/o Interlaken Tourismus, Höheweg 37, CH–3800 Interlaken (☎ 033 828 37 47 **info@berneroberland.ch www.berneroberland.ch**)
Embassies:	Swiss Embassy, 16–18 Montagu Place, London W1H 2BQ (☎ 020 7616 600)
	Swiss Embassy, 6 Aylesbury Road, Ballsbridge, Dublin 4 (☎ 0353 1218 6382/3)
	Swiss Embassy, 633 Third Avenue, 30th Floor, New York, NY 10017–6706 (☎ (212) 599 5700)
	Swiss Embassy, 154 University Avenue, Suite 601, Toronto ON M5H 3Y9 (☎ (416) 593 5371)

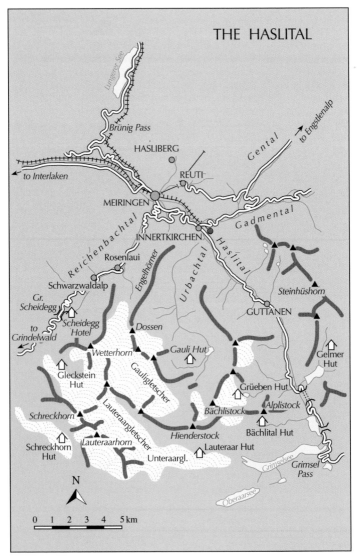

THE HASLITAL

Lungerer See

Brünig Pass

HASLIBERG

to Interlaken

REUTI

MEIRINGEN

Gental

to Engstlenalp

INNERTKIRCHEN

Gadmental

Reichenbachtal

Rosenlaui

Engelhörner

Urbachtal

Haslital

Schwarzwaldalp

Gr. Scheidegg

Steinhüshorn

to Grindelwald

Scheidegg Hotel

GUTTANEN

Dossen

Gleckstein Hut

Wetterhorn

Gauli Hut

Gelmer Hut

Gauligletscher

Grüeben Hut

Schreckhorn

Lauteraargletscher

Bächlistock

Alplistock

Hienderstock

Bächlital Hut

Schreckhorn Hut

Lauteraarhorn

Unteraargl.

Lauteraar Hut

Grimselsee

Grimsel Pass

N

Oberaarsee

0 1 2 3 4 5km

HASLITAL

As a base for a walking holiday, or as the starting point for an exploration of the Bernese Alps, the flat-bottomed, deeply cut Haslital has much to commend it. In its upper reaches near the Grimsel Pass, it has all the raw, semi-barren features of the high mountains, but at its lower, northern end where it curves to meet the gleaming expanse of the Mediterranean-like Brienzer See , it's broad and open with low-lying meadows and chalets with flowers at their balconies. The Grimsel Pass is at 2165m, the Brienzer See a modest 564m. Between the two extremes the valley descends in a series of steps exhibiting a rich variety of landscapes with lush pastures, dazzling cascades, deep shadowed gorges and several tributary glens worth exploring.

ACCESS AND INFORMATION

Location	At the eastern end of the Bernese Alps, draining north from the Grimsel Pass to the Brienzer See.
Maps	LS 255T *Sustenpass*, 265T *Nufenenpass*, 254T *Interlaken* at 1:50,000
	Wanderkarte Oberhasli at 1:50,000 available locally
Bases	Innertkirchen (625m), Meiringen (595m)
Information	Tourist Information Innertkirchen, CH–3862 Innertkirchen (☎ 033 972 12 20 **www.innertkirchen.ch**)
	Tourist Information Meiringen-Haslital, Bahnhofstr. 22, CH–3860 Meiringen (☎ 033 972 50 50 **info@alpenregion.ch www.alpenregion.ch**)
Access	By train to Meiringen via Interlaken or Lucerne. The rest of the valley is served by postbus.
	In summer a postbus service operates several times a day between Meiringen and Andermatt across the Grimsel Pass (reservations obligatory).

The Haslital has been used as a major transit valley for centuries, and the old mule trail to the Grimsel Pass still exists in places. As early as 1211 the Bernese marched along it and crossed the Grimsel to invade the Valais, but in more peaceful times it became an important trade route to Italy. Today there are no fewer than four road passes feeding into the valley: the Brunig, Susten, Grimsel and Grosse Scheidegg – the last-named open only to local permit holders and buses travelling between Meiringen and Grindelwald. And walkers, of course.

The main peaks, whose glaciers carved valleys feeding into the Haslital, are located in a great arc to the south, east and northeast. Titlis (3238m) heads both the lovely Gental and the Gadmental. Then there's the Sustenhorn (3503m) above the pass of the same name, and the big glacial mass of the Winterberg, Tieralplistock and the Gelmerhörner curving above the Furka and Grimsel passes. To the west of the Grimsel the Oberaar and Unteraargletschers sweep out of the arctic-like heartland of the Bernese Alps, while the western wall of the Haslital begins with the Bachlistock (3247m) and Ritzlihorn (3263m) before being sliced by the peaceful Urbachtal with the Hangendgletscherhorn (3292m) and the great east-facing slabs of the Engelhörner rising from it.

There's enough in the Haslital to keep a mountaineer or mountain walker quietly content for many a long day.

General tourists based here will find enough to satisfy a holiday too. There are associations with Sherlock Holmes around Meiringen, for example, for Conan Doyle was sufficiently impressed with the area that he brought the fictitious Holmes to the town for a final battle with Professor Moriarty at the nearby Reichenbach Falls. There's the Aareschlucht too, an imposing narrow limestone gorge with a walkway through it (fee charged for entry), midway between Meiringen and Innertkirchen. There are yet more cascades to be seen in the Gental which leads to the honeypot of the Engstlensee, and a cableway that carries visitors up to the Hasliberg terrace and beyond for gentle strolls with memorable views.

To restate the obvious, the Haslital makes a fine start to an exploration of the Bernese Alps for visitors of all persuasions. But perhaps the very best is reserved for the walker, for there's a rich vein of routes to be tapped in a surprisingly diverse set of landscapes.

MAIN BASES

INNERTKIRCHEN (625m) lies in the bed of the valley about 6km southeast of Meiringen in an upper grassy plain. Reached by postbus, or by train from Interlaken via Brienz and Meiringen, the village has two campsites, five hotels and a variety of chalets and apartments for holiday let. It has limited shopping facilities, but there's a PTT and tourist information office. To the east the Susten Pass road cuts into the Gadmental, which in turn forks soon after with one of its branches delving into the Gental. Innertkirchen, therefore, is conveniently situated to make the most of several very fine walking districts.

MEIRINGEN (595m) is the main tourist centre of the valley. Although old, little remains of the original town, for two serious fires destroyed much of it in 1879 and 1891. (A total of 293 houses were burned in the two fires.) Napoleon was here in 1810; other visitors have been Conan Doyle, Gertrude Bell, Hilaire Belloc and King Albert of the Belgians. Melchior Anderegg, one of the great mountain guides of the Golden Age, had a farm at nearby Zaun. The church, with its 14th-century Romanesque tower topped by a wooden spire, is worth a visit. Served by railway from Interlaken, Meiringen is very much a modern resort with no shortage of shops, restaurants, banks, PTT, sports facilities and a tourist information office. There are a dozen or so hotels ranging from small family-run establishments to the five-star Parkhotel du Sauvage where Conan Doyle used to stay. For lower-priced accommodation try Simons Herberge on Alpbacchstrasse (77 beds, 49 dorm places; ☎ 033 971 17 15 **info@simons-herberge.ch www.simons-herberge.ch**), or the small Hotel Brunner (nine beds) on Bahnhofstrasse (☎ 033 971 14 23 **cafe.hotel-brunner@freesurf.ch**). The nearest campsite is 2km to the west; Camping Balmweid (☎ 033 971 51 15 **www.camping-meiringen.ch**), and there's a cableway to Reuti on the Hasliberg terrace above the resort.

OTHER BASES

On a prosperous sunny terrace above Meiringen, **HASLIBERG** (1000–1100m) consists of a scattered collection of hamlets and hotels made accessible by cableway from the valley, with more cableways continuing up to the high bowl of Mägisalp, and from there to Planplatten – a ski area with splendid views, which also gives plenty of opportunities for the walker. Hasliberg has more than a dozen hotels, as well as holiday apartments and chalets. For detailed information contact Tourist Information Hasliberg, CH–6084 Hasliberg Wasserwendi (☎ 033 972 51 51 **info@alpenregion.ch www.alpenregion.ch**).

Northeast of Innertkirchen, on the Susten Pass road, **GADMEN** (1205m) is a small village with several fine old wooden chalets, a campsite, and accommodation in Hotel Steingletscher (☎ 033 975 12 22 **info@sustenpass.ch www.susten-pass.ch**), while 150 dormitory places are available at the Alpine Center, Chalet Ochsen at the Susten Pass (same contact details as Hotel Steingletscher).

Elsewhere, at the head of the Gental which feeds into the Gadmental above Innertkirchen, mention must be made of **HOTEL ENGSTLENALP** (1834m). With beds and dormitory places, it's open from May to the end of October (☎ 033 975 11 61 **hotel@engstlenalp.ch www.engstlenalp.ch**). Reached by postbus from Meiringen, it makes a popular excursion with the lake of Engstlensee nearby, the Joch Pass above (accessible by chairlift or footpath), and several very fine walks leading from it.

The Lauteraar Rothorner directs the way to the Lauteraar Hut

In the upper Haslital, **GUTTANEN** (1057m) has the family-run Hotel Bären (☎ 033 973 12 61 **info@baeren-guttanen.ch www.baeren-guttanen.ch**); there's also Hotel Handeck with 67 beds further towards the Grimsel Pass (☎ 033 982 36 11 **grimselhotels@kwo.ch www.grimselhotels.ch**), and at the pass itself the Grimsel Hospiz, set above the dam, has 64 beds (☎ 033 982 46 11 **www.grimselhotels.ch**).

Southwest of Meiringen, on the way to the Grosse Scheidegg, several hotels, inns and *gasthofs* in the Reichenbachtal offer accommodation in gentle surroundings. Details are given in the text where walks lead to or past them.

MOUNTAIN HUTS
Although there are several mountain huts in the district covered by this chapter, only two are visited on walks described.

LAUTERAAR HUT (2392m) This SAC hut is located above a confluence of glaciers in wonderfully wild country west of the Grimsel Pass. With places for 50 and a resident guardian in July and August (meals provided) it's reached in about 4–4½hrs from the Grimsel Hospice. (☎ 033 973 11 10 **lauteraar@bluewin.ch**).

GAULI HUT (2205m) Near the head of the Urbachtal, this 65-place hut is owned by the Bern Section of the SAC, and has a resident guardian from April to early October (☎ 033 971 31 66 **schild.re@bluewin.ch www.gauli.ch**).

ROUTE 1

Engstlenalp (1834m) –
Schwarzental (1369m)

Grade:	1
Distance	5km
Height loss	465m
Time	1–1½hrs
Location	Northeast of Innertkirchen

Engstlenalp lies at the head of the lovely Gental, in a location reckoned by Professor John Tyndall, the scientific Irishman and a Vice-President of the Alpine Club, as 'one of the most charming spots in the Alps.' What he wrote in 1866 is still true today. There's a Victorian hotel, gentle pastures, a clutch of timber chalets and barns, and the clear blue-green Engstlensee walled to the south by a huge mass of slabs topped by a ridge linking the Mähren and Wendenstöcke which continues over the Reissend Nollen to the summit of the Titlis. Cattle graze along the shores of the lake, and much of the area is a designated nature reserve. A track goes to the lake from the hotel and car park, and when it narrows, a path rises to the Joch Pass (2207m), and over to Engelberg. There's also a chairlift to the pass from the eastern end of the lake. (See Central Switzerland, a walking guide in the same series as the present book, for additional routes.)

Southwest of Engstlenalp runs the long, deep valley of the Gental – forested here and there, but with open meadows and tiny hamlets lining the narrow road that climbs through it. As you gaze along the valley, eyes are drawn to the big mountains of the Oberland where the Wetterhorn presents an unmistakable profile.

Postbuses go as far as Engstlenalp from Meiringen and Innertkirchen, and the car park there is often very busy in summer. From the alp there are three ways back to the Haslital; the particular route which follows is the shortest and easiest, but has some spectacular landscape features to enjoy.

From Hotel Engstlenalp cross the approach road and join a path which descends ahead among trees, keeping left of a stream which soon cuts a channel below. It's an easy path to follow, in and out of woods with wild fruits in season and plenty of wild flowers too. There are open glades and rough pastures to cross, and at Point 1535m (on the map) you pass a tiny huddle of alp huts. The path continues without difficulty, crossing the occasional side stream and with the woods thinning to give more open views into the valley stretching ahead as it falls away in natural terraces, or steps, of pastureland.

Near the huts of Under Graben (1468m) by a large old sycamore tree, you have a superb view of a number of cascades showering from limestone cliffs ahead and to the left. It's a lovely sight, but it becomes even better as you pass below them.

Restaurant Schwarzental is a converted dairy built in 1799. As well as meals and refreshments, accommodation is available with 18–20 dormitory places (☎ 033 975 12 40 or 033 971 48 31).

The path swings to the right, then resumes its former direction to take you beneath the waterfalls, crossing their drainage stream by way of a footbridge. Shortly after this you cross the valley to the hamlet of **Schwarzental** (*accommodation, refreshments*) from which point you can catch a postbus down to Innertkirchen or Meiringen. ◀

NOTE

Should you wish to walk all the way to Meiringen, follow the road until it forks just beyond a small settlement reservoir. Take the right fork for about 10mins, then bear left on a minor road which soon becomes a track. At a left-hand hairpin break ahead beside a solitary farmhouse into mixed woodland. Waymarked paths then continue, and eventually lead down to **Meiringen**, about 4hrs after leaving Engstlenalp.

ROUTE 2

Engstlenalp (1834m) –
Hinderarni (1459m) –
Reuti (1061m) – Meiringen (595m)

Grade	3
Distance	16km
Height gain	87m
Height loss	1239m
Time	4½–5hrs
Location	Northeast of Innertkirchen

This is a high-level route that follows a belvedere course along a hillside above the Gental, and is used on the classic Alpine Pass Route. There's nothing particularly difficult about the walk, save for its length, and it is the distance, rather than severity, that rates it Grade 3. All along the high path there are fine views to enjoy. There are features in the valley below to study from a distance, and the all-absorbing scene ahead of Oberland peaks growing larger and more prominent by the minute. By the time you reach Hasliberg-Reuti, you will have a fresh respect for this stunning landscape. From Reuti there is a steep descent through forest to Meiringen, although there is the option of cablecar for those who prefer it.

With no refreshment possibilities between Engstlenalp and Reuti (other than fresh water at Underbalm), make sure to fill water bottles before setting out, and carry a packed lunch.

Facing the Gental with your back to Hotel Engstlenalp, take the path heading to the right (northwest) signed to Hasliberg and Melchsee which leads past the haybarns and farm buildings, then swings westward over a stream. When it forks ignore the upper branch which leads to the Tannensee and Melchsee-Frutt, but continue ahead on a

The alp of Hinderarni is visited on the high trail to Meiringen

lovely balcony path. This is a delight of long views to the Wetterhorn, of wild flowers and shrubs. It's not a well-walked path, so there is a good chance you will be able to enjoy a certain amount of solitude. In places narrow and a little exposed (though never dangerously so), in an hour from Engstlenalp the path brings you to the handful of buildings of **Baumgarten** (1702m), which has a narrow farm road leading down to the valley. Walk along this road for about 200m, then resume on a footpath at the first bend.

On reaching the solitary farm of **Underbalm** (1551m) you can refill water bottles from a spring-fed pipe. The way leads on to **Hinderarni** (1459m; 2hrs 10mins) and another dirt road. To the east big snow peaks crowd the horizon above the unseen Susten Pass. The way now

Hasliberg-Reuti is expanding from a small village into a sunny resort 400m above the Haslital. Linked by cablecar with Meiringen, another cable lift extends to Bidmi and Mägisalp, where a gondola continues up to Planplatten at 2245m for some fine walks options. Accommodation can be had at Hotel Reuti (beds & dorm places, ☎ 033 971 18 32), Hotel Viktoria (beds & dorm places, (☎ 033 971 11 21) and Gasthof Weber (**gasthof. weber@freesurf.ch**).

curves to the right above the Haslital, through patches of forest and out between pastures again. Losing height wander past a few farms and chalets and come to **Reuti** (1061m *accommodation, refreshments*) about 1hr 15mins from Hinderarni.

At the entrance to Reuti signposts direct the continuing path across pastures, then into forest where the route becomes steep on the sharp descent to **Meiringen** which it reaches not far from the cablecar station about 1hr from Reuti.

ROUTE 3

Engstlenalp (1834m) – Tannenalp (1974m) – Melchsee-Frutt (1902m)

Grade	1–2
Distance	7km (one way)
Height gain	140m
Height loss	72m
Time	1½–2hrs
Location	West of Engstlenalp

This popular walk is not too demanding, but visually delightful. It begins by using the initial section of Route 2, then crosses the northwestern wall of the Gental to enter a high, gently sloping pastureland that leads down to the small resort of Melchsee-Frutt. Down there the valley has patches of limestone pavement and a rich alpine flora. There are two lakes in the pastureland, and the small alp village of Tannenalp. A choice of routes will return you to Engstlenalp.

From Hotel Engstlenalp wander along the path round the western edge of the alp, then veer westward on a clear

The Wetterhorn can be seen quite clearly from Engstlenalp

trail (as for Route 2) which soon takes you across a stream below a cascade. Soon after this the path forks and you take the right branch rising steadily southwestward now with views along the Gental. On a rising traverse below cliffs that wall the valley, the path brings you above them onto a grassy crest with fine views, and over this to descend slightly towards **Tannenalp** after about an hour. Refreshments can be had here.

From Tannenalp bear left along a narrow road, and on coming to the Tannensee, pass round either side of the lake; path to the left, roadway to the right. Continue downvalley, so to reach **Melchsee-Frutt** where there's accommodation, refreshments and shops. ◄

The lakes of Tannensee and Melchsee lie in the geographical heart of Switzerland, and the pastoral basin in which they are set is very popular with walkers. →

To return to Engstlenalp either reverse your outward route (2hrs), or head south from the lake at Melchsee and climb up to Balmeregghorn (2255m) following the line of a cableway. Once on the ridge between the Gental and Melchsee bear left and follow the ridgepath to Tannensee, where you can re-join the outward route back to **Engstlenalp**.

Other routes from Engstlenalp

- One of the classic walks from here is along the path to the **Joch Pass** (2207m) in about 1hr 10mins. It is a busy path and somewhat devalued by the close proximity of the chairlift. That being said, it is still a fine walk, with the possibility of extending it all the way to **Engelberg** – a walk of about 4hrs from Engstlenalp.
- Another good route, somewhat strenuous but rewarding, is that which crosses the ridge of the Tällistock – the mountain wall dividing the Gental from the Gadmental – and descends to the village of **Gadmen** on the far side. This is a walk of a little over 5hrs, with the option of breaking it with an overnight stay in the **Tälli Hut.**
- A Grade 3 extension to Route 3 leads across the **Balmeregghorn** to **Planplatten** and **Meiringen** in 6½hrs. From Engstlenalp to Tannenalp the route is the same as in Route 3, but thereafter the ridge dividing the two valleys is gained and followed southwestward across the slopes of Ezegg, then over the Balmeregghorn to Planplatten (2245m) where you have a choice of continuing routes to Meiringen. One option involves taking the Eagle Express gondola to Mägisalp and down to Meiringen.

← Accommodation can be found at **Berghaus Tannalp** (☎ 041 669 12 41 **www.tannalp.ch**) and **Sporthotel Kurhaus Frutt** (☎ 041 669 17 12), both of which have dorm beds as well as hotel rooms. See *Central Switzerland: a walking guide* also published by Cicerone.

ROUTE 4

Innertkirchen (625m) –
Urbachtal – Gauli Hut (2205m)

Grade	3
Distance	13km (one way)
Height gain	1580m
Time	6hrs
Location	South of Innertkirchen

Cutting into the mountains south of Innertkirchen, the Urbachtal is an unin-habited pastoral valley rising here and there in gorge-like narrows between high walls of rock. Its western wall is a stupendous flank of limestone – the Engelhörner – which divides the Urbachtal from that of Rosenlaui. This strenuous walk goes all the way through the valley to its inner recesses below the Gauligletscher which, with other icefields, forms a glacial cirque containing the valley's headwall. Set upon a remote alp the Gauli Hut commands fine views of the Ewigschneehorn and Hienderstock.

From Innertkirchen follow the narrow road which cuts away to the south of the Aare river to Grund, and then climbs in a long series of hairpins among forest, eventually levelling above a rocky cleft to enter the Urbachtal. There are footpath short-cuts in places. The road then crosses the Urbachwasser and heads into the valley proper after about 1hr 20mins.

On the trail to the Gauli Hut, great slab walls flank the Urbachtal

Continue along the road heading southwest, passing a string of farmhouses and haybarns dotted on either side among the meadows. The vast Engelhörner wall on the right is streaked with slender waterfalls and the whole

scene is reminiscent of parts of Norway. High above, at the head of the valley, modest glaciers and snowfields may be seen draped from the Hangendgletscherhorn.

The road ends and becomes a stony track that winds upvalley, passes the little hut of Röhrmatten (seen to the left) and continues as a footpath. Ahead the valley narrows almost to gorge-like proportions and is heavily wooded. The path takes you up into the woods, gaining height steeply in places, then rounds a bend below a solitary cabin at 1364m and eases across a steep gully with a stream pouring through it. (Early in the season this gully may be choked with snow; in which case you should proceed with caution.) Beyond the gully the way becomes a gentle terrace, now out of the trees.

The valley has broadened again, opening to a wide stream-sliced basin. Shortly after, you come to Schrätteren, a rough pasturage with a handful of alp huts above to the left. The path leads on, crosses the Urbachwasser stream and soon forks. Take the left-hand path which climbs on over increasingly rough terrain to gain another 300m or so before making another fork at 1850m.

Both the ongoing trails lead to the **Gauli Hut**, but the left branch swings round to take the shaft of river-cut valley to visit the hidden tarn of the Mattensee before climbing on to reach the hut. This is perhaps of more interest than the shorter, direct route which climbs over the lower reaches of the TËlligrat (2222m) before making a steady descending traverse to the hut itself, set in a remote alp at the head of the Urbachtal. ▶

Other routes in the Urbachtal

If Route 4 seems to be rather longer or more demanding than you'd care to tackle, don't despair, for the valley is well worth a visit no matter what your demands may be. It's also possible to drive there from Innertkirchen, thus reducing the time and effort otherwise required to explore it. Should you decide to drive into the valley, park with discretion in its lower reaches soon after entering. You should be able to find a space to park just off the road in order not to block it.

With places for 65 in its dormitories, the **Gauli Hut** has a guardian in residence in April and May, and from July to mid-October (sometimes wardened in June), when meals and refreshments are available. It is owned by the Bern Section of the SAC. For reservations (☎ 033 971 31 66 **schild.re@bluewin. ch www.gauli.ch**)

- By following Route 4 a very pleasant walk may be had to **Schrätteren** (allow 3–4hrs for the walk there and back; Grade 2). Or, if this is still too far, simply wander to **Röhrmatten** and back for an overview of a valley that is practically unique in the Bernese Alps.

ROUTE 5

Innertkirchen (625m) – Guttannen (1050m) – Grimsel Hospice (1980m)

Grade	2–3
Distance	19km (one way)
Height gain	1355m
Time	6½ hrs
Location	Southeast of Innertkirchen

The Grimsel Pass has been used for centuries; in times both of war and of peace. It has been used by traders transporting goods from the north of Switzerland to Italy – and vice-versa – and by mountain peasants, hunters, mercenaries and pilgrims. A mule track was the first 'road' to cross it, and when the specially engineered highway (mostly used today) was opened in 1895, there were some 300 horses stabled in Meiringen for use in drawing the post coaches over it. Parts of the old mule track through the Haslital are still in evidence, and this walk follows it wherever possible. There are paths in other places, sometimes the walk is on the road itself, but from Handegg, midway between Guttannen and the Pass, a Bergweg is taken through the wild upper part of the route. Note that there is a slight danger of avalanche early in the season.

From the start it is necessary to follow the path which climbs in zig-zags south of Innertkirchen through the woods towards the entrance to the Urbachtal. This leads to the narrow road serving the valley, but almost as soon as the road takes you across the Urbachwasser at Vordertal, break away on the route signed to Understock. Here you join a track leading along the southern slopes of the Haslital. In and out of woods it makes a steady traverse of these slopes and eventually brings you to the hamlet of **Boden** (869m), a little under 2hrs after setting out.

Go onto the main road here and walk a short distance downvalley to join the old mule track on the true right bank of the Aare, then follow this upstream. The way now leads uphill to **Guttannen**, the highest village in the Haslital – Handegg is little more than a hamlet. (Noted for its crystals, Guttanen is actually on the opposite bank, but may be reached by a bridge. Refreshments are available there.)

Beyond Guttannen the route becomes more interesting and wild, the mountains crowding overhead. About 2½km above it the track brings you onto the road which you wander along for the next 3–4km as far as Handegg, gained in a little over 4hrs from Innertkirchen. Handegg is the home of a hydro-electric station, the lakes above having been dammed to serve it. Off to the right are seen the cascades of the Handeggfall. Shortly after this you will see a path breaking away from the road on its right-hand side. This is the one to take; it leads up to the Räterischboden reservoir, skirts the lake's western edge, and comes to the **Grimsel Hospice** (*accommodation, refreshments*) overlooking the Grimselsee. ▶

This is an astonishing place; drab yet enticing, eerie but vibrant. There is evidence of past glaciations everywhere. Grey granite slabs scarred by long-gone ice, and the hint of icefields far-off that suggest highways into the heart of the mountains. A wild place it certainly is, and it's interesting to speculate on the influence the region had on the pioneers of mountaineering – and of the study of glaciology – who came this way more than 150 years ago. See Route 6 below for a route into the heart of the mountains from the Hospice to the Lauteraar Hut. But to return to Innertkirchen, take the postbus.

Accommodation (beds and dormitory places) at the **Grimsel Pass** is available at the **Grimsel Hospice** (☎ 033 982 46 11).

Other walks from Innertkirchen

Walkers based in Innertkirchen need not run short of ideas. There's something here for every taste; short, easy valley strolls and long and arduous mountain trails to follow.

- The **Aareschlucht** is one of the valley's features which will no doubt attract many walking visitors. It's a deep and narrow gorge, 1400m long and 200m deep with a walkway (fee charged) leading through it. The gorge is open daily between April and the end of October – weather permitting – and is floodlit on Wednesdays and Fridays in July and August from 9.00–11.00pm. (For information: **www.aareschlucht.ch**)

- A high route, nearly 1000m above the valley, can be achieved by going from Innertkirchen to Guttannen along a farmers' trail linking several isolated alps. First you climb towards the **Blattenstock** (1849m), then along the path high on the northern flanks of the valley to **Holzhus** (Holzhausalp; 1931m) and Steinhus (Steinhausalp; 1942m) before descending a knee-shattering zig-zag path to **Guttannen**. This Grade 3 route will take about 8½hrs to achieve.

- A long Grade 2 walk may be had through the Gadmental towards the Susten Pass. Three hours along a variety of footpath, track and road will lead to **Gadmen** among charming scenery. Served by postbus from Innertkirchen, or by using Gadmen as a base, the **Gadmental** has many fine outings worth exploring, among them the 2½hr walk from Nessental through the alps of Staldi and Birchlaui to the **Tälli Hut**. (Grade 2–3) There is also a steep haul up to **Sättelli** on the Tällistock ridge for a choice of fine views – either to the east to the Sustenhorn and its glacier-clad neighbours, across the depths of the Gental, or south towards the giants of the Oberland. This Grade 3 route from **Furen** will require a little over 3hrs.

- **Furen** (sometimes spelt Führen) is also the starting point for a demanding cross-country route over the

mountains to **Guttannen**, high in the Haslital. This
Grade 3 walk goes south from Furen into the valley
of the Triftwasser and up to the little alp of **Underi
Trift**. From here 1½hrs will lead to the Windegg
Hut, followed by a southwestward scramble to gain
the **Furtwangsattel** (2568m) before dropping very
steeply to Guttannen. This magnificent route is for
experienced mountain trekkers only, and will take
7½–8hrs.

ROUTE 6

*Grimsel Hospice (1980m) –
Lauteraar Hut (2392m)*

Grade	3
Distance	10km (one way)
Height gain	483m
Height loss	71m
Time	4–4½ hrs
Location	West of the Grimsel Pass

Originally known as the Pavilion Dolfus, the Lauteraar Hut sits on a grassy
shelf overlooking the concordia of two major glacier systems; the
Lauteraargletscher and the Finsteraargletscher which combine to become
the Unteraargletscher. This serves as a highway into the very heart of the
Bernese Alps. As their names suggest, the Lauteraar Glacier is headed by
the Lauteraarhorn, the Finsteraar Glacier by the Finsteraarhorn. Also in
view are the Schreckhorn and Oberaarhorn and a range of mountain walls
and pinnacles.

This approach route skirts the dismal-looking Grimselsee, then heads
along the rubble-strewn Unteraargletscher through a landscape more reminiscent of the barren Karakoram than of the pastoral Alps. But this raw, →

← monochrome mountainscape has great attraction for many of us, and serves as a direct contrast to that enjoyed on the vast majority of walks included in this guide. Although the route wanders along a glacier, it should be pointed out that this glacier is likely to be roughly carpeted with morainic debris. No crevasses were detected when the walk was researched, but it is important to follow marker poles and cairns (not always easy to see) for the precise up-to-date route. In poor visibility the correct point at which the glacier is left may be difficult to locate.

From the Grimsel Hospice (reached by postbus from Meiringen) go down a series of steps and across the top of the reservoir's dam wall. Climbing up the far side the path takes you high above the northern side of the Grimselsee, through a tunnel and out to steep, shrub-covered hillsides heading west. It's a fine walk, much of it among clusters of alpenrose, passing below cascades, then the Eldorado slabs that are very popular with climbers.

Buddhist prayer flags bring a touch of the Himalaya to the Unteraargletscher

At the far end of the lake (2–2½hrs) the path takes you onto the moraine-covered Unteraargletscher. From

here the way is marked with poles and cairns on the right-hand (northern) side of the glacier, meandering to find the easiest route. On the glacier has been built a huge chorten, complete with prayer flags, which adds to the Himalayan, or Karakoram-like atmosphere.

The SAC-owned **Lauteraar Hut** has 50 places and a resident guardian during July and August →

In the first half of the 19th century the Swiss glaciologist, Louis Agassiz, built a shelter on the Unteraargletscher as a base for his studies. The so-called Hôtel des Neuchatelois consisted of 'a large cave on a rock-island in the middle of the glacier, formed by a huge overhanging block of mica schist, made more weatherproof by a wall of stones, and more comfortable by layers of grass and oilcloth'. In the summer of 1841, James David Forbes, the young Scots geologist, adopted the 'hotel' as his base not only for scientific studies, but also to make the fourth ascent (and first British ascent) of the Jungfrau.

About an hour or so along the glacier you come to a point where you can see the valley's right-hand wall has a shallow indent with grass-covered slabs at its western end. A sign and marker poles direct you off the glacier here, then with painted waymarks on rocks you pick a route up rough slopes to find a clear path leading upvalley. Crossing one or two streams gain a grassy knoll and at last come to the **Lauteraar Hut**, which is not seen until just before you reach it. ▶

← when a full meals service is offered (☎ 033 973 11 10 **lauteraar@bluewin.ch**). Views are remarkable and justify the effort involved in getting here.

ROUTE 7

Meiringen (595m) – Rosenlaui (1328m)

Grade	2
Distance	8km (one way)
Height gain	733m
Time	3hrs
Location	SSW of Meiringen

Rosenlaui has a magical ring about it. Snug among the trees at the foot of the Wellhorn on the way to the Grosse Scheidegg, it is very much a climbing centre, with the big walls of the Engelhörner nearby. This approach walk, though steep at first, is none too arduous, and is just one section of a longer crossing to Grindelwald. Since much of the valley is hemmed in by steep mountains and forest, it's preferable to choose a bright day to tackle this outing, otherwise it can seem unnecessarily gloomy.

Leaving Meiringen take the main valley road out of town and across the Aare river to enter the neighbouring village of **Willigen**. About 50m beyond Hotel Tourist turn right along a narrow road between a house and a barn. When the road ends take a grass path rising steeply ahead. This brings you onto another minor road which you follow briefly before cutting away again on the continuing path. Several times this path leapfrogs the road, but is waymarked with precision so there is little chance of missing it. It leads over pastures and soon reaches the hamlet of **Schwendi** (792m; 40mins). Accommodation may be had here at Hotel Schwendi (☎ 033 971 28 25).

Continue along the road for a short distance until a footpath cuts off to the right, enters forest and becomes a paved mule-track that brings you to Gasthaus Zwirgi

(☎ 033 971 14 22 **gasthaus@zwirgi.ch**), located near the Reichenbach Falls. A signpost here suggests it will take 45mins to reach Kalterbrunnen. The path leaves the road on the left and takes you through more forest and meadow before rejoining the road near Berggasthof Kaltenbrunnen (1210m) about 1¾hrs from Meiringen (beds & dorm accommodation: ☎ 033 971 19 08). ▶

By now the gradient has eased with the valley stretching ahead, steep-walled and forested. Keep to the road until it makes a left-hand hairpin, where you keep ahead on a footpath alongside the stream all the way to Rosenlaui. As you approach **Gschwantenmad** – a group of old barns and farmhouses at 1304m (2¼hrs) – the valley opens to reveal the Engelhörner peaks above to the left, the broken snout of the Rosenlaui Glacier, and the Wetterhorn at the head of the valley. Remain left of the stream, and in another 15mins or so you will arrive at **Rosenlaui**, with the massive Victorian Hotel Rosenlaui (beds & dorm places; ☎ 033 971 29 12 **welcome@rosenlaui.ch www.rosenlaui.ch**). ▶

A 4hr circular walk from **Kaltenbrunnen** breaks away to the northwest, visits Kaltenbrunnen Alp and Stafel, and continues to the Hochmoor – Europe's highest protected upland moor at around 1800m.

While visiting Rosenlaui a recommended side-trip goes to the **Gletscherschlucht** (entry fee), a narrow glacier-carved gorge with spectacular cascades just a few minutes' walk from the hotel.

ROUTE 8

Meiringen (595m) – Schwarzwaldalp (1458m) – Grosse Scheidegg (1962m) – Grindelwald (1034m)

Grade	2–3
Distance	21km
Height gain	1367m
Height loss	928m
Time	7½hrs
Location	Southwest of Meiringen

This is the classic walker's route to Grindelwald; a trek that's well worth tackling, either in its entirety or, if you consider the distance too far for one day, by breaking the journey with an overnight spent at some midway point (several *gasthofs* are passed en route). Alternatively you could take the bus to Rosenlaui or Schwarzwaldalp and walk from there. The whole route between Meiringen and Grindelwald is served by bus, so with several halts along the way, it's perfectly feasible to cut the walk short at almost any given point, should the weather turn bad or you become too tired to continue.

Follow Route 7 as far as **Gschwantenmad**, where you have two routes to choose from on the way to Schwarzwaldalp. The first continues (as per Route 7) to Rosenlaui, wanders on towards the Glescherschlucht glacier gorge, then swings to the right above the road. Shortly before reaching **Schwarzwaldalp** (1454m; 45–50mins from Rosenlaui) the path forks by a bridge. For refreshment or accommodation cross the bridge to Hotel Chalet Schwarzwaldalp (beds & dorm places ☎ 033 971 35 15 **www.schwarzwaldalp.ch**), otherwise remain left of the stream and continue ahead.

ALTERNATIVE ROUTE: GSCHWANTENMAD TO SCHWARZWALDALP

At Gschwantenmad leave the road and take the farm track off to the right across the pastures. A footpath soon leaves this, heads through a collection of trees, crosses more pasture and rejoins the farm track at Rufenen, an open region of grazing land with fine mountain views. A signpost now directs you away across the meadows on the left in the direction of Broch and Schwarzwaldalp. Meadowland leads to forest, and out again to rejoin the valley road at the hamlet of **Broch**. Bear right and follow the road a short distance to **Schwarzwaldalp**. A few paces beyond the hotel leave the road, cross a bridge over the Reichenbach stream and turn right on the main path which leads to Grosse Scheidegg.

A pleasant stretch of path continues upvalley among trees and shrubs, then over rough pasture before crossing the stream once more. Here you wander up a track to meet the road yet again. Here a continuing path mounts the slope ahead beside the road, before crossing and recrossing it several times on the way to **Grosse Scheidegg** (1962m; 5hrs). This is a true saddle on a grassy ridge between the massive Wetterhorn on the left, and insignificant-looking Schwarzhorn to the right. From it you gaze across the rich meadowland basin in which Grindelwald is scattered, to the Männlichen ridge, while the Eiger is seen side-on in profile. Beside the road on the pass stands Berghotel Grosse Scheidegg which has both hotel beds and dormitory accommodation (☎ 033 853 67 16 **grossescheidegg@bluewin.ch www.grossescheidegg.ch**).

The way down to Grindelwald needs little description. It begins directly below the hotel, and is adequately signed and waymarked all the way to Hotel Wetterhorn. On the way it cuts through pastures and crosses the twisting road on a number of occasions, as well as keeping to the road here and there. About 1hr 15mins from Grosse Scheidegg you come to **Hotel Wetterhorn** opposite a parking area. The hotel has beds and dormitory places (☎ 033 853 12 18 **wetterhorn@grindelwald.ch www.hotel-wetterhorn.ch**).

At the bottom left-hand corner of the car park follow a track sloping downhill through mixed woodland. After about 8mins turn right on a path which descends to a footbridge. Across this the way rises, emerges from woodland and crosses a meadow with glorious mountain views. Turn left at a crossing tarmac path, then right between buildings. Through more pasture and a strip of woodland, cross another stream and shortly come to a narrow service road. Follow this all the way down to **Grindelwald** among chalets bright with petunias and geraniums at their windows.

Other routes from Meiringen

The proximity of the Hasliberg cableway complex adds much to Meiringen's appeal as a walking centre, but even without exploiting this attractive upland area there will be no shortage of outings to consider. Leaflets are available from the tourist information offices in Meiringen and Hasliberg, which outline some of the possibilities. But even a brief study of the map of the area shows the vast range of outings for walkers of all degrees of commitment here.

- One full day's walk makes a high traverse of the southern wall of the valley to the west of the town. It visits the quaint scattered hamlet of **Zaun**, goes to the terrace of **Wirzenalp** (1246m) and the secluded tarn of **Hinterburgseeli** (1514m) and on to **Axalp** (1535m) where the postbus can be taken down to Brienz. This walk, graded 3 on account of its length and height gain, will take about 5hrs to complete.

- A less strenuous walk, keeping in the bed of the valley throughout, goes to **Brienz** by way of **Unterheid** and **Unterbach**. This Grade 1 outing will take about 3½hrs.

- On the Hasliberg terrace there are no end of walks to be made with tremendous panoramic views. Try the *Panoramaweg* that leads in 3hrs from **Reuti** to the **Brünig Pass** by way of **Wasserwendi**. Higher still, the so-called *Murmeliweg* between **Käserstatt** and **Mägisalp** (1hr), and the Giebelweg which goes from **Käserstatt** to **Giebel** and steeply down to **Lungern** on the edge of the Lungernsee on the far side of the Brünig Pass. This last is a route of about 3½hrs. And, of course, there are others; study the map for ideas.

- As for the Reichenbachtal (the valley which leads to Rosenlaui and on to the Grosse Scheidegg), there are plenty of options here too. One fine loop trip goes to the **Kaltenbrunnen Alp** and up to **Oberer Stafel**, then on a little further to a famed moorland region on the northern slopes of Tschingel. Return once more to the huts of **Oberer Stafel** where you veer left to **Seilialp** (1465m) to find the trail leading back down to Kaltenbrunnen once more. This Grade 3 circuit will take about 4hrs, with a height gain of something like 600m.

LÜTSCHENTAL

Grindelwald's valley is probably the busiest in the Bernese Alps. Opening at its head to a great bowl of pastureland dotted with chalets, rimmed with evergreen forest and blocked in the south by an impressive wall of mountains, it is no wonder that tourists of every persuasion flock here. The Wetterhorn forms a multi-turreted cornerstone. The sharply pointed Schreckhorn and delicate stiletto of the Finsteraarhorn stand back above their glaciers. The Fiescherwand dominates a glacial basin just behind Grindelwald, but offers to the village little more than a hint of its beauty. But the Eiger, which is one of the main attractions, is much more brazen, standing bold and defiant above the meadows of Alpiglen. Leaving Grindelwald by any one of its numerous trails will gently unfold the landscape and lead the walker to scenes of startling grandeur. Here is mountain walking at its very best.

ACCESS AND INFORMATION

Location	Southeast of Interlaken. Headed by Grindelwald's mountain-girt basin, the valley flows roughly west and north to the Brienzer See .
Maps	LS 254T *Interlaken* at 1:50,000
	Kümmerly & Frey *Jungfrau-Region Oberhasli* at 1:60,000
	A 1:25,000 scale wanderkarte, *Grindelwald* is available from Grindelwald tourist office
Bases	Wilderswil (584m), Grindelwald (1034m)
Information	Wilderswil Tourismus, CH–3812 Wilderswil (☎ 033 822 84 55 **mail@wilderswil.ch www.wilderswil.ch**) Grindelwald Tourismus, Postfach 124, CH–3818 Grindelwald (☎ 033 854 12 12 **touristcenter@ grindelwald.ch www.grindelwald.com**)
Access	By train via Interlaken Ost. By road head south from Interlaken, drive through Wilderswil then branch left when the road forks at Zweilütschinen.

South of Interlaken the first village of note is Wilderswil which occupies the open 'gateway' to the steep-walled valley of the Lütschine. Here the abrupt

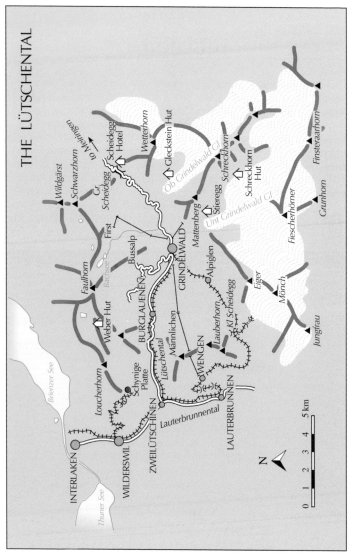

mountain slopes are dark with forest, but from certain angles and in certain lights a flash of snowpeak or hanging glacier can be seen far ahead, apparently floating among the clouds.

Continue along the true left bank of the river into the narrowing confines of the valley. Then, at the hamlet of Zweilütschinen, the valley, road and railway all fork at the confluence of two streams: the Weisse Lütschine coming from the south, the Schwarze Lütschine from the east. The valley of the Weisse (or White) Lütschine is better known as the Lauterbrunnental, the Schwarze (or Black) Lütschine is the Lütschental with Grindelwald at its head.

The Lütschental is a lovely green vale that saves its best till last. Daily through summer and winter alike, cars, coaches and crowded trains wind up the valley in a centuries-old pilgrimage that shows no sign of abating. Grindelwald, of course, is the Mecca, for its peaks, pastures and glaciers create an almost idyllic setting for one of the major resorts of the Alps.

From Grindelwald you look through a glacier gorge to the soaring face of the Fiescherwand

As you draw near so the Wetterhorn comes first into view, immediately recognisable with its turreted summits appearing somewhat like a crown. The valley steepens, then opens out as a huge pastoral basin liberally spattered with chalets and haybarns, strung about with cableways and blocked at its head not only by the Wetterhorn, but by the blank-faced Mättenberg which stubs the northern end of the Schreckhorn's ridge, and by the dark brooding walls of the Eiger to the right. Between the Eiger and Mättenberg is the gorge cut by the Unterer Grindelwaldgletscher; between the Mättenberg and Wetterhorn the blue-green motionless cascade of the Oberer Grindelwaldgletscher holds a touch of winter all year through.

These three mountain walls, interspersed with glaciers, are impressive enough in themselves, yet the finest peaks of all in the vicinity may only be seen properly by those prepared to foresake the village streets and immediate pastures of the valley. By going up to Bussalp, Bachsee or onto the easily-gained Faulhorn, one of the most beautiful mountain vistas to be had anywhere in Europe is laid out in a panorama of almost unbelievable loveliness. The Schreckhorn, Finsteraarhorn and Fiescherhorn habitually hide themselves behind Grindelwald's immediate backdrop, but from any one of these walkers' view-points they appear as sharks' teeth of stone and ice, delicate fins that project from snowfields, walls that shine with glacial armoury, ridges that lace one summit to another. All this on the horizon with a foreground of deep rich greenery. With wild flowers and cowbells near to hand, and glaciers draped down the mountains ahead, it is in such contrasts that the very essence of the Alps is revealed.

Visitors were first drawn to the head of the Lütschental as long ago as the early 18th century. Then it was the glaciers that served as the lure, drawing among others, William Burnet in 1708, Sir Horace Mann in 1723 – who wrote that an exorcist had been employed to halt the advance of the glaciers that were threatening Grindelwald – Thomas Pennant in 1765, William Coxe and Goethe who walked on the ice in 1779. These were but a handful of a steadily growing stream of visitors, and a hundred years later there was even a colony of English here.

In the early 19th century mountaineers became attracted by the peaks themselves. The Finsteraarhorn's lofty summit was first reached in 1829, the Wetterhorn in 1844, the Eiger in 1858 and Schreckhorn three years later. When Alfred Wills climbed the Wetterhorn during his honeymoon in 1854 he did so unaware at the time that it had already received its first ascent, and the oft-told account of his climb which appeared in *Wanderings Among the High Alps*, effectively marked the start of the Golden Age of Mountaineering.

More recently, of course, public attention has focussed in grim fascination – inspired no doubt by a certain amount of media myopia – on the Eiger's Nordwand, probably the single major alpine face known to non-mountaineers. Its history has been highlighted by presumed nationalism and public tragedy, yet there have been some magnificent climbing achievements played out upon it. The Eiger is, though, just one piece of the jigsaw; one ornament in the backdrop to some of the best walking to be found anywhere in the Bernese Alps.

MAIN BASES

WILDERSWIL (584m) is a busy place in summer, and not only with those staying in the village, for its railway station is the main valley terminus of the Schynige Platte funicular, as well as being one of those that serves the Lauterbrunnen–Wengen–Jungfraujoch–Grindelwald rail system. The village has some interesting features, including a 17th-century church (re-built in 1673 using the materials of a much older place of worship) standing across the river and reached by a covered bridge. A short distance away stands the ruin of a 16th-century castle, setting for Byron's *Manfred*, and within the village itself there are a few attractive old houses. For accommodation Wilderswil has 15 hotels and *pensions* (1–3 star rated), more than 600 beds in holiday apartments, and a camp-site with superb facilities. One of the benefits of using Wilderswil as a base is its ease of access to so many other areas – both in and on the edge of the mountains. Another is its climate which is somewhat less prone to the storms that are attracted to north-facing mountains upvalley.

GRINDELWALD (1034m) needs little introduction. Used as a mountaineering base for over 150 years, it is now an all-year-round resort as well known for its skiing as for its summer attractions. There are several cableways of use to walkers. These include gondolas to First and Männlichen, and the short cablecar leading to Pfingstegg. There's the rack-and-pinion railway to Kleine Scheidegg, Grindelwald Bus to Grosse Scheidegg and Bussalp, and Europe's highest railway (albeit a very expensive one) which goes to the 3454m Jungfraujoch for an unforgettable view worth sampling on an off-day from walking. The village is layered on a steep hill-side. It has one main street with shops of every kind; there are banks, PTT, restaurants and a large and helpful tourist information office. There is also a mountain guides' bureau which, in addition to providing private guiding services, also arranges climbing and ski-touring tours (*Bergsteigerzentrum* ☎ 033 854 12 80 **www.gomountain.ch**). There are numerous sports facilities, including a swimming pool, tennis courts etc. Accommodation is available in all degrees of comfort. With around 50 hotels (ungraded up to five-star), a number of which also have dormitory places; about 7000 beds in apartments and chalets; a youth hostel on the Terrassenweg (☎ 033 853 50 29 **grindelwald@youthhostel.ch**), a Naturfreundehaus also on the Terrassenweg (☎ 033 853 13 33) and no less than five campsites, Grindelwald can meet most accommodation needs.

OTHER BASES

Away from the valley proper several mountain inns (berghotels) and restaurants provide accommodation in more peaceful surroundings. The following is a selection. Above Wilderswil, and reached by funicular, **SCHYNIGE PLATTE KULM** enjoys a stunning panoramic view at about 2000m (☎ 033 822 34 31 **hotel@schynigeplatte.ch www.schynigeplatte.ch**). With 36 beds and simple dormitory accommodation nearby, it is located at the start of one of the district's finest walks – see Route 9. That walk visits the Faulhorn, on which stands Switzerland's oldest mountain hotel, **BERGHOTEL FAULHORN** (2681m). It has 16 beds and 80 dormitory places (☎ 033 853 27 13 **www.berghotel-faul-horn.ch**). At the First gondola station (2186m) 90 dormitory places are available in **BERGGASTHAUS FIRST** (☎ 033 853 12 84 **berghausfirst@grindelwald.ch www.berghausfirst.ch**).

Below and southwest of First, the **WALDSPITZ** restaurant has 35 dormitory places (☎ 033 853 18 61), while the midway gondola station of Bort (1570m) can accommodate 70 people in beds and dormitories at **BERGHAUS BORT** (☎ 033 853 36 51 **info@berghaus-bort.ch www.berghaus-bort.ch**).

BERGHOTEL GROSSE SCHEIDEGG, as its name implies, is set upon the Grosse Scheidegg saddle between the Reichenbachtal and Lütschental, and has both bedrooms and dormitories (☎ 033 853 67 16 **grossescheidegg@bluewin.ch www.grossescheidegg.ch.vu**). Midway between Grosse Scheidegg and Grindelwald, **HOTEL WETTERHORN** has 15 beds and dormitory accommodation for 30 (☎ 033 853 12 18 **wetterhorn@grindelwald.ch www.hotel-wetterhorn.ch**).

Set on a shrinking meadow within the glacial basin of the Unterer Grindelwaldgletscher, **STIEREGG** (1650m) has 18 dormitory places (☎ 033 853 43 14 hr. **burgener@freesurf.ch www.stieregg.ch**) and a magical outlook. **BERGHAUS DES ALPES, ALPIGLEN** also has a magical outlook from its position directly below the Eiger. There are 12 beds in the main building, and 40 dormitory places in an annexe (☎ 033 853 11 30 **mail@alpiglen.ch www.alpiglen.ch**). By the entrance to the Jungfraujoch railway tunnel, **GASTHAUS EIGERGLETSCHER** has dormitory accommodation (☎ 033 855 22 91). Below it, **KLEINE SCHEIDEGG** has several hotels with a total of 96 beds (☎ 033 855 12 12 **www.scheidegg-hotels.ch**), and the nearby **GRINDEL-WALDBLICK** on the path to Männlichen, has 90 dormitory places and a direct view of the Eiger, Mönch and Jungfrau (☎ 033 855 13 74 **grindelwaldblick@grindelwald.ch www.grindelwaldblick.ch**). Farther along the path beyond the Grindelwaldblick, **BERGGASTHAUS MÄNNLICHEN** has 28 beds and is easily reached by gondola from Grindelwald (☎ 033 853 10 68 **berggasthaus@maennlichen.ch www.maennlichen.ch**).

Grindelwald, backed by the Wetterhorn

MOUNTAIN HUTS

GLECKSTEIN HUT (2317m) Base for climbs on the Wetterhorn, but also a challenging destination for walkers, this hut may be reached in about 3½hrs from Hotel Wetterhorn. Owned by the Burgdorf Section of the SAC it has 100 places, and a resident guardian from July to the end of September, and is partly wardened in June and October. Meals are provided (☎ 033 853 11 40 **info@gleckstein.ch www.gleckstein.ch**).

SCHRECKHORN HUT (2520m) Standing at the base of the Schreckhorn, and overlooking the Obers Eismeer glacier, this remote hut has places for 90. There is a resident guardian from late June to the end of September, when meals may be provided. It is owned by the Basle Section of the SAC (☎ 033 855 10 25), and reached by a crumbling path from Stieregg (4½hrs from the Pfingstegg cablecar).

The Wetterhorn dominates the head of the Lütschental

WEBER HUT (2344m) This small, privately-owned hut is set in a minor saddle on the classic Schynige Platte to Faulhorn path. Known also as the Männdlenen-Weber Hut (or Berghütte Männdlenen) it is manned from late June to mid-October with a full meals service, and can sleep 30 in its dormitories (☎ 033 853 44 64).

ROUTE 9

Schynige Platte (1987m) –
Faulhorn (2681m) –
Faulhorn (2681m) – First (2167m)

Grade	3
Distance	15km
Height gain	694m
Height loss	514m
Time	5–6hrs
Location	Southeast of Wilderswil

No book of walks in the Bernese Alps would be complete without this one. It is, quite simply, one of the classic walks of the Alps, and it doesn't matter how often you walk it, nor how many others have done so before you, it is always worth tackling. Its main feature is the constantly changing panorama, for it begins with one of the Alps' finest views, with Eiger, Mönch, Jungfrau and Lauterbrunnen Breithorn, then changes to a steep overview of the Brienzer See and the northern hills; changes again to one of an intimate little glen, and then grows in glory with the Wetterhorn, Schreckhorn, Finsteraarhorn and Fiescherhorn shimmering in the clear waters of the Bachsee.

But if the views keep changing, so too does the very nature of this high route. Variety is of the essence. But do choose a day with the weather full of promise, for there are long sections away from shelter. In any case, you will want good visibility and sunshine to bring out the full glory of the landscape. (**Note:** In July and August guided moonlight tours are arranged along this path, aiming to capture sunrise from the Faulhorn and having breakfast at the First restaurant. Enquire at the tourist office in Wilderswil for details.)

On the classic walk from Schynige Platte to First,
a ridge path gives direct views onto the Brienzersee

The funicular was built in 1893 to enable visitors to admire the breathtaking views. Above the Schynige Platte station there's a well-known alpine garden with somewhere in the region of 500 different plant species – worth a visit (fee payable). There's also a hotel; see details above under Other Bases.

Take the funicular from Wilderswil to Schynige Platte. It's a slow but entertaining ride. ◄

To begin the walk, descend from the station platform where a sign directs you onto the path to the Faulhorn. Shortly after, it forks. Both options will do, but the preferred route bears left for the Panoramaweg, passes below the alpine garden, and forks once more. Take the right branch across a bowl of pasture towards the Oberberghorn, skirt below it and join the alternative lower path from Schynige Platte. Keep ahead and you will shortly come onto a grass-covered crest that plunges steeply on its northern side. The path is quite safe, but the views down to the Brienzer See are dramatic, while gazing westwards Interlaken is seen far below with the Thunersee shimmering beyond it.

Follow the crest northeastward, descend a steel ladder, and at a path junction go up a slope to the base of the Laucherhorn. The way angles below this mountain to cross a ridge spur, then makes a traverse of a steep slope to gain a narrow pass at 2025m. Now cross a desolate hidden region of rocks, limestone ribs and cliffs to another minor col between the Laucherhorn and Ussri

THE SCHYNIGE PLATTE PANORAMAWEG

The Panoramaweg makes a worthwhile outing of about 2½hrs for those who balk at the long walk to First. Start by walking up the track from the station to the Schynige Platte Kulm hotel. The Panoramaweg path continues from here to zig-zag up to the vantage point of Tuba (2076m). The way then goes along the crest towards the Oberberghorn and is joined by the main walk almost as far as the Laucherhorn, before returning to Schynige Platte through the Oberberg pastures.

Sägissa. This takes you into the moorland-like Sägistal with a small tarn at the far end of the valley.

Grazed by sheep, this little glen is almost entirely circled by ridges, and the path keeps along the slopes of the right-hand wall. Much of the way goes along a series of limestone terraces, then veers right, rising gently across more bare ribs before coming to the narrow cleft of the Männdlenen saddle in which is found the tiny **Weber Hut** (2344m *accommodation, refreshments*) at a junction of paths. This is gained about 2½–3hrs from Schynige Platte. (The right-hand path here makes a long descent to Burglauenen in the valley.)

The continuing route climbs steeply beyond the hut, then eases along a natural terrace below the Winteregg ridge with the Faulhorn rising ahead. Coming onto the ridge, new views open again to the Eiger, Mönch and Jungfrau; yet another splendid vantage point from which to study these lovely mountains. Soon the path offers a choice. Either continue directly up to the Faulhorn summit, or break away on the right-hand path which makes a traverse across the face of the mountain.

Views from the top of the 2681m Faulhorn are certainly worth the extra effort involved in reaching it. There is also the prospect of refreshment at **Berghotel Faulhorn** (*accommodation, refreshments*) just a few metres below the summit.

From the summit, or the lower option, you then descend to an obvious saddle (Gassenboden; 2553m) and bear left, winding down among rocks and over more rough grass slopes to reach the **Bachsee** with its stunning panorama of big mountains and glaciers. The path skirts the left shoreline of this delightful lake with views drawing you on, and then continues down to the gondola lift station of **First** *(accommodation, refreshments)*. Take the gondola down to Grindelwald.

ROUTE 10

Saxeten (1103m) – Wilderswil (584m)

Grade	1–2
Distance	5km
Height loss	519m
Time	1hr 15mins
Location	Southwest of Wilderswil

Draining down to Wilderswil, the Saxettal is reached by a winding road served by an infrequent postbus. Wooded in its lower reaches, and distinctly pastoral higher up, the valley is largely hidden from view from below. Scooped out by a long-vanished glacier, it is blocked by an amphitheatre formed by the converging ridges of the Lobhörner, Schwalmere and Morgenberghorn. It has just one village; Saxeten is a modestly pretty place in a sheltered position set among pastures midway through the valley, with walking routes leading up to and across the high encircling ridges. This route makes a pleasant morning's walk, giving a brief glimpse of the valley after taking the postbus to Saxeten. Saxeten has one hotel, the Alpenrose (☎ 033 822 1834 **alpenrose@saxeten. net**), a restaurant, and post office.

At the T-junction in the centre of Saxeten a sign gives 1hr 15mins for the walk to Wilderswil. Pass alongside Hotel Alpenrose and continue on the road until it ends. A track then takes you between pastures from which you can catch a glimpse of the Brienzer See ahead. After passing a couple of barns, leave the track and fork right to slope down through the pastures to a single barn where the path enters the Sytiwald forest. Descend in zig-zags, and after passing a few barns within the forest, cross the Saxetbach on a wooden bridge. The path is more substantial on the right bank of the river, and soon becomes a forest track.

Making progress down the right bank all the way to Wilderswil, you occasionally come onto the road, then revert to footpath or track. At one of the road entries you cross through a small memorial park that recalls 21 young people who lost their lives nearby in a canyoning tragedy in 1999.

A brief section of path continues from here, then returns you to the road once more. Just after passing the **Wilderswil** sign, turn left to cross the river by a covered bridge, on the far side of which stands the village museum (note the water wheel). Signs now lead the way through quiet side streets to the railway station.

Other routes from Wilderswil and Saxeten

Although the Wilderswil district lies on the outer edge of the mountains, it would be worth remembering some walks possibilities for those days when, perhaps, the weather is not conducive to tackling high routes. However, there are also some enticing prospects for more challenging walks too.

*   Mention should be made of a short riverside walk alongside the Lütschine leading from Wilderswil to **Bönigen** on the southern shore of the Brienzer See; an undemanding Grade 1 that could be extended by continuing along the lake shore.
*   Another riverside walk from Wilderswil heads upvalley on the true right bank (east side) of the Lütschine to Gsteigwiler, continues to Zweilütschinen and through the confines of the Weisse Lütschine to **Lauterbrunnen**. This is a 2½hr walk, Grade 1.
*   There's a short (1½hr) ascent from Wilderswil to the 1135m viewpoint of **Abendberg** (or Aabeberg)

situated on the spur of mountain almost due west of the village at the end of the long Darliggrat ridge. This is mostly a woodland walk on a good path (Grade 2), with views along the lakes of Thun and Brienz.

- A more challenging proposition is the path that begins on the east side of Wilderswil station and climbs all the way to **Schynige Platte** – a Grade 2–3 walk of 4–4½hrs.
- As for trails from Saxeten, one fairly demanding route begins by heading up the road out of the village for a short distance, then breaks off to climb through forest and pasture towards the **Rengglipass** at 1879m. From the pass another trail strikes roughly northward to the 2249m summit of the **Morgenberghorn**; an easy mountain with a wonderful summit panorama. (Grade 3; about 5–6hrs for the round-trip.)
- Another long route crosses the Rengglipass, descends steeply to the Latrejebach's valley (the Suldtal) and follows the stream downvalley to the delightful village of **Aeschi**, more than 1000m lower than the pass. Reached in 6–6½hrs from Saxeten, Aeschi overlooks the Thunersee and has an infrequent bus link with Spiez. From there it's possible to return to Wilderswil by train via Interlaken Ost.

ROUTE 11

Grindelwald (Bussalp: 1780m) –
Faulhorn (2681m)

Grade	2–3
Distance	4 km (one way)
Height gain	901m
Time	2½–3hrs
Location	Northwest of Grindelwald

As has already been noted, the Faulhorn is one of the classic vantage points above Grindelwald. It provides a highlight of the walk between Schynige Platte and First, and makes a worthwhile destination on its own count. There are three obvious ways of approaching it from Grindelwald; from Bussalp, from the upper station of the First gondola, or from Grosse Scheidegg – the last two going by way of the Bachsee lake. All three routes are described in due course. Bussalp itself is a large and pleasant bowl of pastureland reached either by footpath in 2½hrs, or by the local Grindelwald Bus from the village. It is better to take an early bus, spend time enjoying the views, and then make an unhurried descent to the valley via Bachsee and the First gondola lift.

The bus journey terminates at Bussalp Mittelläger where there is a restaurant. At once there are views to enjoy towards the Eiger, Mönch and Jungfrau, and the long Männlichen ridge marking the valley's limits to the south. Walk up the continuing road to Oberläger (2020m) where the Faulhorn path begins its climb over pastures and rough slopes ahead. There is no difficulty following the route, although it is a little rough under foot in places,

Below the Faulhorn the Gassenboden saddle focuses attention on the Wetterhorn (Routes 9, 11, 12, 13)

and as you gain height so the eastward panorama unfolds to reveal the Finsteraarhorn and Schreckhorn complementing one another amid a sea of jutting peaks.

In a little under 2hrs from Mittelläger you come onto a bare saddle (**Gassenboden**; 2553m) below and to the southeast of the Faulhorn. Here you bear left and follow a well-trodden path that winds up to the summit of the mountain, steepening in its final pull, in about 20 minutes. The simple Berghotel (*accommodation, refreshments*) is tucked just below the **Faulhorn** summit. From the top you gaze steeply north and west to the Brienzer See and off to the Thunersee. But south and east there is a tremendous vista of snow-capped peaks of immense charm, making the ascent well worthwhile.

NOTE

To descend, retrace your steps to the Gassenboden saddle, then bear left to follow a clear path down to the Bachsee, and beyond that to the upper station of the First gondola in 1hr from the summit.

ROUTE 12

Grindelwald (First; 2167m) – Faulhorn (2681m) – Bussalp (1780m) – Grindelwald (1034m)

Grade	3
Distance	15km
Height gain	514m
Height loss	1647m
Time	5½hrs
Location	Northeast of Grindelwald

This, the second Faulhorn route from Grindelwald, is probably taken by most walkers, the First gondola reducing much of the effort of height gain. The valley station for this cableway is found just off the main street towards the eastern end of the village, midway between the railway station and the church. It is, of course, well signed. The gondola rises in several stages, although you do not have to change, and throughout there are wonderful views of the big mountains to the south. Once you leave the gondola at First, however, you turn away from those views, so it's necessary to keep stopping on the path to enjoy the mountains behind you.

On arrival at the upper station, a signpost directs you onto the broad Bachsee path which needs no description. From a viewpoint above the gondola station, you can see a waterfall pouring from the Milibach pasture whose stream drains the Bachsee lakes. A colony of marmots inhabits the rough hillocks and hollows near the path and you stand a good chance of seeing some of these creatures as you wander along.

In 45mins you arrive at the **Bachsee**, and continue along the shoreline path to the far end to gain one of the classic views of the Bernese Alps, with reflections of the Wetterhorn, Schreckhorn and Finsteraarhorn dancing in the

With Schreckhorn (left) and Finsteraarhorn mirrored in its waters, the Bachsee is one of the most beautiful lakes in the Alps

water. No matter how many postcards you may have seen of this view in Grindelwald, the reality is breathtaking.

Beyond the lake the path begins its ascent of the grass slope that leads to the saddle of Gassenboden (2553m), gained in about 1½hrs from First. Just below it there's a small shelter. Bear right and follow the clear path up to the **Faulhorn** summit (*accommodation, refreshments*).

When you can tear yourself away, retrace your steps to the saddle, and then branch right on a path that takes you down to **Bussalp**. First to the alp huts of Oberläger, then either on a farm road to Mittelläger (*refreshments*), or break away from this onto a steep and narrow path that drops over pastures in a short-cut to reach the road below the Mittelläger restaurant. If you decide to return to Grindelwald by bus, wait at the restaurant. If, however, you prefer to walk all the way (a little under 2hrs from here), wander along the road for a few paces, then cut off to the right on a continuing path that crosses pastures and streams and comes to a track. There are several choices of route between here and Grindelwald, each of which is adequately signed and waymarked, leading through patches of forest with views between the trees to the Männlichen ridge opposite, and chalets speckling the hillsides below. It's a fine walk.

ROUTE 13

Grindelwald (Grosse Scheidegg; 1962m) – Bachsee (2265m) – Faulhorn (2681m)

Grade	2–3
Distance	10km (one way)
Height gain	719m
Time	3½ hrs
Location	Northeast of Grindelwald

The very fine contouring path from Grosse Scheidegg to First at the start of this walk, is known locally as the *Höhenweg 2400*. It provides a constantly-evolving panorama which is more than simply a prelude to the day's sights. Take an early bus to Grosse Scheidegg then enjoy every step, but only take this walk if there's a settled weather forecast.

At Grosse Scheidegg turn your back to the Wetterhorn and follow a clear track heading northwards along the broad ridge dividing Grindelwald's valley from that of the Reichenbachtal. On reaching a junction of tracks at a

Viewed from the 'Höhenweg 2400' path, the Schreckhorn shows its graceful ice-tapered summit

small hut (Kuhmattenschärm), ignore that which veers left and take the footpath above it. This is the *Höhenweg 2400*. It curves left, crosses a stream and later passes above the alp buildings of Grindel Oberläger, to which it is linked by another path. All the while the Oberland wall of mountains off to the left teases with new peaks that gradually appear one by one, until a magnificent panorama spreads as far as the eye can see. Keep on the *Höhenweg 2400* path which leads directly to the **First** gondola station (refreshments) in about 1½hrs from Grosse Scheidegg. Now follow directions as for Route 12 up to the Bachsee and on to the **Faulhorn**.

ROUTE 14

Grindelwald (First; 2167m) –
Bachsee (2265m)

Grade	1
Distance	3km (one way)
Height gain	98m
Time	45mins
Location	Northeast of Grindelwald

This route is included in an effort to remind casual holidaymakers that it is not essential to dedicate several hours to an energetic walk in order to capture some of the most magical views. By riding the First gondola and then following the broad and easy path to the **Bachsee** (mentioned in Route 12), a superb morning can be spent without getting out of breath. Take a picnic lunch and laze by the lake with the long views. As for an alternative return to Grindelwald, consider reversing the *Höhenweg 2400* path to the **Grosse Scheidegg** from First (1¼hrs), as described in Route 13. From Grosse Scheidegg you can take the bus down to Grindelwald.

ROUTE 15

Grindelwald (First; 2167m) –
Uf Spitzen (2390m) – Bussalp (1792m)

Grade	3
Distance	9km
Height gain	223m
Height loss	598m
Time	3hrs
Location	Northeast of Grindelwald

Between the hanging valley in which the Bachsee is found, and that of Bussalp, a ridge crest extends southeastward from the Faulhorn. It has no great peaks projecting from it, but bearing in mind the beauty of the views from both Bachsee and Bussalp, it will be evident that from this crest there will be an even more extensive panorama to enjoy. This walk, sometimes known as the Höhenweg 2200, links the two hanging valleys by crossing that ridge.

From the upper station of the First gondola lift walk along the path to the **Bachsee**, but instead of continuing along the right-hand shore, break away to the left on the footpath crossing between the two lakes. The path bears left and forks soon after. The path which goes straight ahead descends into the grasslands split by the Milibach stream, while ours (the main, right-hand trail) begins to rise up the hillside. In a little over ½hr from the lake you will come onto the crest where the path forks again. (Superb views.)

Take the right-hand branch over the top of **Uf Spitzen**, then begin the descent, heading west. Above the alp huts of Feld you come to yet another trail junction. Take the right-hand path to make a steady hillside traverse, coming down at last to Oberläger, the upper

Bussalp Oberläger looks across rolling pastures to the Eiger

section of **Bussalp.** Now follow the track down to Mittelläger where there's a restaurant (*refreshments*), and the possibility of catching the bus back to Grindelwald. (Should you choose to walk all the way, follow directions at the end of Route 12; an undemanding walk with several options – allow about 2hrs.)

ROUTE 16

Grindelwald (First; 2167m) –
Waldspitz (1918m) – Bussalp (1792m)

Grade	2
Distance	9km
Height gain	250m
Height loss	375m
Time	3hrs 15mins
Location	Northeast of Grindelwald

Known as the *Höhenweg 2000*, this walk makes an undulating contour of the sunny lower slopes of the crest running south from the Faulhorn. It is, in fact, a more modest version of Route 15, but with magnificent views practically every step of the way.

From the First gondola station take the Bachsee path uphill, but branch left after about 2mins, where a way-marked path makes a steep zig-zag descent (some well-made steps), then crosses pastures to the alp of **Bachläger** (1980m). Note the fine waterfall on the right, which drains the Bachsee lakes. Over a stream the way becomes a track that contours across the hillside as far as **Waldspitz** (accommodation, refreshments); about 40mins from First.

Easily reached from First, the Bachläger alp is watered by a cascade draining from the Bachsee

The way continues, but instead of following the broad track down to Grindelwald, about 6mins after leaving Waldspitz take a footpath on the right which rises among shrubs of juniper and alpenrose. Going through a tree-fringed hollow the path curves right to a junction. Bear right, and ignoring other path options descend slightly, then go up towards some alp buildings. Just before reaching these the path swings sharply to the right and climbs in sweeping curves to the upper alp huts of **Spillmatten** (1863m).

Though narrow, the path above the huts is way-marked as it ascends above the treeline and crosses a hillside littered with rocks and boulders. Gaining a high point go through a gate (wonderful views from here) and make a traverse of hillside ahead, then rise again to turn a grassy spur. On coming to a major path junction at 2200m, continue ahead and slope down to a ridge spur and another junction overlooking alp Feld. Bear right, cross the pastures, go over a stream in a gully, then down through more pastures to yet another junction. Take the left-hand option which descends to **Bussalp Mittelläger** (*refreshments*), for the bus to Grindelwald.

ROUTE 17

*Grindelwald (First; 2167m) –
Hagelsee (2339m) – Wildgärst (2890m) –
Grosse Chrinne (2635m) – First*

Grade	3
Distance	17km
Height gain	723m
Height loss	723m
Time	5½–6hrs
Location	Northeast of Grindelwald

A long and fairly demanding walk, this route explores a wild and seemingly remote patch of country. It goes behind the ridge running roughly eastward from the Bachsee where a couple of tarns are found. There are screes and bleak rock-scapes, but pastures too, and long vistas of magical alpine peaks. There are no opportunities for refreshment, nor for shelter in case of bad weather. In inclement weather with poor visibility there could be difficulties with route finding. Choose a good day, take a packed lunch and a drink, and enjoy the rich and varied terrain along the way.

From the First gondola station take the Bachsee path for about 30mins until at a junction of trails a sign directs you onto a right-forking path to Hagelsee and Wildgärst. (The sign also gives directions to Axalp and Brienz for another long walk.) Wander up the slope to pass a small pool (Standseeli) and come to a modest saddle. The way now descends among boulders round the northern end of the Ritzengratli at about 2400m, and swings eastward behind the low rocky ridge into the Hinterberg hanging valley.

Here the **Hagelsee** is often partly covered with ice and snow even in the early summer, and is passed along its northern shore. Continue in the same direction, the route rising and falling among rocks and scree to reach the second tarn, Häxenseeli. Red-white *Bergweg* waymarks

Caught in a hidden valley below the Wildgärst, the little Hagelsee lies in an untamed landscape

lead you on, rising to the saddle of Wart (2706m) between the Schwarzhorn to the right, and Wildgärst to the left. Ahead the mountains curve in an arc, with the Reichenbachtal spreading away to the Haslital.

NOTE

For an alternative return from the saddle of Wart, cross over and go down the left-hand side of the Blaugletscher, a small remnant of glacier with no need for roped precautions. The descent is steep, however, and continues below the glacier veering southeastward to cross snow patches, scree and rough grass slopes. The path heads down the left-hand side of the Geissbach stream and comes upon a crossing farm track. Follow this to the right, heading southwest now and soon coming to the alp huts of Oberläger (1941m). Beyond this you come to another broad track (a farm road) which leads to Grosse Scheidegg where you can catch a bus for Grindelwald.

Bear left and wander up to the 2890m summit of the **Wildgärst** (reached in about 3½hrs from First) where three ridges converge. Fine panoramas extend in all directions; a contrast of lake and snowpeak, of meadow and glacier, forest and rock wall.

Return to the saddle and down along the route towards Häxenseeli, but halfway to the tarn look for waymarks breaking left (southeast) and follow these up to the little pass of **Grosse Chrinne**. The ridge is very narrow – note the *via ferrata* ladders fixed to the ridge on the left to facilitate a route on the Schwarzhorn. Do not attempt to descend directly on the south side, but bear right on the ridge for a few paces, then follow blue-white waymarks down. The way is steep, but a series of fixed chains safeguard the initial descent until a path leads down, eventually reaching pastures and the head of the Chrinnenboden ski-lift. Continue down to the main path, then bear right to First.

Other routes from First
The First gondola gives access to a wonderland of trails, a number of which have already been described. There are

many more possibilities, a few of which are briefly outlined below.

- The ascent of the 2928m **Schwarzhorn** on the watershed ridge northwest of Grosse Scheidegg makes a popular Grade 3 outing (4½–5hrs there and back) via the Chrinnenboden pastures. **Note:** there's also a *via ferrata* route on the Schwarzhorn, accessed from the Grosse Chrinne (see Route 17), but this should only be attempted by experienced scramblers.

- Promoted locally as the Marmot Valley Trail (*Murmeltiertal-weg*), a devious walk leading to **Grosse Scheidegg** also heads through the Chrinnenboden pastures towards the Schwarzhorn, but then breaks away behind the impressive block of Schilt to descend a little hanging valley to meet the *Höhenweg 2400* trail above Oberläger. It then cuts round to Grosse Scheidegg (1½–2hrs).

- A 2–2½hr walk takes the path from First to the **Bachsee**, then descends below the two lakes to the Bachlager alp, takes the track round to the **Waldspitz** restaurant, then descends to **Bort** for the gondola descent to Grindelwald.

ROUTE 18

Grindelwald (Hotel Wetterhorn; 1228m) – Gleckstein Hut (2317m)

Grade	3
Distance	5km (one way)
Height gain	1089m
Time	3½–4hrs
Location	East of Grindelwald

Base for climbs on the Wetterhorn and Schreckhorn, the Gleckstein Hut is situated in a very dramatic position high above the Oberer Grindelwaldgletscher on the slopes of the Wetterhorn. The approach to it is steep and somewhat arduous, and should not be tackled by inexperienced walkers. Whilst it's perfectly feasible to walk all the way from Grindelwald, most hut visitors take the bus (or drive) as far as Hotel Wetterhorn on the way to Grosse Scheidegg. This is as far as private vehicles are allowed to go, and there's a large parking area opposite the hotel.

Note: An alternative start to the Gleckstein Hut approach can be made by taking the Grosse Scheidegg bus as far as Loichbiel (Unter Lauchbühl). A signed path begins at the hairpin bend, with a time given of 2hrs 40mins. This path is joined by the trail from Hotel Wetterhorn at Pt. 1590m

From Hotel Wetterhorn (*accommodation, refreshments*) walk along the road towards Grosse Scheidegg, but at the first sharp left-hand bend leave it for a signed path that cuts off ahead. Crossing a stream it swings to the right with the Wetterhorn looming directly ahead, crosses a second stream and continues to rise up the Ischboden pastures to meet another path at 1590m. ◀

Turn right to angle southwestward up a series of limestone terraces (the Ischpfad), with occasional handrails for safety. Turning sharply to the south round a corner at Engi (1670m) the angle eases above the east side of a gorge, then steepens again high above the glacier. Steep zig-zags lead up through rocky bluffs, and on to scant pastures at 2151m. The final approach, turning first northeast then northwest, continues at a fairly steep angle, but by comparison with the earlier path is easy-going. The **Gleckstein Hut** is found on a grassy shelf

The **Gleckstein Hut** has a wonderful outlook. To the northeast the crags of the Wetterhorn rise in a confusion of rock and snow, while to the southeast the Schreckhorn appears above a turmoil of ice. Owned by the Burgdorf Section of the SAC it can accommodate 16 in four-bedded rooms, and 80 in dormitories. There is a resident guardian from the end of June to the end of September, when meals are available. For reservations ☎ 033 853 11 40 **info@gleckstein.ch www.gleckstein.ch**. From the hut there are marked routes southeast to Beesibärgli for an intimate view of the glaciers (2hrs); and north for the ascent of the 2737m Chrinnenhorn in 1½hrs.

overlooking the Oberer Grindelwald glacier. Ibex can often be seen in the vicinity.

ROUTE 19

Grindelwald (Hotel Wetterhorn; 1228m) – Milchbach (1348m) – Pfingstegg (1392m)

Grade	1–2
Distance	3km (one way)
Height gain	164m
Time	1hr 20mins
Location	Northeast of Grindelwald

The Grindelwald-Pfingstegg cableway gives a 7min ride to a choice of balcony trails on the flanks of the Mättenberg. The most popular of these cuts above a gorge carved by the Oberer Grindelwaldgletscher and eventually comes to Stieregg in a huge glacial amphitheatre. This is described as Route 20. The other high trail heads northeastward to the glacier gorge of the Unterer Grindelwaldgletscher. Whilst this last-mentioned gently descending path makes an easy walk, it is offered here in reverse for those who may have been enticed to Hotel Wetterhorn by bus. It's not a demanding walk, except in the early stages of the climb through woodland to the Milchbach restaurant. But thereafter it follows an undulating course high above the valley with good views over Grindelwald.

Begin at the upper right-hand corner of the parking area opposite Hotel Wetterhorn where a broad track enters woodland, then forks in 2mins. Take the right branch, and at a second junction continue ahead to cross a glacial torrent on a bridge. On the other side turn left, and a few minutes later the track forks. Both lead to Chalet-Restaurant Milchbach; the right-hand option is the easier and more gently-inclined, while the left branch is favoured for its surprise view into the glacier gorge.

Taking the left-hand trail the way climbs to a T-junction of paths where you turn right, and climbing through woodland you'll come to a view of the ice-smooothed slabs at the entrance to the Oberer Grindel-waldgletscher's gorge. About 2mins later you reach **Chalet Milchbach** (*refreshments*). ◀

Pass in front of the restaurant and go briefly down a track, then left at a signed junction. At a four-way junction keep ahead, and when the track forks again keep ahead once more to descend on a woodland path. Once again there's a junction with the right-hand option descending to Grindelwald. Remain on the upper path and soon contour across an open stony section with clear views over Grindelwald, before passing through more fingers of woodland on the way to a series of glacial slabs which the path crosses on a natural ledge. This area is known as **Breitlouwina**, and an information board records its geological history.

The path continues across a footbridge, passes among more trees, and across a little meadow (lovely views back to the Wetterhorn). On the final approach to Pfingstegg come onto a track near the foot of a summer toboggan run (Rodelbahn). Wander up the track to the cablecar station and small restaurant of **Pfingstegg** (*refreshments*). Either ride the cablecar down to Grindelwald, or take the high path which continues from it (see Route 20) for about 10mins, then descend by an alternative path to Marmorbruch and on a minor road back to Grindelwald (about 45mins).

A popular tourist attraction, the **glacier gorge** is accessible from Hotel Wetterhorn in 15mins, followed by the ascent of 890 wooden steps to the glacier's snout and a small refreshment bar.

ROUTE 20

Grindelwald (Pfingstegg; 1392m) –
Stieregg (1650m)

Grade	1–2
Distance	2.5 km (one way)
Height gain	258m
Time	1hr
Location	South of Grindelwald

There can be few easier walks in the Alps that give such a close view of high mountains, glaciers and snowfields, than this one. It's a real gem of a walk along a path carved out of the steep mountain wall above the gorge of the Unterer Grindelwaldgletscher. Astonishing views are gained of the eastern (Mittellegi) ridge wall of the Eiger, of the icefalls and glaciers that flow from the Finsteraarhorn's arctic basin, and near-views to the huge ice-plastered face of the Fiescherhorn. Stieregg is a restaurant on a tiny oasis-like meadow in a sea of ice and snow; a sun-trap that's difficult to drag yourself away from.

With the massive Fiescherwand as a backdrop, Restaurant Stieregg nestles on a crumbling moraine-top meadow

Note: Stieregg's little meadow is on a levelling of old moraine. The effects of global warming are not only shrinking the glaciers, but the permafrost which held the moraine in place is melting, and each summer large chunks fall away. Do not stray too close to the edge.

From the upper station of the Pfingstegg cablecar bear right and follow the well-trodden path across a little meadow, then among trees. In 10mins another path breaks away to the right at the Wysseflue junction for a descent to Grindelwald. Keep ahead, rising a little more steeply with views growing of the big Fiescherwand wall at the head of the gorge. Working along the upper edge of the glacier gorge the path climbs, then contours, then climbs again. In places it's a little exposed, but there's a length of fencing and a handrail for safety. In any case the trail is broad enough to enable those tending towards vertigo to move comfortably away from the edge. Then the gorge is passed and you turn a corner to see **Restaurant Stieregg** (*accommodation, refreshments*) just ahead. ◀

Instead of riding the cablecar to Pfingstegg, consider walking all the way from Grindelwald; an extra 1¼hrs. Make your way via the church to the Pfingstegg cablecar station. Cross the river below it and walk along the road until a path cuts away to Marmorbruch (20mins). From here a good trail climbs the wooded slope to join the Pfingstegg–Stieregg path at the Wysseflue junction (1386m).

ROUTE 21

Grindelwald (Pfingstegg; 1392m) –
Stieregg (1650m) –
Schreckhorn Hut (2529m)

Grade	3
Distance	7km (one way)
Height gain	1137m
Time	4½hrs
Location	South of Grindelwald

This continuation of Route 20 is a much more demanding affair and should only be attempted by experienced mountain walkers. **Under certain conditions there is some avalanche danger**. Between Stieregg and the Rots Gufer the path is subject to change as the moraine bank continues to crumble, while the Rots Gufer cliffs that border an ice-fall, demand a good head for heights. Although safeguarded with fixed ladders, cables and metal pegs, the cliffs are somewhat exposed. As for the Schreckhorn Hut itself, this makes a fine destination for a walk. It sits below the Schreckhorn's broken west face and overlooks a vast sweep of glacier with the Finsteraarhorn rising like a delicate fin to the south. The whole walk is a stunning exposé of the forces at work to create a wonderland out of the bare bones of the mountains.

Follow directions outlined in Route 20 as far as **Restaurant Stieregg** (*accommodation, refreshments*). Beyond this, blue–white waymarks indicate a potentially hazardous Alpine Route. The path curves leftward to avoid the crumbling moraine edge, loses then gains height and enjoys a fascinating view ahead to the ice-fall of the Obers Eismeer. Then it makes towards the ice-fall where the cliffs of the Rots Gufer rise to its left.

At the end of a challenging 4½ hour walk, the Schreckhorn Hut is found below the Schreckhorn's broken west face

The way up the cliffs is well-marked and made safe with various aids, although caution must always be exercised. Roped parties are not uncommon here; the additional safeguard of a rope may be helpful as a slip could be serious.

Above the Rots Gufer rock barrier the path continues, a little easier now, to cross streams and old snow patches (beware avalanches early in the season, or after snowfall). Then you come to a cone of moraine and rocks spreading from the left. There are the ruins of a stone hut and beyond these the way seems to be blocked by converging glaciers. The path forks and you bear left to see the **Schreckhorn Hut** directly above. The final approach is along a slope of moraine.

Built to replace the Strahlegg Hut which was destroyed by avalanche, the **Schreckhorn Hut** is owned by the Basle Section of the SAC and has a resident guardian from late June to the end of September. There are 90 dormitory places and meals provided; for reservations ☎ 033 855 10 25.

ROUTE 22

Grindelwald (1034m) – Alpiglen (1616m)

Grade	3
Distance	7km
Height gain	800m
Height loss	240m
Time	3hrs
Location	Southwest of Grindelwald

The huddle of barns, hotel and railway station at Alpiglen are set among pastures at the foot of the Eiger, and it is from here that many epics on the North Face have begun. This walk actually works its way along the lower flank of the Eiger, and is fairly strenuous but interesting throughout. It climbs above the gorge of the Unterer Grindelwaldgletscher, weaves a route through steep woodland and follows a belvedere of a trail across open slopes with big views, before sloping down through pastures to Alpiglen. Since the hamlet is on the Grindelwald to Kleine Scheidegg railway, a return to base can be made by train. **Note**: an alternative route to Alpiglen is given as Route 23.

From Grindelwald make your way below the village church to the Pfingstegg cablecar station, and continue to the foot of the slope where you cross the river and veer right along a road to the Gletscherschlucht (glacier gorge). On coming to **Hotel–Restaurant Gletscherschlucht** (1016m *accommodation, refreshments*) pass alongside it on a footpath which takes you into forest. Climbing steadily, come to a junction and turn right, then left at the next junction a couple of minutes later. On emerging from the trees you cross an open slope of rocks and boulders from which you have a direct view across the valley to Grindelwald. (There's a small shelter on the left, with views through the gorge to the Fiescherwand.)

The path works its way among alpenrose and dwarf pine to a barrier of smooth slabs, which you ascend by a series of narrow terraces, then climb a steel ladder that brings you into forest once more. The way continues to gain height, but the steepest sections of path are eased by wood-braced steps. About 1½hrs after leaving Grindelwald you come to **Boneren** (1508m), a forest glade in which there's a log cabin shelter.

Here the trail angles to the right and the gradient eases, and just before turning a spur to leave the gorge, you pass alongside a band of cliffs in which there are several small caves. There's a fine view of the Wetterhorn, a slightly exposed section of path and a flight of steps, but then you come out of the trees into an open area

Towards the end of the high route to Alpiglen, the path crosses a short footbridge where a stream has sliced through the limestone

(Schüssellauenen, 1545m) to gain a view up to the Eiger's Hörnli-Mittellegi ridge.

Over this open section, return briefly to another strip of trees, then out again to a hillside patched with old snow and scree. Where the path crosses a shallow gully there seems always to be a large cone of compacted snow; a fixed rope has been placed here to aid the crossing. Shortly after you come to the highest point of the walk (1773m) immediately above a tiny hut. This is a splendid vantage point from which to study Grindelwald's pastoral basin below, the Lütschental funnelling off to the west, and the Wetterhorn back in the northeast.

The way now begins its steady descent to Alpiglen, and in another 10mins or so you cross a footbridge that spans a narrow limestone runnel whose racing stream is smoothing and moulding the rock into fantastic shapes. A few minutes later come to a signed junction of paths (1725m). The upper path here is the popular Eiger Trail (see Route 24), while the continuing route suggests 20mins to Alpiglen. Over an open hillside there's another embedded stream to cross, after which the descent has a steep section to negotiate before a final easy stroll into **Alpiglen** (*accommodation, refreshments*).

Alpiglen's situation is very fine. With the Eiger behind, a sweep of pasture and forest below, the Männlichen ridge to the west, and a direct view of the Wetterhorn in the northeast (the alpenglow on the Wetterhorn is something to witness from here) it's tempting to spend a night or two away from the crowds that gather in Grindelwald. **Berghaus Des Alpes** has rooms, and dormitory accommodation in an annexe (☎ 033 853 11 30 **mail@alpiglen.ch www.alpiglen.ch**).

ROUTE 23

Grindelwald (1034m) –
Grund (943m) – Alpiglen (1616m)

Grade	2
Distance	4km
Height gain	673m
Height loss	91m
Time	2¼hrs
Location	Southwest of Grindelwald

Although this approach to Alpiglen is shorter and more direct than that described as Route 22, it is nonetheless a very steep walk in places. However, there's nothing difficult about it, and for much of the way you'll be either walking on tarmac or farm track.

Begin by making your way from Grindelwald *bahnhof* (railway station) to the station at Grund which lies at the foot of the slope. The way is well signed. At **Grund** cross the railway line and the Schwarze Lütschine just beyond it, and turn left. You will soon cross the railway line that climbs to Alpiglen and Kleine Scheidegg, and just beyond this come to a crossing road. Keep ahead on a

steeply climbing tarmac path between chalets and meadows. Eventually the chalets are mostly left behind and
you continue through open meadows, the steep gradient
being maintained most of the way, and the railway line
never far off to your right. Shortly after coming to woods,
the tarmac way curves sharply to the right on the
approach to Brandegg. At this point break away to walk
directly ahead (signed to Alpiglen) up through the woods,
then across the railway line which is then followed all the
way to **Alpiglen**.

ROUTE 24

Alpiglen (1616m) – Eiger Trail –
Eigergletscher (2320m) –
Kleine Scheidegg (2061m)

Grade	3
Distance	8km
Height gain	704m
Height loss	259m
Time	3½–4hrs
Location	Southwest of Alpiglen

Linking Alpiglen and Eigergletscher Station (where the Jungfraujoch railway
tunnels into the mountain) the Eiger Trail, as its name suggests, has been created along the lower slopes of the infamous mountain; not on the mountain
itself, of course, but where the abrupt face turns to scree and scant pastureland. It's a very fine trail that affords some far-reaching panoramic views.
Most walkers naturally tackle it from Eigergletscher down to Alpiglen (this is
outlined below as Route 25), but my preference is for the upward walk. But
if you have the time, it would be worth walking it in both directions!

Follow the signed path which leaves Alpiglen heading
southeast across rising pastures, then more steeply in zig-
zags before easing again to reach a path junction at 1725m
after 25–30mins. The Eiger Trail breaks to the right, and
slants up and across the hillside towards the Eiger's north
wall. Crossing flat limestone slabs the path makes long
winding zig-zags up the slope with tremendous views back
to the Wetterhorn, Grosse Scheidegg, Schwarzhorn etc.

After crossing scant high pastures the trail then
strikes across screes at the foot of the North Face. At the
top of the screes the way leads round a basin, then up
again to a splendid grassy shoulder with stunning views
in all directions. Ahead, across the unseen depths of the
Lauterbrunnen Valley, can be seen Mürren with the
Schilthorn above it, and backed by the Gspaltenhorn,
Büttlassen and more distant Blüemlisalp massif. Nearer to
hand the graceful, snowy Silberhorn on the face of the
Jungfrau looks beautiful in the sunlight.

Over the western side of the shoulder, the path
descends, then curves left to climb once more in a long
slant across a final slope of scree, at the top of which you
come to the complex of buildings at **Eigergletscher**
(2320m; 3hrs *accommodation, refreshments*). Apart from
the railway station on the Kleine Scheidegg to
Jungfraujoch line, there's a restaurant here with a direct
view of the Eiger's glacier, and down through the deep
shaft of the Trummeltal. There's also dormitory accommodation to be had at the Eigergletscher Gasthaus (☎ 033
855 22 91) close to the railway tunnel entrance. ▶

There are three ways to reach Kleine Scheidegg from
here. The first merely takes the train. The second is a
direct route on a path that parallels the railway line
(35mins), while the third option is the recommended one
to take, as follows.

Go down to the restaurant which stands beside the
railway line. On its uphill side a path strikes off between
buildings and descends to the moraine wall that flanks
the Eiger's glacier. Walk down the crest path for about
10mins where you come to a signpost. Veer right here on
the trail signed to Fallboden and Kleine Scheidegg. After

Above the first build-
ing, at the top of a
short grass slope,
there sits the original
Mittellegi Hut
brought here to be
used as a tiny
museum. Formerly it
stood on a rocky
knoll on the Eiger's
Mittellegi Ridge at
3355m, but was
winched off the
mountain when a
larger replacement
hut was needed.

Kleine Scheidegg, a collection of hotels and railway buildings backed by stupendous mountains

a brief descent from the moraine the path contours across a grass slope, then rises to a shoulder with a fabulous view back to the Jungfrau. An easy, gentle path now winds round the hillside, crosses the railway line and brings you directly to **Kleine Scheidegg** (*accommodation, refreshments*). From the station trains go to Grindelwald in one direction, the Jungfraujoch in another, and Lauterbrunnen via Wengen to the northwest.

ROUTE 25

Kleine Scheidegg (Eigergletscher; 2320m) – Eiger Trail – Alpiglen (1616m)

Grade	2
Distance	5km
Height loss	704m
Time	2hrs
Location	South of Kleine Scheidegg

The Eiger Trail is most often walked in this direction, but as there's only one path with no alternative options to consider until you've almost reached Alpiglen, a basic outline only is given here. For more information please see Route 24.

Make your way from Kleine Scheidegg to the Eigergletscher Station at the entrance to the Jungfraujoch railway tunnel. You can do this by either riding the Jungfraujoch train, or following the signed path alongside the railway for 50mins.

From the station go up the paved footpath to the upper buildings where you walk along a brief track towards the Eiger's north wall, then on a clear footpath that goes down a slope at the foot of the mountain. After losing height the trail eases round to the left, then climbs a steepish slope to gain a high grassy shoulder with wonderful views. Over this cross a basin, then down and across screes to continuing high pastureland, the Wetterhorn directly ahead. The path is clear throughout, and it soon winds downhill, over flat slabs, and eventually comes to a signed junction at 1725m. Turn left for Alpiglen, which you reach in another 20mins.

Return to Kleine Scheidegg on the train, or walk up the broad track which parallels the railway for part of the way – a Grade 1 walk of 1½hrs.

NOTE

At the path junction above Alpiglen, it would be perfectly feasible to continue down to Grindelwald on another high trail (described in the reverse direction as Route 22) to complete a traverse of the Eiger's flank. This crosses the mountain's lower northeast slopes, goes through forest to Boneren (1hr 10mins), followed by a steep 30min descent to the Gletscherschlucht; then on to Grindelwald in 2½hrs. Grade 2–3 – recommended.

ROUTE 26

Grindelwald (1034m) –
Grund (943m) – Männlichen (2343m)

Grade	2
Distance	9km (one way)
Height gain	1400m
Height loss	91m
Time	4½–5hrs
Location	West of Grindelwald

Grindelwald's great basin of pastureland is contained in the west by a ridge that extends northward from the Kleine Scheidegg saddle. On the Grindelwald slope this ridge sweeps down in meadows, but on its western side a barrier of cliffs plunges dramatically to the mid-height terrace of Wengen before dropping again into the depths of the Lauterbrunnen Valley. This ridge then, effectively divides the valleys of the Weisse Lütschine and the Schwarze Lütschine, and at its northern extremity rises to the minor summit of Männlichen, a noted viewpoint. Below it cableways and ski tows rise to a large hotel and restaurant. The gondola lift that comes from Grindelwald is claimed to be the longest in Europe (6.2km and 1200m altitude difference) and takes about 30mins for the journey. But there are other, pedestrian, ways to reach Männlichen, of course, that will take much longer, and give plenty of opportunities to admire the great Eiger Nordwand rising from the pastures – a face that is never seen better than from this walk.

Leave Grindelwald and descend to the railway station at **Grund**. Cross the railway line and the river beyond it, and turn right. Passing the Eigernordwand campsite go left at a fork by a ski lift. The narrow service road rises among pastures and a number of attractive chalets, and although it would be possible to follow this all the way to

The Eiger's great North Face is seen to good effect from the pastures leading to Männlichen

the Männlichen hotel, clearly marked footpaths break from it, go through patches of woodland and across meadows, rising all the time – sometimes quite steeply. It's unnecessary to give precise directions because of the options available, and the generous amount of signposts at junctions. But as you progress up the hillside, so fine views left show the North Face of the Eiger soaring above the pastures. Look back too, to see the graceful Schreckhorn to the southeast. The main path veers towards the line of the gondola lift, then up the slope parallel to it.

Once you arrive at the **Männlichen** hotel (footpaths converge here), bear right and wander along the ridge path to the modest summit (20mins from the hotel). A glorious view looks steeply down to Lauterbrunnen's almost gorge-like valley, and up to the Jungfrau and a long line of snowpeaks dazzling from the south. To return to Grindelwald, either ride the gondola, follow Route 27 to Kleine Scheidegg for the train, or Route 28 for a 3hr walk back via Alpiglen.

ROUTE 27

Grindelwald (Berggasthaus Männlichen; 2229m) – Kleine Scheidegg (2061m)

Grade	1
Distance	4.5km
Height loss	168m
Time	1hr 20mins
Location	South of Männlichen

This has to be the easiest, and one of the busiest, walks in the book on account of the direct views to the Eiger's great Nordwand, to the Mönch and Jungfrau and, way beyond Grindelwald, to the Wetterhorn and Schreckhorn. It's a gentle, easily-angled walk, suitable for young and elderly alike, and there is transportation available at both ends: gondola lift from Grindelwald, cablecar from Wengen, and train to both places from Kleine Scheidegg. In the early summer the path is flanked by a rich assortment of alpine plants, but please don't be tempted to pick any.

No directions are required beyond simply saying head south on the broad, clearly marked path which takes you along the Grindelwald side of the ridge. It makes a steady curve to round a spur coming from the peaklet of Tschuggen (rising from the ridge), passes below the Lauberhorn (famous for the annual downhill ski race held there) and beside the Grindelwaldblick restaurant (*accommodation, refreshments*), before arriving at the cosmopolitan complex of hotels and railway station of Kleine Scheidegg – complete with brimming crowds, souvenir stands and alpenhorns. The peace of the mountains will not be found here, but Kleine Scheidegg is, nonetheless, one of those places that all who visit Grindelwald should make a pilgrimage to see.

ROUTE 28

Grindelwald (Berggasthaus Männlichen;
2229m) – Alpiglen (1616m) – Grund
(943m) – Grindelwald (1034m)

Grade	1–2
Distance	12km
Height loss	1286m
Height gain	91m
Time	3hrs
Location	Southeast and east of Männlichen

As with Route 27, this walk begins at the Männlichen hotel by the gondola station and, like that walk, enjoys a privileged view of the Eiger's great North Face. In fact you wander directly towards it, then virtually beneath it, for Alpiglen stands at the base of that notorious wall, which is somewhat foreshortened from this angle. The paths are mostly clear, well-trodden and popular; the first, as far as Alpiglen, being known locally as the *Höhenweg 1900*.

Leaving Männlichen, take the broad path heading south towards Kleine Scheidegg, then break away left at the first junction, reached after 10–15mins. Descending past a little pool, keep ahead on a hillside traverse going southeast with the Eiger luring you on. In a little over 1hr from Männlichen come to the farm buildings of Bustiglen, with views down to Grindelwald and across to the Wetterhorn. Ignoring alternatives continue on the main path as it heads south, crosses a stream, then swings round towards the Kleine Scheidegg–Grindelwald railway line. Losing height you reach **Alpiglen** (*accommodation, refreshments*) about 40mins beyond Bustiglen.

The continuing route to Grindelwald is straightforward from here. It goes down the left-hand side of the railway, then crosses back through forest. Eventually it comes onto a steep tarmac path (which can be a strain for tired legs) and descends among chalets and meadows. This leads directly to the bed of the valley where you cross the river and come to Grund railway station. Bear right on a road that leads uphill to **Grindelwald**.

ROUTE 29

Grindelwald (1034m) –
Grund (943m) – Kleine Scheidegg
(2061m) – Wengen (1275m)

Grade	2–3
Distance	15km
Height gain	1118m
Height loss	877m
Time	5½hrs
Location	Southwest of Grindelwald

The Kleine Scheidegg has naturally been adopted by the Alpine Pass Route, for it's a classic crossing without difficulties or complications. While other Oberland passes may be higher, more challenging or remote, Kleine Scheidegg is a bustle of train-bound tourists and the path on either side will invariably be trailed by other walkers. What makes this crossing special is the close proximity of so many magnificent high peaks. First, of course, there's the Eiger, and looking back from Alpiglen, for example, the Wetterhorn looks very fine. Then, at Kleine Scheidegg, the Mönch is a powerful neighbour, while descending to Wengernalp the glorious Jungfrau rises in snow-draped splendour – tossing down her excesses in avalanche after avalanche on warm summer days, but ahead across the Lauterbrunnen Valley the Gspaltenhorn shows its long cock's comb ridge. From Grund below Grindelwald, the climb to Alpiglen is an extremely steep one. Thereafter the angle eases, and the descent to Wengen from the pass takes a comfortable gradient.

The route from Grindelwald to **Alpiglen** via Grund (2¼hrs) was described as Route 23. Refreshments and accommodation are available at the Berghaus Des Alpes near Alpiglen station. Beyond the Berghaus the track rises easily, soon crosses to the right-hand side of the railway line and continues with a steady ascent below the Eiger to reach **Kleine Scheidegg** (*accommodation, refreshments*) about 1½hrs after leaving Alpiglen.

On the left of the busy railway station, cross the Jungfraujoch line and descend an easy track beside the railway which goes to Wengen and Lauterbrunnen. Views are now dominated by the Mönch and Jungfrau, and very impressive they are, too. For 30mins the track keeps company with the railway line, then at **Wengernalp** (4hrs 20mins; *refreshments*) you leave the main track to cut left on a narrow path across a steep patch of pasture heading towards forest. Continue into the trees, and you will shortly come to a farm track that in turn leads to the sunny pastures of Mettlenalp. From here you gain views of the Gspaltenhorn above Mürren, and to the Breithorn at the head of Lauterbrunnen's valley. Continue along the track as it curves round the hillside and leads all the way to **Wengen**, reached about 1hr 10mins after leaving Wengernalp.

(For details of Wengen, please refer to the appropriate section in the Lauterbrunnental chapter that follows.)

Other routes from Grindelwald

In addition to those routes described above, Grindelwald has so many more walks available – and variations of walks – that a fortnight's holiday could easily be spent here without duplicating an outing. The tourist information office publishes a sheet of suggested walks in the neighbourhood. These are mostly short and easy strolls, but with a few more demanding outings included as well. There are also walking maps available with suggestions and varying degrees of detail.

- One worth considering by fit walkers (a Grade 3 route) goes from First towards Hagelsee (Route 17), then breaks away to the north to explore the pre-alpine countryside of **Axalp** (a 4hr walk). Buses link Axalp with Brienz, where connections are made for the journey back to Grindelwald.

- Mention should be made of the **Jungfraujoch** (3454m), reached by the famous (and very expensive) railway that tunnels through the Eiger and Mönch. A visit to this tremendous vantage point is a highlight for many visitors to Grindelwald. There are modest ascents possible from that elevated position, but these are for experienced mountaineers only. The **Mönch**, for example, may be ascended in about 2½–3hrs from the Jungfraujoch Station; the **Jungfrau** (by a much-crevassed route) in 3hrs. Most visitors here, of course, are content with the magnificent arctic-style views, or at most with a visit to the **Mönchsjoch Hut** (3650m), 1hr from the station. Again, these are only for adepts. For most, the views will be breathtaking enough in every sense of the word.

LAUTERBRUNNENTAL

The Lauterbrunnental (Lauterbrunnen Valley) is one of the finest examples of a glacier-carved valley in all the Alps. A steep-walled, U- shaped cleft, it takes its name from the many feathery waterfalls that shower down its vertical sides, one of which (the Staubbach) is probably the most famous in Switzerland. On both flanks of the valley, forest and meadow spread back from the head of the walling cliffs in natural terraces well-supplied with walking trails. Panoramic views are outstanding, and with Wengen, Mürren and Gimmelwald set upon these terraces, it's possible to spend a complete holiday up there without once descending to the valley. But this would be a mistake, for the bed of the valley has its own undeniable appeal, and beyond the roadhead a magical 'hidden' region invites exploration.

Travelling south into the Lauterbrunnental the visitor is at first blinkered by its steep and narrow confines, but as the forest withdraws mountain walls begin to reveal themselves, and views gradually unfold to be highlighted by the Breithorn at the very head of the valley. Then the Breithorn's neighbouring peaks – each one snow-draped and girded with hanging glaciers – swell into the scene, topped overall by the beautiful Jungfrau; a superbly proportioned and graceful mountain

The great shaft of the Lauterbrunnental, seen from Wengen

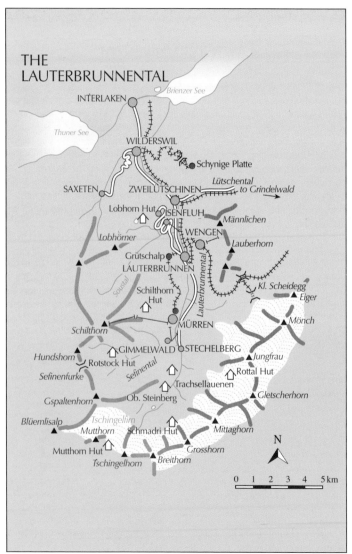

THE
LAUTERBRUNNENTAL

Brienzer See

INTERLAKEN

Thuner See

WILDERSWIL

Schynige Platte

SAXETEN   ZWEILÜTSCHINEN   *Lütschental*
                                    to Grindelwald

Lobhorn Hut   ISENFLUH   Männlichen
                WENGEN
Lobhörner   Lauberhorn

Grütschalp
LAUTERBRUNNEN

Soustal

Schilthorn
Hut   Kl. Scheidegg
                            Eiger

Schilthorn   MÜRREN   Mönch

Hundshorn   GIMMELWALD STECHELBERG   *Jungfrau*
              Rotstock Hut   Rottal Hut
Sefinenfurke *Sefinental*
                            Trachsellauenen
Gspaltenhorn Ob. Steinberg   *Gletscherhorn*

Blüemlisalp   *Tschingellirn*
       Mutthorn Schmadri Hut   *Mittaghorn*
Mutthorn Hut   N
   Tschingelhorn *Breithorn* *Grosshorn*

0 1 2 3 4 5 km

ACCESS AND INFORMATION

Location	South of Interlaken, and southwest of the Lütschental
Maps	LS 254T *Interlaken*, and 264T *Jungfrau* at 1:50,000 Kümmerly + Frey *Jungfrau-Region Oberhasli* at 1:60,000 A 1:40,000 scale wanderkarte, *Lauterbrunnental* is available locally
Bases	Lauterbrunnen (795m), Wengen (1275m), Mürren (1638m), Gimmelwald (1380m), Stechelberg (910m)
Information	Tourist Information, Bahnhofplatz, CH–3822 Lauterbrunnen (☎ 033 856 85 68 **info@lauterbrun- nen.ch www.wengen-muerren.ch**) Tourist Information, Dorfstrasse, CH–3823 Wengen (☎ 033 855 14 14 **info@wengen.ch www.wengen- muerren.ch**) Tourist Information Mürren, CH–3825 Mürren (☎ 033 855 86 86 **info@muerren.ch www.wengen-muerren.ch**) Verkehrsbüro, CH–3826 Gimmelwald (☎ 033 855 33 81 **info@gimmelwald.ch www.wengen-muerren.ch**) Verkehrsverein, CH–3824 Stechelberg (☎ 033 855 10 32 **info@stechelberg.ch www.wengen-muerren.ch**)
Access	By train to Lauterbrunnen via Interlaken Ost. From Lauterbrunnen change trains for Wengen and Kleine Scheidegg. A funicular rises from Lauterbrunnen to Grütschalp to connect with a short train ride to Mürren. Postbuses run throughout the valley as far as Stechelberg, where a cablecar connects with Gimmelwald and Mürren.

best seen from one of the natural terraces that edge the upper walls of the valley. To the left (east) one of these terraces is occupied by Wengen, to the right Mürren has its own shelf, with Gimmelwald perched on the lip of the slope a little lower; a slope from which a whole series of delicate waterfalls tip over to streak the cliffs. But behind Mürren, and further to the north, Isenfluh, another magnificently set village, enjoys one of the best of all views of the Jungfrau – from its glinting snow crown to its grey stony feet more than 3000m below, seen in one tremendous sweep of the eye.

The Jungfrau's feet rest in the level pastures of Stechelberg where the valley's road ends. South of this small village there are more scanty pastures and patches of forest, and above these the stony ankles of the mountains, sliced with glacial streams that feed the Weisse Lütschine. This upper basin contains several scenically interesting walks, including a desperately steep haul to the Rottal Hut on the southwest flanks of the Jungfrau, and another that crosses the high ridge dividing the upper valley from the Sefinental.

But the whole Lauterbrunnental is a walker's delight; especially on those mid-height terraces where alp clusters are inhabited for the summer by farmers grazing their cattle and making cheese. There are mechanical aids to reach these upper regions, too; funicular links with Wengen and Mürren, and cableways to the famed Schilthorn (2960m) from Stechelberg, Gimmelwald and Mürren.

MAIN BASES

LAUTERBRUNNEN (795m) is virtually a one-street thoroughfare with a busy railway station on the Interlaken–Wengen–Jungfraujoch line. Its handsome church has a large bell set before it. It is said it was carried over the mountains from the Lötschental several centuries ago when the inhabitants of that valley sought to escape the severity of their church rulers in favour of a more relaxed regime in the Lauterbrunnen Valley. This migration involved a number of families who crossed with their cattle by way of the glacial Tschingel Pass. Today Lauterbrunnen has a large multi-storey car park by the station, and several hotels in the main street. For the budget traveller, dormitory accommodation is available at the Valley Hostel (☎ 033 855 20 08 www.valleyhostel.ch) and the two large campsites, the Jungfrau (☎ 033 856 20 10 www.camping-jungfrau.ch), and the Schützenbach (☎ 033 855 54 54 www.schutzenbach-retreat.ch). The village has a small selection of shops, restaurants, banks and a tourist information office. Postbuses run from here to Isenfluh and Stechelberg; and there are rail links with Interlaken, Wengen, Kleine Scheidegg and the Jungfraujoch, and with Mürren via Grütschalp.

Typical Oberland house in Wengen

WENGEN (1275m) is noted as much for its skiing as for its summer attractions, but is thankfully spared the intrusive mechanisation that so marks many other ski resorts. In fact Wengen sits prettily on its shelf, bright with window boxes and a

The Gspaltenhorn is seen from many trails around Mürren

privileged near-view of the Jungfrau. Reached by train from Lauterbrunnen (or by steep woodland paths), it is a traffic-free village – free of traffic, that is, except for a fleet of electrically-powered, softly buzzing vehicles that serve its hotels and shops. There's an abundance of accommodation; almost 30 hotels and pensions, together with 2500 beds in apartments and chalets as well as several low-priced dormitories, including the Bergheim (☎ 033 855 27 55 www.jungfraublick.com) which is managed by the Hotel Jungfraublick; Eddy's Hostel (☎ 033 855 16 34), and the Hot Chili Peppers (☎ 033 855 50 20 chilis@wengen). There are plenty of shops, restaurants, banks and a tourist information office; also a cinema and discos. A cablecar links Wengen with Männlichen high above, and the railway serves Kleine Scheidegg for the Jungfraujoch, and/or Grindelwald.

MÜRREN (1638m) complements Wengen from its location on the sunny western shelf of the valley. Behind it a broad plateau rimmed with an arc of high mountains makes for fine walking. There are summits to aim for, passes to cross, meadows to amble through. And all the time with astonishing views of Eiger, Mönch and Jungfrau, of the Breithorn and Gspaltenhorn and, from some places, the Wetterhorn way off beyond the Eiger. Like Wengen, Mürren is also famed as a ski resort, and it was here that Arnold Lunn introduced the modern slalom in 1922. It was in Mürren that the Kandahar Ski Club was founded two years later, and the now world-famous Inferno race from the Schilthorn's summit to the depths of Lauterbrunnen had its first outing in 1928. (Arnold Lunn is remembered with a memorial stone placed in a small garden near the railway station.) But for users of this guidebook there can be no doubt that as a centre for a mountain walking holiday, Mürren takes a lot of beating. Although on the expensive side, it has no shortage of accommodation – hotels, holiday apartments and chalets. Cheaper accommodation is available in a couple of rustic mountain inns 30mins above the village in the peaceful Blumental; Pension Sonnenberg (☎ 033 855 11 27 **sonnenberg@bluewin.ch**), and the older and delightfully atmospheric Pension Suppenalp (☎ 033 855 17 26 **suppenalp@spectraweb.ch www.suppenalp.ch**), both of which have dormitory places as well as bedrooms. Beds and dormitory places may also be found at Pension Spielbodenalp (☎ 033 855 14 75), about an hour's walk from Mürren on the trail to the Sefinenfurke. Mürren has various shops, banks, restaurants and sporting facilities, and a tourist information office. A cablecar links Mürren with the Schilthorn where a revolving restaurant looks out on a wonderful panorama; there's also a funicular from the village to Allmendhubel for walking possibilities. Like Wengen, Mürren is traffic-free, and reached by funicular from Lauterbrunnen to Grütschalp, followed by a short ride by railway.

GIMMELWALD (1380m) is considerably smaller and much less developed than its more illustrious neighbour, Mürren, and occupies a steep slope of hillside a short distance below it to the south, near the entrance to the Sefinental. It has no public access by road, but a cableway links the village with Stechelberg. The only accommodation is to be had in Pension-Restaurant Gimmelwald which has both beds and dormitory places (☎ 033 855 17 30 **pensiongimmelwald@tcnet.ch www.gimmelwald.ch**), Esther's Guesthouse (☎ 033 855 54 92) which also has a barn in which guests can sleep in the hay; and the former youth hostel, now known as the Mountain Hostel (☎ 033 855 17 04 **mountainhostel@tcnet.ch**) with self-catering facilities.

STECHELBERG (910m) marks the Lauterbrunnental's roadhead. A quiet, unobtrusive place, it makes a fine walking centre in its own right with a network of footpaths heading up into the mountains, or along the valley bed. Reached by postbus from Lauterbrunnen, the village has accommodation in the 30-bed Hotel Stechelberg (☎ 033 855 29 21 **hotel@stechelberg.ch www.stechelberg.ch**), and the simple but welcoming Naturfreundehaus Alpenhof (☎ 033 855 12 02 **www.naturfreunde.ch**). There's also a campsite, and the valley station for the Gimmelwald-Schilthorn cablecar.

OTHER BASES

South of Stechelberg paths explore the hidden upper reaches of the valley, where three mountain inns provide simple but atmospheric accommodation in peaceful surroundings. First of these is **BERGHAUS TRACHSELLAUENEN** (☎ 033 855 12 35) set in woodland 45mins from the roadhead; then an hour or so further upvalley **HOTEL TSCHINGELHORN** (☎ 033 855 13 43) with lovely views, and lastly, another 20mins walk away, the delightful **BERGHOTEL OBERSTEINBERG** with beds and dormitory accommodation (☎ 033 855 20 33), which proudly boasts no electricity or running water in the rooms; after dark all meals are candelit, and a jug of water is placed in your room for washing.

On a remote natural terrace high on the south flank of the Sefinental, and reached only by a very steep path, the little dairy farm of **BUSENALP** has (at the time of writing) up to 5 beds in a separate guest-room – no electricity or running water. There's no meals provision, other than basic refreshments, so guests must take their own food. But its situation is among the most beautiful in all the Bernese Alps. With no permanent telephone at the farm, it's not possible to make prior reservations. The farm is usually operational from July to mid-September.

Midway between Stechelberg and Lauterbrunnen, there's a campsite at **SANDBACH**, while to the north of Lauterbrunnen, on a hillside shelf high above the valley, **ISENFLUH** (1081m) has accommodation at Pension-Restaurant Waldrand (☎ 033 855 12 27 **hotel_waldrand@bluewin.ch www.wal-drand.com**), superb views and some grand, if steep, walking country on its doorstep.

MOUNTAIN HUTS

ROTTAL HUT (2755m) Standing high above Stechelberg, from which it is reached by an excessively steep trail in about 5½hrs, this hut, owned by the Interlaken Section of the SAC, looks on the Ebnefluh, Mittaghorn, Grosshorn, Breithorn and Tschingelhorn. There are 45 places and a resident guardian only at weekends at the end of June to mid-September, when simple meals may be available (☎ 033 855 24 45).

SCHMADRI HUT (2263m) This is also accessible from Stechelberg; a small unmanned hut with places for 14 located below the Grosshorn at the foot of the valley's headwall. Owned by the Academic Alpine Club of Bern, the hut is equipped with self-catering facilities – but take your own food.

ROTSTOCK HUT (2039m) Situated on the Boganggen alp on the approach to the Sefinenfurke, this hut is owned by the Stechelberg Ski Club. It has dormitory places for 52, and a resident guardian with meals provision from June to the end

The Rottal Hut

of September (☎ 033 855 24 64 **www.rotstockhuette.ch**). The hut is reached in a little over 2hrs from Mürren.

SCHILTHORN HUT (2432m) As its name suggests, this hut serves the Schilthorn and is found in the little hanging valley of the Engital below the Schwarzgrat. Owned by the Mürren Ski Club, it has 40 places and a resident guardian from December to April for skiers, and from July to September for walkers (☎ 033 855 50 53).

SULS-LOBHORN HUT (1955m) With a truly spectacular view of the Eiger, Mönch and Jungfrau, this is a small timber-built hut reached in about 3hrs from Isenfluh, or 2hrs from Grütschalp. It belongs to the Lauterbrunnen Section of the SAC, has just 24 places and a guardian from June to mid-October, with meals provision. As space is limited reservations for overnight accommodation are recommended (☎ 079 656 53 20).

ROUTE 30

Isenfluh (1081m) – Sulsseeli (1920m) –
Suls-Lobhorn Hut (1955m)

Grade	3
Distance	5km (one way)
Height gain	874m
Time	2hrs 45mins
Location	West of Isenfluh

Mürren's view of mountains at the head of the Lauterbrunnental is justifiably famous. Less well-known are Isenfluh and Sulwald, yet they also command a magnificent vista of big mountains; the Eiger, Mönch and Jungfrau in particular, seen from a hillside terrace high above the valley near its junction with that of the Lütschental. This walk makes the most of those views as it visits a shallow tarn and an idyllically-situated mountain hut. It's a steep walk that could be eased by taking the cablecar from Isenfluh to Sulwald, thus saving about 560m of height-gain and 1¼hrs of walking time.

Reached by postbus from Lauterbrunnen, Isenfluh is a small village with limited accommodation. Steep meadows rise above it, while forests cling to cliffs that plunge to the valley below; views to the Jungfrau are stunning. The path to Sulwald is well-signed from the village; it climbs through meadows and between farm buildings at a severe gradient from the very start. Soon going through forest, work your way ever-upward with clear directions at all trail junctions. After about 1hr 15mins emerge from the woods onto the open pastures of **Sulwald** (1540m), a scattered hamlet of chalets and haybarns with views that will stop you in your tracks.

Follow a narrow roadway past the top station of the Isenfluh cableway and then cut up to the right through

The Suls-Lobhorn Hut has an amazing view of the Jungfrau

more meadows (rich with flowers in the early summer) on a path signed to Sulsalp and the Lobhorn Hut. It soon enters forest again and climbs on until coming to a clearing where you see just below the alp buildings of Kühbodmen (Chüebodmi on the map). One path drops to it, but we continue uphill and before long leave the forest in favour of a sloping meadowland with ribs of white limestone jutting from it. An obvious saddle is seen ahead, and on the hilltop above it to the right, the Lobhorn Hut can be made out.

Wandering up and across this meadowland yet more extraordinary views will be enjoyed. These include the Wetterhorn, as well as Eiger, Mönch and Jungfrau, and the deep Lauterbrunnental now some 1200m below.

Now narrow, the path goes through the saddle and a little valley beyond, following the Sulsbach stream. The smooth rock face of the unfortunately-named peak of Ars rises above to the left, and beyond that the five prongs of the Lobhörner. In the little valley you come to the **Sulsalp** (1910m) with its farmhouse and cattle byres (cheese and butter for sale).

From here you have a choice of routes to the Lobhorn Hut. A direct path cuts back half-right for a 20min approach; the alternative first visits the **Sulsseeli** tarn and is described here. Take the signed path which heads to the right, rises over a bluff, and comes to the lake 5mins later (1hr 15mins from Sulwald). For views of distant mountains, with the tarn in the foreground, you'll have to go round the western shoreline, but to reach the hut keep ahead on the path for another 2mins, then break away to the right at a marked junction. A narrow trail now cuts across a meadow with exposed limestone ribs, and brings you to the **Suls-Lobhorn Hut** with its commanding panorama; not only to the well-known Oberland peaks to the south, but southwest to the five fingers of the Lobhörner. It's a wonderful location. ▶

The **Lobhorn Hut** is small but cosy. Owned by the Lauterbrunnen Section of the SAC, it has just 24 places and meals provided when the guardian is in residence, from June to mid-October. Reservation recommended (☎ 033 656 53 20). A view of alpenglow on the Jungfrau is spectacular from here.

ROUTE 31

Isenfluh (1081m) – Bällehöchst (2095m) – Saxeten (1103m)

Grade	3
Distance	14 km
Height gain	1014m
Height loss	992m
Time	6hrs
Location	West and northwest of Isenfluh

This is a long and somewhat tiring day's walk which crosses the mountain ridge forming a divide between the Sulstal and the Saxettal. It could, of course, be shortened by taking the cablecar from Isenfluh to Sulwald (thus saving 1¼hrs), or by staying overnight at the Lobhorn Hut. Between the Sulsseeli and a saddle below the Bällehöchst, the path traverses the headwall of a steep hanging valley, which could be dangerous if snow-covered. Do not attempt this walk until snow has cleared the paths.

Follow Route 30 as far as the lake of **Sulsseeli** (1920m; 2½hrs), continue along its right-hand (eastern) side, then up a grass slope to a saddle which overlooks the steeply-plunging Sylertal, flanked by abrupt limestone cliffs. The way now makes a traverse of this valley's headwall (caution if wet, and do not attempt to cross if snow covers the path), beyond which you rise to another grass saddle at 1998m, about 40–45mins from the lake. A 15min walk up the broad right-hand ridge leads to the vantage point of **Bällehöchst** (2095m; 3½hrs) where the views are impressive.

Return to the saddle, then briefly down a grass slope where the way is confused by cattle paths. Low marker posts soon direct you on a rightward contour to a point just above the red-roofed alp building of Unter Bällen (1883m), then downhill left of the building on a more pronounced path. About 10mins later you come to the alp buildings of **Hinder Bällen** at 1769m.

Take the left-hand trail signed to Saxeten in 1hr 40mins. It rises a little, comes to a spur, and over this descends a slope of pasture (more waymark posts) before crossing a stream in a gully. After this continue down forested slopes, then over more pasture to cross a second stream, after which the gradient eases, as a clear path takes you towards the head of the valley. Cross the main Saxetenbach stream to its true left bank, come onto a farm road and pass alongside the dairy buildings of **Underberg** (1460m).

After about 2mins on the road, take a footpath on the right. This leads through forest, soon crosses a track and continues down the wooded slope to emerge to a view of a waterfall ahead. Rejoin the road at a hairpin bend. (Another fine waterfall pours through a narrow limestone ravine on the right.) Now keep on the road all the way to **Saxeten** (1103m *accommodation, refreshments*) from where there's an infrequent postbus service to Wilderswil. (Take the train from Wilderswil back to Lauterbrunnen.)

Should you still have enough energy to walk down to Wilderswil (another 1hr 15mins), or decide to spend a night in Saxeten at Hotel Alpenrose (☎ 033 522 18 34 **alpenrose@saxeten.net**) and walk down next day, see Route 10 for directions.

ROUTE 32

Isenfluh (1081m) – Soustal (1700m) –
Grütschalp (1486m)

Grade	3
Distance	10km
Height gain	822m
Height loss	417m
Time	4–4½hrs
Location	South of Isenfluh

This is one of those quiet walks that leads into a fine valley somewhat off the beaten track, where the daily life of alpine farming goes on without much tourist disturbance. It enjoys many of the long views noted in the two previous routes, but also rewards with viewpoints of its own.

The Soustal is visited on the way from Isenfluh to Grütschalp

Follow directions towards the alp of **Suls** (2hrs 20mins) as given in Route 30. Just before reaching it, however, cross the stream flowing through the narrow valley and bear left on the path on the opposite side. This heads eastward to round a spur of mountain in a lengthy traverse, soon delving among trees and shrubbery with tantalising views. The path swings round the steep mountainside into the mouth of the Soustal, but high above it. The trail is muddy in places, being regularly churned by cattle.

Keep towards the head of the valley, by now heading southwest with the summit of the Schilthorn seen clearly some way ahead. (Interesting to speculate on the number of visitors crowded up at that point while you have the valley virtually to yourself.) Ignore an alternative path that breaks away left to descend into the valley by a series of tight zig-zags, but continue ahead to pass the alp buildings of Naterwengli (1776m). Beyond these enter woods again, where the path takes you easily down into the valley. ▶

Once in the Soustal proper wander downvalley on the stream's left bank. Passing the first farm a bridge takes you over to the right bank where you continue on a farm track. Drawing level with another bridge over the stream, turn right on a path which brings you up past a log-built chalet to a junction of paths at Flöschwald/Sousmatten (1680m). Turn left on the path signed to Grütschalp in 1hr (nearby you can buy basic refreshments of milk, tea or coffee at one of the farm buildings). Passing a tarn and more farm buildings below to your left, the clear trail takes you mostly through forest all the way to **Grütschalp**, a station where you can either ride the funicular or follow the steep signed path which descends through forest to Lauterbrunnen (1hr), or catch a train ahead to Mürren.

The **Soustal** is soft, green and pastoral; a back-country valley with isolated farms, a clear-running stream and charming views. At its head the Kilchfluh Pass gives access to the valley of Spiggengrund, which in turn leads to the lovely Kiental.

ROUTE 33

Lauterbrunnen (795m) –
Grütschalp (1486m)

Grade	3
Distance	3km (one way)
Height gain	691m
Time	2hrs
Location	West of Lauterbrunnen

This extremely steep walk to the first shelf of hillside above Lauterbrunnen is an alternative to the Grütschalp funicular. It's a stiff, lung-stretching pull that should be taken at an easy pace. Practically the whole way is through forest.

The path begins near a bakery in Lauterbrunnen's main street a short distance upvalley from the railway station. It takes you past a number of houses, over a stream and on a traverse towards the right. Ignore a left-hand alternative, go under the railway and then in tight zig-zags uphill through the forest. After about 50mins come to Alpweg (1086m) and a junction of trails. Take the left-hand option which continues its steep upward route, crosses the funicular again and with more zig-zags eventually brings you to another crossing path. Go right here to the other side of the railway yet again, then bear left for the final winding uphill to **Grütschalp** Station.

ROUTE 34

Grütschalp (1486m) – Mürren (1638m)

Grade	1
Distance	4km (one way)
Height gain	152m
Time	1hr 10mins
Location	South of Grütschalp

A delightful, easy walk, on a good path with magnificent views, this makes an excellent introduction for newcomers to the area, a prelude to many walks worth tackling. From Grütschalp to Mürren is the gentlest kind of walking you may hope to find in the Alps – almost without any steep ascent, but with an exquisite panorama that takes in the Jungfrau, Ebnefluh, Mittaghorn, Grosshorn and Breithorn. There's also the spear wedge of the Eiger and the snowy bulk of the Mönch and, as you draw nearer to Mürren, the lovely Gspaltenhorn too. The valley plunges away in a spectacular gulf; there are forests alive with birdsong and pastures rich in flowers.

Either take the funicular from Lauterbrunnen to Grütschalp, or walk up the steep path as per Route 33. Leaving the upper station, cross the railway tracks and take the footpath heading left, signed to Mürren. No further descriptions are necessary, except to say that at every path junction adequate signs are given and it's almost impossible to lose the way. At **Winteregg**, an intermediate halt, refreshments are available. For some of the way the path runs parallel with the railway, and eventually brings you directly into **Mürren** at its northern end by the station.

Pastures backed by the Gspaltenhorn near Mürren

ROUTE 35

Grütschalp (1486m) –
Mürren (1638m) – Gimmelwald
(1380m) – Stechelberg (910m)

Grade	2
Distance	9km
Height gain	152m
Height loss	728m
Time	2½hrs
Location	South of Grütschalp

Another first-rate introductory walk, this would make a good initial outing after arrival in the area. There's nothing difficult about it, although the descent from Gimmelwald to Stechelberg has a few steep stretches to tighten muscles unaccustomed to such gradients. Views are breathtaking and there's little doubt that the basic walking time will be considerably exceeded by virtue of the need to keep stopping to gaze at the scenery.

Take Route 34 to **Mürren**. At the station the street forks ahead and you take the left branch. (For tourist information bear right.) As you wander along the street look for a signpost near the post office directing you left down a narrow service road towards Gimmelwald. The way soon descends out of the village between steeply sloping meadows with stunning views, and comes to the tiny huddled village of **Gimmelwald** (*accommodation, refreshments*) about 30mins or so from Mürren.

Wander through the village on a path signed to Stechelberg, passing the Mountain Hostel on your left. The path descends very steeply past farms and haybarns, then over a stream flowing through the Sefinental where you bear left. Continue down, now through forest and nearly always quite steeply. Eventually it brings you out at **Stechelberg** (*accommodation, refreshments*), at the valley's roadhead. Either catch a postbus back to Lauterbrunnen, or wander downvalley on the left-bank of the river for a pleasant 1½hr extension to the walk.

ROUTE 36

Lauterbrunnen (795m) – Stechelberg (910m)

Grade	1
Distance	7km (one way)
Height gain	115m
Time	1hr 45mins
Location	South of Lauterbrunnen

A very gentle walk that gives plenty of opportunities to enjoy the valley at leisure, with the dazzling smoke of numerous waterfalls cascading from the steep walls, and consistently lovely views of the big peaks ahead. This is especially fine on a summer's evening when the snow peaks at the southern end of the valley catch the alpenglow – although you'll probably have to walk back again as no doubt the last postbus will have left Stechelberg long before.

Walk along Lauterbrunnen's main street heading south, ignoring the left-hand sweep of the road where it forks just before the village church. The Staubbach Falls are seen showering from the right almost from the start. Continue ahead along a peaceful lane cutting through meadows and passing several attractive chalets, with the Breithorn looking particularly handsome directly before you. At Stegmatten the lane crosses the Weisse

Lütschine to join the main valley road, but here you take the riverside footpath, remaining on the true left bank (west side). Continue to **Stechelberg** (*accommodation, refreshments*).

ROUTE 37

Lauterbrunnen (795m) – Wengen (1275m)

Grade	2–3
Distance	3km (one way)
Height gain	480m
Time	1½hrs
Location	East of Lauterbrunnen

In many ways this route matches the steep walk from Lauterbrunnen to Grütschalp (Route 33), but more views are shown through the trees on this walk and, just below the village, there's a splendid little alpine meadow thick with wild flowers in the early summer. It is a steep walk, but an enjoyable alternative to the often-crowded train that winds its way up the hillside.

The walk begins by the railway station in Lauterbrunnen and goes between the station and its nearby multi-storey car park, crosses the river, passes chalets and then starts to climb the hillside. Where there are junctions signposts direct the way. Soon zig-zags gain height in the shade of trees, sometimes with the railway for company. Then the forest gives way to an open meadow and you gaze across it to the top of the Staubbach Falls. A fine view. Now **Wengen** is seen just above you and the way enters the village, still quite steeply, past a number of houses with the Jungfrau gazing down in a gleam of snow and ice.

ROUTE 38

Wengen (1275m) – Leiterhorn (1525m) – Burglauenen (896m)

Grade	1
Distance	7.5km
Height gain	305m
Height loss	684m
Time	2½ hrs
Location	North and northeast of Wengen

This gentle walk links Wengen's hillside terrace with the Lütschental, which is joined some way downvalley from Grindelwald, and provides a number of scenic contrasts. Much of the route is in forest, but there are several outstanding viewpoints, especially on the approach to Spätenalp where the Wetterhorn suddenly appears ahead like some misplaced Himalayan giant. Simple refreshments are available at the Spätenalp farm.

From the heart of Wengen find your way to the cinema (Kino), then turn left in front of Hotel Jungfraublick where a road rises steadily between chalets and hotels. When it forks on the outskirts of the village, bear right, then go left at a group of buildings at Flüelenboden to follow a track rising through a strip of woodland and between more chalets, haybarns and open meadows. Come to the forest edge and a crossing path (the Rundweg). Bear left, and a minute later go up a narrow path on the right, climbing in and out of forest to a junction marked as Untere Lische (1510m). The Burglauenen trail goes off to the right, but before taking this it is worth diverting for a few moments to the viewpoint of **Leiterhorn** which overlooks the confluence of the Schwarze and Weisse Lütschine valleys far below, and off to Wilderswil and Interlaken. Leiterhorn is signed from this path junction.

Taking the Burglauenen path the way continues through forest, crosses a track and joins another shortly after. This soon curves to the right high above the Lütschental, with Schynige Platte seen on the far side. After gaining a high point the track reverts to footpath and begins an undemanding descent, sloping down among trees, then over open pastures with the Wetterhorn in view at the head of the valley. Reach the lone farm of **Spätenalp** (*refreshments*) in about 1½hrs from Wengen, and bear left. A large wooden cross here has a bench seat below it – a good place for a picnic.

The trail returns to forest and becomes narrow and tricky in places, climbing and descending steeply at times before reaching the alp of Ritten (1358m). Beyond this you eventually arrive at a track which is followed all the way down to **Burglauenen** (*refreshments*).

Nearing Burglauenen on the walk from Wengen, the Wetterhorn appears to block the valley

Return to Wengen by train either via Lauterbrunnen (change at Zweilütschinen) or Grindelwald. If the latter is chosen continue across Kleine Scheidegg, or catch the Männlichen gondola. Alternatively, an easy walk downvalley on the right-hand side of the road leads to Zweilütschinen (in 1hr 35mins), then alongside the Weisse Lütschine to Lauterbrunnen (1hr 15mins from Zweilütschinen). From Lauterbrunnen either take the train uphill to Wengen, or follow Route 37.

ROUTE 39

Wengen (Männlichen; 2229m) –
Wengen (1275m)

Grade	2
Distance	4km
Height loss	954m
Time	2hrs
Location	East of Wengen

There are just a few reasonably level walks to be had from Wengen. These wander along the hillside shelf across pastures and through the woods. There are fine viewpoints to be visited too, but it must be said that with the mountainsides being so steep and high above the Lauterbrunnental, it is inevitable that many of the best outings will require either steep ascents or descents. This is one of them. High above Wengen the Männlichen–Lauberhorn ridge makes a formidable wall, crusted here and there with avalanche protection fences. A path links the village with this ridge, but so steep and arduous is it in places that it may be better to walk it from top to bottom. The views are every bit as enjoyable after all. So the suggestion is to take the cablecar from Wengen to Männlichen, wander from the upper station to the Männlichen summit (a short and easy stroll), then descend back to the village. On the way up by cablecar one gains a tremendous respect for the power of glaciers that carved Lauterbrunnen's deep valley, while from the Männlichen ridge the panorama overlooking Grindelwald's pastoral basin is seen in all its glory – with Wetterhorn, Schreckhorn, Eiger, Mönch and Jungfrau all competing for favour. Männlichen is used as a launch-pad by paragliding enthusiasts, and you may see a number of brightly-coloured parachutes sailing over the valley as you walk.

On leaving the cablecar bear left for the **Männlichen** summit (20mins), or turn right for the return to Wengen.

Before coming to the hotel and restaurant with its fine view, cut through the ridge on a descending path that drops steeply at first, then slopes off a little more easily beside avalanche fences and beneath the cableway, with the valley bed a very long way down. (At this point you are more than 1200m above it.) Initially the descent is northward, the gradient quite comfortable. Then the path zig-zags steeply to a junction (Parwengi; 1864m) where you can either continue northwards again before dropping once more through woods to reach Wengen via the alp huts of Ussri Allmi, or bear left for a longer hillside traverse above the treeline before cutting down to the village. If the latter route is chosen, add another 20mins to the overall time.

ROUTE 40

Wengen (Männlichen; 2229m) – Kleine Scheidegg (2061m) – Wengernalp (1874m) – Wengen (1275m)

Grade	2
Distance	11km
Height loss	954m
Time	3hrs
Location	East and southeast of Wengen

This walk is a variation of Routes 27 and 29, both of which were described under the previous chapter covering Grindelwald and the Lütschental, but is given here in order to remind visitors to Wengen of the possibilities available to them. It is one of the classic walks of the region.

Wengernalp station

Ride the Männlichen cablecar from Wengen, and on leaving the upper station turn right along the clear, broad path that runs along the left-hand edge of the ridge with the Eiger's North Face directly ahead. Passing the large Männlichen hotel and restaurant, and the gondola lift from Grindelwald, the path will invariably be busy, and in the early weeks of summer is bordered by masses of alpine flowers. It makes a long curve round the slopes of Tschuggen, passes below the Lauberhorn and reaches **Kleine Scheidegg** (*accommodation, refreshments*) after about 1hr 20mins.

Veer right to cross the railway line just to the left of the main station buildings and follow a broad track that goes down beside the railway. The towering Mönch and Jungfrau dominate the scene. Just before you reach **Wengernalp Station** (*refreshments*) 30mins below Kleine Scheidegg, cut left on a narrow path that crosses a rough slope of pasture. You will come to woodland and a track that leads to more open pasture at Mettlenalp. The track continues now, rounds a spur of hillside and at an easy angle makes a steady approach to Wengen, which is reached in a little over an hour from Wengernalp.

ROUTE 41

Wengen (1275m) – Wengernalp (1874m)

Grade	2
Distance	4km (one way)
Height gain	599m
Time	2hrs
Location	South of Wengen

'Surely the Wengern Alp must be precisely the loveliest place in this world,' wrote Leslie Stephen in *The Playground of Europe*. 'It is delicious to lie upon the short crisp turf . . . to watch a light summer mist driving by, and the great mountains look through its rents at intervals from an apparently impossible height above the clouds.' The Wengernalp is indeed a wonderful place from which to gaze at the great mountains. It is a great place, too, from which to watch avalanches peel off the face of the Jungfrau almost hourly on a summer's afternoon.

From Wengen railway station walk along the street which runs parallel to the Kleine Scheidegg line on its left-hand side, then bear right beneath the line and continue past several hotels and flower-bright chalets, steadily gaining height. You soon ease out of the village with the Jungfrau drawing you on. A broad track leads without difficulty or diversion among pastures and through patches of forest, heading roughly southward and rising all the time at a comfortable angle. Rounding a spur of mountain high above the cleft of the Trümmeltal you come to the pastures of **Mettlenalp**. Here you bear left, taking a path away from the track, over pasture and into woods that lead directly to **Wengernalp**, with its farm buildings, railway above and big mountains hanging overhead. Return to Wengen by the same path, or by railway from Wengernalp station.

The Mönch looms above Mettlenalp

ROUTE 42

*Wengen (Eigergletscher; 2320m) –
Prechalp (1320m) – Trümmelbach –
Lauterbrunnen (795m)*

Grade	2–3
Distance	12km (one way)
Height loss	1525m
Time	4½–5hrs
Location	Southeast of Wengen

The steep, knee-crunching descent from the Eiger glacier near Kleine Scheidegg, to the depths of the Lauterbrunnen Valley where the drainage of the glacier (and those of the Mönch and Jungfrau) spills out, is full of interest. It begins along a moraine wall, passes through meadow and woodland, descends steep pasture, visits a lonely alp farm, and then twists down the abrupt wall of the Lauterbrunnental alongside the famed Trümmelbach Falls. Don't tackle this walk if you have knee problems! Trekking poles will be an advantage, for they will not only act as a brake where the gradient is very severe, but they'll also help to reduce muscle-strain. Simple refreshments are available at Prechalp (shown as Preech on some maps).

Take the train to Kleine Scheidegg, and change there for Eigergletscher Station on the Jungfraujoch line. Alternatively you could walk from Kleine Scheidegg to Eigergletscher on a signed path that parallels the railway line for much of the way, adding about 50mins to the walk.

From Eigergletscher Station walk along the platform to the restaurant, just beyond which a path cuts off to the right and descends to the right-hand lateral moraine walling the Eiger's glacier. Walk down the crest path with

Eigergletscher and the moraine crest path used at the start of the long descent to the Lauterbrunnental

a long view ahead through the Trümmeltal to a hint of the Lauterbrunnen Valley. After about 10mins the path forks. Remain on the crest path, but this soon eases off the moraine to descend steep grass slopes, eventually bringing you onto a saddle (Haaregg; 1990m). Keep on the ridge here with small cairns marking the route among juniper and low-growing conifers.

Descending among trees come to a signed junction where you curve left into woodland. In another 6mins bear left at the Weisse Fluh junction in the direction of Biglenalp and Mettlenalp. It's a narrow path that goes down through more woodland, then onto rough pastures with alp buildings seen across a stream. Do not cross here, but bear right and a few minutes later pass alongside the **Biglenalp** farmhouse and dairy. Crossing pastures, through patches of forest and over three streams, you come onto a track at **Mettlenalp** (1725m).

Keep along the track to pass alp buildings (direction Stalden and Wengen), and about 10–15mins later leave the track on a path which descends left into a small meadow where there's a path junction. This is Stalden (1665m). Turn left for Prechalp. The path soon descends a very steep forested hillside with occasional views between the trees onto rooftops far below in the Lauterbrunnental.

About 2hrs 15mins from Eigergletscher you come to the lonely alp farm of **Prechalp** (1320m *refreshments*) set in a sloping pasture with huge rock walls soaring ahead.

Another alp building is passed about 10mins below Prechalp, soon after which you descend a metal ladder and a series of wood-braced steps. The path continues its descent and takes you over a bridge spanning the Trümmelbach in a very narrow and lightless ravine, through which the river thunders, smoothing and refashioning the rocks as it does.

Over the bridge the path climbs a little to gain a narrow shelf (cable protection), then plunges downhill again among trees, twisting this way and that. Near the foot of the slope you make a sloping traverse of rock slabs (fixed cable for aid), and at last reach the flat meadows of the valley bed, just left of the **Trümmelbach Falls**.

> The **Trümmelbach Falls** are listed as a Swiss National Monument. Ten waterfalls carrying 20,000 litres of water per second, pour through a narrow defile in the Lauterbrunnental's east-flanking wall – the meltwater of the Eiger, Mönch and Jungfrau's glaciers. Accessible to the public (fee charged), stairs and walkways take visitors on a noisy, damp, but spectacular journey 'inside' the mountain to view the corkscrew effects of so much liquid energy.

Walk across the meadows to the road and turn right. A short distance along the road bear left to cross the Weisse Lütschine, and soon after turn right and wander along a peaceful route into **Lauterbrunnen**. Ride the train back to Wengen.

ROUTE 43

Stechelberg (910m) – Rottal Hut (2755m)

Grade	3
Distance	6km (one way)
Height gain	1845m
Time	5–5½hrs
Location	Southeast of Stechelberg

The Rottal Hut is situated high above the upper basin of the Lauterbrunnental under the Jungfrau's southwest arête; a remarkable position, not least for the beauty of its views. Whilst around the hut there are slopes of boulder and rubble, the little hanging valley of Rottal is cupped in a horseshoe of high peaks adorned with ice. Glaciers hang from near-vertical walls, cornices make sharp lips to the ridges, while just below the hut more icefields are imperceptibly carving out new valleys, new landscapes for tomorrow. This route of approach is by way of a very steep path – severe even – and with one section depending on a fixed rope to aid the ascent of a gully that splits a sheer rockface. There's also a steep snowslope to negotiate.

This is probably the most demanding route in the book, but one that is highly recommended to those who are fit, have a head for heights and experience of high mountain wandering. There are some objective dangers to face, though, and you should be aware of them. Stonefall could be a hazard on the ascent of the gully, and a snowslope below the hut could be dangerous in melting – or icy – conditions. If you have an ice axe with you, take it.

From the valley roadhead follow a broad paved footpath upvalley between meadows and trees with the Weisse Lütschine to your right. After about 8mins come to a side stream where a path branches left, signed to Stufenstein and the Rottal Hut.

Climbing steeply with a number of zig-zags, the path then bears right on a rising traverse with lovely views ahead to the Breithorn. When you come to an alp hut at 1585m, head left to enter a broad gully steepening into a tight wedge. Going through a fenced enclosure bear right to cross a stream coming down the gully. The path then resumes its steep ascent, now with the icefall of the Rottal's glacier seen way above, and the glistening ice face of the Mittaghorn off to the right. Stony wastes are relieved by shelves of pasture, but these soon give way to a wilderness of scree and rock, with vertical crags running in a line above.

The route heads up to the base of these crags and wanders along them to the right until coming to a gully with a fixed chain hanging down it. If there are others on the cliffs above, take shelter until all danger of stonefall is passed. The ascent of the gully is straightforward with the aid of the chain and/or fixed ropes, but a number of narrow ledges are littered with grit and stones.

Once above the gully the path resumes in easy windings up a boulderscape of old moraine, then along

Happy walker below the Rottal Hut

The **Rottal Hut** belongs to the Interlaken Section of the SAC. With a guardian at weekends from late June to mid-September, it has 45 dormitory places. For reservations ☎ 033 855 24 45.

the crest of a moraine wall above the glacier. Wander along this crest heading east into the little Rottal basin, the hut now seen some way ahead, and come to a rock wall heading a steep but short snow slope. Cross the slope at its upper edge, then scale a small cliff with another fixed rope. Emerging at the top you will see the **Rottal Hut** nearby. (Return to Stechelberg by the same route – about 3hrs.) ◀

ROUTE 44

Stechelberg (910m) –
Obersteinberg (1778m)

Grade	2
Distance	5km (one way)
Height gain	868m
Time	2½hrs
Location	Southwest of Stechelberg

Obersteinberg has a wonderfully remote location in the upper basin of the Lauterbrunnen Valley, nestling among an amphitheatre of peaks that crowd the valley head. To the northeast there's the Jungfrau, to the south the Breithorn and southwest the Tschingelhorn with the rock towers of the Lauterbrunnen Wetterhorn standing proud. The outlook is one of glacier and rock; moraine tip, pine and alpenrose; a raw land tamed and tended only in rare patches. Berghotel Obersteinberg (with a small farm nearby) commands some of the best views, and a night spent there would be one to remember.

Although rather steep in places, the walk is given a Grade 2 since there are no difficulties, nor is the route too long, and there are opportunities for refreshment along the

Berghotel Obersteinberg, at the head of the Lauterbrunnental

way. From the roadhead, wander upvalley to the left of the Weisse Lütschine on a paved footpath. Rising between meadow and woodland, it soon brings you to a bridge across the river. Over this come to a broad crossing track where the path continues ahead, meets the track again, then follows it uphill to the right until after about 200m another path breaks to the right, signed to Trachsellauenen. This is the one to take.

Crossing rough pasture with a small farm, 20mins later come to **Berghaus Trachsellauenen** (1203m *accommodation, refreshments*) – this is about 45mins from Stechelberg. At a major crossing track, turn right and when it ends 5mins later, a footpath continues ahead, rising among trees. Wandering through woods the path forks by a water trough (1260m). Both options lead to Obersteinberg. (The right-hand path climbs steeply in zig-zags, the left-hand trail is less demanding.) Bear left and continue on the path which becomes almost a stairway of rocks among damp and lush vegetation.

At the next junction continue straight ahead and leave the woods to cross an open area littered with avalanche debris, following the stream into an amphitheatre of mountains – the Schmadri Falls look particularly splendid as they spray down the hillside ahead. After passing the farm of Scheuerboden (1379m) a long and steepish climb through more woods brings the path to another junction at Wildegg (1560m) where you branch right for Obersteinberg. The final section of the walk (about 40mins) brings you into the open on a steeply winding path with **Berghotel Obersteinberg** seen above.

BERGHOTEL OBERSTEINBERG

Berghotel Obersteinberg is a romantic old mountain inn, dating from the 1880s, whose rooms have neither electricity nor running water. After dark candlelight is a necessity, not an effect. Dormitory accommodation is also available here in an adjacent building. The seemingly remote location within the UNESCO World Natural Heritage Region is magnificent. (For reservations ☎ 033 855 20 33 www.stechelberg.ch)

ROUTE 45

*Stechelberg (910m) – Obersteinberg
(1778m) – Stechelberg*

Grade	2–3
Distance	9km
Height gain	868m
Height loss	868m
Time	4½hrs
Location	South of Stechelberg

This walk is a loop trip which, coupled with a side journey to the Oberhornsee (Route 46), or a lengthy lunch stop at Berghotel Obersteinberg, would make a rewarding full day's outing.

Follow Route 44 to **Obersteinberg** (2½hrs *accommodation, refreshments*) and continue along the path beyond the hotel heading northeast over pastureland. After about 15mins you come to **Hotel Tschingelhorn** (1678m *accommodation, refreshments*), another rustic mountain inn standing in an isolated position on the edge of woodland (☎ 33 855 13 43). The path forks just beyond the hotel, and both options lead to Stechelberg.

Ignore the right-hand path and continue ahead. The trail loses height, steeply in places, but always clear. Eventually you will come to another junction of tracks. One leads to the Sefinental and Gimmelwald, the other cuts down to Stechelberg. Take the descending path to the right. On the way down you cross an open bluff of pastureland with a farm and barn upon it, and with fine views down into the Lauterbrunnental. Shortly after this you rejoin the path used on the upward route and wander down the familiar trail to **Stechelberg.**

ROUTE 46

Obersteinberg (1778m) –
Oberhornsee (2065m)

Grade	2
Distance	2.5 km (one way)
Height gain	287m
Time	1hr 10mins
Location	South of Obersteinberg

This short walk could easily be tacked onto Route 45 for added interest, if the plan is to do a loop trip from Stechelberg. (See Route 47 for a continuation from Oberhornsee back to Stechelberg.) Oberhornsee is an attractive little tarn trapped among boulders and green moraine below the glaciers that come from the Tschingel Pass, Tschingelhorn and Breithorn. From it there is an unusual view of the southwest flanks of the Jungfrau. The tarn, and a good part of this upper valley, is protected as a nature reserve.

Leaving Berghotel Obersteinberg head to the right and at the nearby signed junction bear right again on a splendid hillside traverse that contours across flower-rich slopes, with a steep drop on the left and the constant boom of cascades in your ears. After a while the path descends to a stream, the Tschingel Lütschine, crosses on a bridge and climbs over rough pastures. Steadily gaining height you pass waterfalls and cross more streams, then finally loop up and over a grassy bluff to find the little tarn of **Oberhornsee** nestling among the boulders. The water is a beautiful deep blue in colour; above it glaciers and moraine banks provide a wild yet lovely scene. (Allow 45–50mins for the return to Obersteinberg, or see the following route for an extension to the walk.)

The Lauterbrunnen Wetterhorn, seen from the path to the Oberhornsee

ROUTE 47

Obersteinberg (1778m) – Schmadri Hut
(2263m) – Stechelberg (910m)

Grade	3
Distance	8km
Height gain	485m
Height loss	1353m
Time	5hrs
Location	South then northeast of Obersteinberg

This alternative return to Stechelberg leads through some wild country and visits a small mountain hut. It should be borne in mind though, that one section of the route passes below glacial séracs that from time to time crash down and send their ice chunks across the trail.

Follow Route 46 to the **Oberhornsee**. Walk along its north shore and down to a spongy plain bordered on either side by rocks and grassy bluffs. Turn left and follow

The wild upper reaches of the Lauterbrunnental, seen from the Schmadri Hut

the stream northward, on its left bank, until you come to a plank footbridge. Cross the stream and follow paint flashes leading steeply up a slope to a knoll with fine views from the top. Above there are glaciers with bands of séracs. Now descend to cross the Schmadribach stream by a second plank footbridge, beyond which the trail climbs among a mixture of pasture and moraine to reach the **Schmadri Hut**. This is a splendid setting for such a small refuge; big mountains tower overhead and there are views over a truly wild landscape. ▶

The route to Stechelberg returns briefly down the approach path, then continues to lose height over stony slopes heading northeastward. It maintains direction to cross avalanche slopes and more streams on the route to the alp farm at **Schwand** (1684m) where there is a junction of trails. The right-hand path continues round the hillside and eventually descends to Trachsellauenen by a circuitous route. The left-hand path descends a grassy rib in steep zig-zags, then slopes off to the north to reach **Berghaus Trachsellauenen** (*accommodation, refreshments*) by a more direct route. From here follow the main valley path to **Stechelberg**.

Owned by the Academic Alpine Club of Bern, the **Schmadri Hut** has no resident guardian, but there are self-catering facilities and dormitory places for 14.

ROUTE 48

*Obersteinberg (1778m) – Tanzbödeli
(2095m) – Stechelberg (910m)*

Grade	3
Distance	9km
Height gain	317m
Height loss	1185m
Time	3¾–4hrs
Location	Northeast of Obersteinberg

This is a tremendous walk which crosses a high ridge and descends into the lovely Sefinental before going down to Stechelberg. It's quite tough in places but has amazing panoramic views. The high point of Tanzbödeli (the 'little dance floor') is gained by a 20min, very steep optional path breaking away from the main trail, which leads to an almost level meadow falling abruptly on three sides. A good head for heights is needed, for the descent is long and steep. But it's a splendid walk.

Leaving Berghotel Obersteinberg turn left (northeast) and walk towards the small farm building nearby. Immediately before it go through a gate on the left and along a narrow track for just 3mins, when you fork right on a path that makes long loops up the steep grass hillside. Gaining height the path is both narrow and a little exposed; there are views of the Tschingelhorn in one direction, the Jungfrau in the other.

After about 40mins turn the spur of the **Busengrat** and come to a path junction (1940m) from where a very fine view is gained along the Lauterbrunnen Valley, across the Sefinental to Mürren and Gimmelwald, to Wengen and Männlichen and Schynige Platte too.

The continuing route to Stechelberg descends from here, but to gain the Tanzbödeli you must break away and take the path which climbs steeply for about 20mins. The little **Tanzbödeli** meadow is at 2095m and from it a stunning 360° panorama greets you. Along the ridge to the southwest the craggy Ellstabhorn partially conceals the Gspaltenhorn, but to the left of that Tschingelhorn, Lauterbrunnen Breithorn, and the long headwall of snow and ice-capped peaks lead round to the Jungfrau. Peeping over a saddle north of the Jungfrau can be seen the spear-like peak of the Eiger. To the northwest stands the Schilthorn, while almost 1200m below lies the deep Lauterbrunnen Valley.

Descend with care to the Busengrat junction and turn left. The steep descent winds among alpenrose and bilberry, then pines stub the hillside, and about 20mins from the junction another narrow path breaks left. This

leads to the **Busenalp Hut** (*accommodation, refreshments*) in a further 15mins. Although it is not on our route, if you have both time and energy, it would be worth making the diversion. ▶

Continue to descend, and 5mins beyond the Busenalp junction, the path turns a spur to gain a view across the Sefinental and up to the Gspaltenhorn. The gradient becomes more severe down wooded slopes, and after a particularly steep section eased with steps, the way tucks below abrupt (and in some places, overhanging) cliffs. Below these the way forks again. Take the right branch, and soon you'll come to a wooden bridge spanning the Sefinen Lütschine. Cross to the north bank and turn right on a broad track which leads all the way to **Stechelberg.**

Steep crags of the Ellstabhorn rise above the Tanzbödeli

The **Busenalp Hut** is really an alp dairy farm in which limited, basic accommodation (up to five places) is sometimes available. Set upon a level of pasture on the south flank of the Sefinental, its situation is idyllic.

ROUTE 49

Gimmelwald (1380m) – Sefinental (1256m) – Tanzbödeli (2095m)

Grade	3
Distance	6km (one way)
Height gain	839m
Height loss	124m
Time	3hrs
Location	South of Gimmelwald

On its crossing of the Busengrat (the dividing ridge that separates the upper Lauterbrunnental from the Sefinental), Route 48 made a diversion to visit the wonderful vantage point of the Tanzbödeli meadow. Visitors to Gimmelwald are also encouraged to make the steep and demanding walk to that vantage point, for it is quite simply one of the finest in the Bernese Alps. Hence the route described here. Before setting out, however, do remember that while the ascent to the Tanzbödeli is very steep so will the descent be on the return to Gimmelwald. It will be a fairly tough but rewarding day.

Follow the tarmac road out of Gimmelwald, and when it makes a sharp hairpin bend, take the track ahead which now slopes downhill into the **Sefinental.** On reaching a junction of tracks in the valley bed (20mins from Gimmelwald), turn left and in another 3–4mins you'll see below on the right a bridge spanning the Sefinen Lütschine. Cross the river and at once you'll begin the sharp uphill climb on a marked footpath. The way is relentlessly steep, through forest for the first hour or so. As the forest thins, so the angle eases and you come to a path junction. The right branch visits the Busenalp (see Route 48 for details), but ours veers leftward.

The ascent resumes with views growing in extent, while the path twists up grass- and shrub-covered slopes, and leads eventually to another junction on the ridge-spur of **Busengrat** (1940m; 2½hrs). Views are magnificent from here, but the panorama is even better from above. Take the right-hand trail and climb the ridge for a further 20mins, until emerging onto the flat meadowland of **Tanzbödeli**. (Return by the same path, taking special care on the initial descent to the Busengrat junction.)

ROUTE 50

Gimmelwald (1380m) – Sefinental (1256m) – Rotstock Hut (2039m)

Grade	3
Distance	6.5km
Height gain	783m
Height loss	124m
Time	3hrs
Location	Southwest and west of Gimmelwald

The Rotstock Hut is popular in summer with walkers and long-distance trekkers. Mostly visited from Mürren, this hut approach from Gimmelwald explores the lovely Sefinental before making a fairly demanding climb over pasture and through forest.

Take the same route out of Gimmelwald described at the start of Route 49. On coming to the track junction in the bed of the **Sefinental** after about 20mins, turn right. At once you have a glorious direct view to the head of the valley where Gspaltenhorn and Büttlassen form an

Gimmelwald huddles on a terrace below Mürren

The **Rotstock Hut** stands on a shelf of pasture next to the Boganggen alp buildings, below the Sefinenfurke. It's a cosy hut with 52 dormitory places, and a resident guardian from June to the end of September; meals provided. For reservations ☎ 033 855 24 64 www.rot-stockhuette.ch

impressive headwall. The track remains on the right-hand side of the Sefinen Lütschine, rising steadily through patches of woodland and beside rock slabs, then narrows to a footpath. About 10mins later the path forks. The left-hand option goes to Kilchbalm at the head of the valley, but for the Rotstock Hut the right branch is taken.

Ascend a long succession of concrete steps, then enter woodland. Above the trees you continue uphill across a slope of pasture with a solitary alp building on the left (Ozen; 1582m) and a splendid view to the right. Beyond this there are more steps and a continuing steep climb that eventually leads to another junction at 1820m from which you can see the Rotstock Hut and adjacent farm buildings on a grassy shelf ahead.

The upper path at this junction goes to Oberberg and Mürren (see Route 51), but we take the left branch to weave among lush vegetation, then up a grassy gully and across a stream, before crossing the final pastures to gain the **Rotstock Hut**. ◀

ROUTE 51

*Gimmelwald (1380m) – Sefinental
(1256m) – Oberberg (1930m) –
Mürren (1638m)*

Grade	3
Distance	11km
Height gain	674m
Height loss	292m
Time	4–4½hrs
Location	Southwest and west of Gimmelwald

Another challenging walk from Gimmelwald, this near-circular route explores a large part of the district and sees familiar mountains from unfamiliar angles. Much of the route shares the tracks and paths used on Route 50, but below the Rotstock Hut it branches away to the alp of Oberberg. Here a note of caution is necessary, for shortly before the path from Oberberg meets a well-made trail by the Brünli viewpoint, it crosses a brief but steep scree-slope and is a bit thin for a few paces. Extra care should be taken on this section. There is, however, an alternative path from Oberberg.

Follow directions given in Route 50 from Gimmelwald as far as the path junction from where you catch a first sight of the Rotstock Hut. This junction is at 1820m. Ignore the left branch which goes to the hut, and continue ahead to reach the four alp buildings of **Oberberg**. There's another path junction here, with the left-hand trail also going to the Rotstock Hut. (That trail leads up to a crossing path which could be used for getting to Mürren, thus avoiding the scree-slope referred to in the introductory paragraph.)

Blocked by Bütlassen and Gspaltenhorn, the Sefinental cuts deep into the mountains below Gimmelwald

Continue past the alp buildings to rise easily over rough pastures, then across a narrow scree-slope. Shortly after crossing the screes the narrow trail climbs up to meet a major path (the Mürren–Rotstock Hut path) where you bear right to the **Brünli** viewpoint at 2020m. You now make a very steep descent to **Spielbodenalp** (1793m *accommodation, refreshments*). Just beyond the restaurant/inn cross a stream and follow signs to Mürren. There are two paths, both of which are straightforward and have their merits. In another 30–40mins you enter **Mürren** near the Schilthorn cablecar station. (Should you need to return to Gimmelwald, either ride the cablecar down, or take the well-signed route near the post office that winds down the linking road.)

ROUTE 52

Mürren (Allmendhubel; 1912m) –
Suppenalp (1852m) – Mürren (1638m)

Grade	1
Distance	3km
Height loss	274m
Time	45mins
Location	West of Mürren

Rising above Mürren the Allmendhubel funicular opens up a fine walking area for visitors. Opened in 1912 the ride lasts for only 4mins but delivers you onto a belvedere with a tremendous panorama laid out before you. Ahead rise all the fabled peaks for which this corner of Switzerland is justly noted, while behind lie the green pastures of the Blumental backed by the Schilthorn. This particular walk makes an easy traverse of the Blumental's pastureland, passes two mountain inns, then descends back to Mürren.

From the upper Allmendhubel station take the left-hand trail that curves round the hillside and soon looks down on the Blumental pastures with their haybarns, chalets and two mountain inns. Take the path down into the pastures and come to a junction. Pension Sonnenberg (*accommodation, refreshments*) is a short step away to the left. However, our route goes to **Pension Suppenalp** (*accommodation, refreshments*) standing next to a one-time dairy at the foot of the slope. Pass in front of the inn, then take the path which descends left into lush vegetation (bilberries and alpenroses). Although there are two or three options on the way down, the preferred route keeps mostly along the edge of woodland and brings you out by the Schilthorn cableway. Turn left into the village.

ROUTE 53

Mürren (1638m) – Suppenalp (1852m) –
Rotstock Hut (2039m) – Mürren

Grade	3
Distance	12km
Height gain	502m
Height loss	502m
Time	4½hrs
Location	Southwest of Mürren

For spectacular views this walk takes a lot of beating. There are a few rather steep sections to it, but some fine level stretches too. It's not a rugged mountain route, but a high walk on soft turf, with flowers and shrubs for company, and a huge panorama to absorb.

Take the upper street through Mürren, and shortly after passing the Allmendhubel funicular station, bear right up a steep and narrow tarmac service road that leads into the lovely Blumental, dotted with chalets and haybarns. Pass Pension Sonnenberge (*accommodation, refreshments*), and continue to **Pension Suppenalp** (*accommodation, refreshments*) with its wonderful views of the Eiger, Mönch and Jungfrau that are especially magical from here with the evening alpenglow on them.

Beyond Suppenalp the path angles up and across the hillside, passes beneath the Schilthorn cableway, goes round a bluff and gains a direct view of the Gspaltenhorn across the Sefinental. The trail eases along a high pastureland and comes to the **Schiltalp** cheesemakers' huts (*refreshments*) in 1hr from Mürren. Keep ahead at a junction of tracks, but a short distance beyond the huts take a narrow path half-left ahead. This contours the hillside and comes to another trail junction by the Schiltbach.

Perched on a shelf of pasture by the Boganggen alp, the Rotstock Hut is a cosy place in which to spend a night.

(The Schilthorn rises at the head of the valley.) Cross the stream and climb the path ahead up a steep vegetated hillside to gain the ridge of Wasenegg. This is another superb viewpoint, elevated and solitary.

A steady descending traverse takes you down to the southwest, into a broad pastureland and a junction of paths at 2050m. Continue ahead for a further 20mins or so to reach the **Rotstock Hut** (*accommodation, refreshments*), set on a shelf of grass by the Boganggen alp huts.

Return to the junction at 2050m and remain on the direct path back to Mürren which goes via the Brünli viewpoint, then steeply down to **Spielbodenalp** (*accommodation, refreshments*) and through the hamlet of Gimmeln with tremendous views all the way.

ROUTE 54

Mürren (1638m) – Spielbodenalp (1793m) – Sprütz – Gimmelwald (1380m) – Mürren

Grade	2–3
Distance	7km
Height gain	413m
Height loss	413m
Time	2½–3hrs
Location	Southwest of Mürren

During this circular walk we visit a small mountain inn, then descend through woodland to tiny Gimmelwald before returning along a winding lane to Mürren. Views are outstanding, of course, but perhaps the most intriguing feature of the walk is where it leads directly behind the Sprütz waterfall, giving the novel experience of standing beneath an overhanging rock to enjoy a view through the veil of a cascade!

Make your way to the Schilthorn cablecar station and continue ahead on the narrow road which crosses the Mürrenbach and rises between steep pastures, now leaving the village behind. The road makes a sharp right-hand bend, but when it curves right again by a wooden chalet, take a narrow footpath ahead. It contours across the hillside, goes through woodland and over one or two minor streams, then through sloping meadows with views ahead to the Gspaltenhorn. In a little under 30mins come to a junction where one trail descends left to Gimmelwald, another climbs to the right to Gimmeln and Schiltalp. Ignoring both of these we continue ahead, rising among more sloping pastures on the North Face Trail.

Wandering past attractive old buildings the path is interrupted by information panels detailing the climbing history of some of the North Faces in view.

After passing typical Oberland chalets the path forks. Although the left branch is signed to Sprütz and Gimmelwald, we continue ahead through strips of forest before coming to a group of buildings and yet another junction. Keep ahead and moments later cross the Schiltbach on a footbridge to reach **Pension Spielbodenalp** (1793m *accommodation, refreshments*) about 40mins from Mürren.

Immediately beyond the inn the path forks again. Take the left branch, cross a brief pasture and go down into woodland. Take the right branch when the way forks yet again, and descend a steeply twisting path which brings you directly to the **Sprütz waterfall** (1hr). Take care as you approach the waterfall, for the steep gritty path may be slippery. ▶

Pass behind it and then climb a flight of steps on the other side. About 5mins from the waterfall come to another woodland junction and keep ahead, now losing height. On emerging from the trees Gimmelwald can be seen below and you descend directly to it on a path that crosses and recrosses the narrow road linking the village with Mürren.

The centre of **Gimmelwald** is reached in about 1½hrs. It's possible to return to Mürren via the Schilthorn cablecar, but if you plan to walk, go alongside the post office, and after a few paces take a footpath which rises between pastures and 5mins later brings you onto the road. Turn right along it (there are footpath shortcuts in several places) all the way to **Mürren**, which you reach by the post office.

The **Sprütz waterfall** occurs where the Schiltbach tips over an overhanging cliff in a steep wooded ravine. After draining the Schilthorn's slopes, the Schiltbach is funnelled into this ravine where it has scoured deep holes and swirls in the rocks via a series of cascades on its way to the Sefinental, about 1300m below its source in the Grauseeli.

ROUTE 55

Mürren (1638m) – Schilthorn Hut (2432m) – Schilthorn (2970m)

Grade	3
Distance	7km (one way)
Height gain	1332m
Time	4½ hrs
Location	Northwest and west of Mürren

A large number of visitors to the Lauterbrunnental ride the cablecar up to the Schilthorn. It's one of the most popular tourist excursions in the Bernese Alps, for the beauty of its summit panorama is known far and wide, not only from local publicity, but from the James Bond movie, *On Her Majesty's Secret Service*, that was partially shot there. Since there is such ease of →

← access, none should imagine that after this long and steep walk to it there will be solitude and peace to be had on the summit. But the walk is a challenge – though there's nothing difficult about it – and it samples the contrast of gentle pasture with the somewhat bleak prospects afforded by the Engital, in which the Schilthorn Hut is based. And the views, of course, are always worth earning.

The **Schilthorn Hut** belongs to the Mürren Ski Club, has 40 places and a resident guardian during the summer season from July to September. For reservations ☎ 033 855 50 53.

Perhaps the most direct start is to follow Route 53 into the Blumental, then veer right to a junction of paths on a grassy saddle at 1912m. From here bear left and go up a broad track or piste which rises through a cleft in the hills known as the 'Kanonenrohr' (Canon Barrel). Through this you enter a basin of pasture, and ease leftward round the north side of the Muttlerehoren to gain the stony wastes of the Engital. Just above to the left the **Schilthorn Hut** (*accommodation, refreshments*) has a fine view of the Jungfrau and its immediate neighbours. ◄

Wander through the Engital, which lies between ridges running west and north from the summit of Birg, and the stony Schwarzgrat above to the right. The Schilthorn tops the valley, with its cablecar swinging between the Birg middle station and the actual summit. Rise to a saddle at 2599m overlooking the Grauseeli tarn and follow an easy track round the head of the basin in which it lies. When the track ends a waymarked path goes up the left-hand (east) ridge, passing a memorial to Alice Arbuthnot (killed by lightning on the Schiltalp in 1865), then more steeply to gain the flat crowded top of the **Schilthorn** (*refreshments*). (Allow about 3½hrs for the descent by the same route or, better still, follow Route 57 back to Mürren.)

SCHILTHORN'S SUMMIT

The **Schilthorn's summit** panorama is impressive. A long wall of snow-crowned peaks includes the wavelike Blüemlisalp massif in the southwest, while the whole of the Jungfrau group is on display in the south and south-east. From a point a short distance below the summit, Mont Blanc can be picked out among a mass of peaks far off in the northwest. Apart from the cablecar station, the summit has a revolving restaurant, shop, and cinema showing clips from the Bond movie *On Her Majesty's Secret Service* filmed in the vicinity. (The mountain experience doesn't come much more bizarre than to make the ascent by one of the Schilthorn's ridges, and minutes after reaching the summit at almost 3000m, to be watching a movie in a cinema!)

ROUTE 56

Mürren (Rotstock Hut; 2039m) –
Schilthorn (2970m)

Grade	3
Distance	5km (one way)
Height gain	931m
Time	2½–3hrs
Location	North of the Rotstock Hut

This, the second of our routes to the summit of the Schilthorn, is more challenging than the first. It also gives a more 'authentic' mountain experience in the wilderness sense, for there's no cablecar sailing overhead, and for much of the way the crowded summit of the mountain is shielded from view. Since parts of the West Ridge, climbed on this route, are narrow, steep and exposed, only experienced mountain scramblers should attempt it. That being said, there are fixed cable safeguards and a section of ladder to ease a particularly steep pitch. It's a fine route.

From the Rotstock Hut take the path towards the Sefinenfurke, heading upvalley, and in 10mins come to a junction with a signpost. Bear right, at first between two minor streams, then along the left-hand side of a little hanging valley. After a while the path cuts across to the valley's east flank, crossing several streams on the way, then zig-zags up the steepening slope before flanking briefly left along a ledge with a view of the Blüemlisalp ahead.

After this steps and cable assistance take you up into a rock tip where waymarks guide the route, then through a basin of shale and grit on the way to the saddle of **Roter Härd** (2668m). This is gained about 1hr 40mins from the hut. Views are impressive from here.

Now turn right along the ridge, at first northeast, then eastward, crossing a high point, then contouring across the right (south) flank of a minor summit to reach a narrow saddle with a view left into the upper Soustal. The way now climbs the right-hand side of the rocky crest, aided in places by fixed cable. A steel ladder and metal rungs also ease the ascent as you then move from one side of the crest to the other, and sometimes on the crest itself. Views become even more impressive and extensive

As the Schilthorn's ridge steepens, the ascent is eased by metal rungs and handrails

as you mount the final section of ridge towards the summit of the **Schilthorn**.

Descent to Mürren could be made by cablecar, or by following Route 57 – this would complete a very satisfactory traverse of the mountain.

ROUTE 57

Mürren (Schilthorn; 2970m) – Schiltalp (1948m) – Blumental – Mürren (1638m)

Grade	3
Distance	8km
Height loss	1332m
Time	3hrs
Location	West and southwest of Mürren

This descent of the Schilthorn is offered as an alternative to using the Engital route, and may be used in order to extend Route 55 into a full loop trip, or to create a traverse of the mountain by those who made the ascent by Route 56. From the summit to the saddle above the Grauseeli tarn the route is the same as that for the final ascent taken on the Route 55, but from the tarn down to Mürren the way follows good paths (very steep in places) into an increasingly green and pleasant landscape.

From the summit descend the eastern arête of the mountain and go down to the saddle at the head of the Engital above the Grauseeli tarn. At the path junction bear right and slope down to the tarn's south shore (wonderful views). From there the way descends steeply to the inner corrie of the Schilttal, bearing left when the trail forks. On an easy traverse of the lower hillside you go through the little hamlet of cheesemakers' huts at **Schiltalp** (*refreshments*). A farm

track descends from here, but we continue ahead (sign to
Blumental; 40mins) along a pleasant green terrace. A path
continues from it, among trees and scrub vegetation, turns a
spur of the Schiltgrat, passes beneath the Mürren–
Schilthorn cableway and comes to **Pension Suppenalp**
(*accommodation, refreshments*) in the Blumental.

It's possible to drop down the hillside here and enter
Mürren near its southern limits, but a better option is to continue across the open pastures of Blumental to Pension
Sonnenberg (*accommodation, refreshments*), then descend
by narrow tarmac service road to the centre of **Mürren**.

ROUTE 58

*Mürren (1638m) –
Grütschalp (1486m) – Mürren*

Grade	1–2
Distance	10.5km
Height gain	426m
Height loss	426m
Time	3–3¼hrs
Location	North of Mürren

An undemanding circular walk across pastures with big views leads to Grütschalp, and back along the shallow terrace in company part of the way with the railway. In the early summer meadows full of flowers add much to the walk; later at the end of August or early September, bilberries should be ripe for picking. There will undoubtedly be marmots on show and, possibly, chamois too.

Walk along Mürren's upper street passing the Allmendhubel funicular station on your right, and shortly after take a narrow service road which climbs steeply between houses, and brings you up into the lovely **Blumental**. Passing Pension Sonnenberg (*accommodation, refreshments*) turn right at a path junction and go up the slope to the Allmendhubel upper station at 1907m (*refreshments*). From here a grass path takes you up the slope heading a little north of west, and soon brings you to an obvious saddle with a path junction and a view left into the Blumental.

Turn right in the direction of Pletschenalp and Grütschalp, and when the path forks about 1min later, ignore the right branch and continue down the slope and wander along the left-hand side of a gentle little valley with Eiger and Mönch seen on the other side of the Lauterbrunnental. At the next trail junction keep ahead (the right branch goes to Winteregg), soon to turn a spur and curve round the edge of a reedy pool. Passing beneath the Winteregg ski lift, you gain a view across the valley to Wengen.

Ignoring other path options remain on the high path across pastureland, brushing against bilberry and wild raspberry as you go, before coming to the **Pletschenalp** junction at 1740m (about 1½hrs). Go ahead through a turnstile, descend a short slope to another junction, and branch right on a path (The Mountain View Trail) that descends directly to **Grütschalp** in another 20mins or so.

On coming to the Grütschalp–Mürren railway line, turn right and follow the clear and easy path back to **Mürren**, arriving by the station. (Refreshments are available at Winteregg, 25mins after leaving Grütschalp.)

ROUTE 59

Mürren (1638m) –
Sefinenfurke (2612m) – Griesalp (1407m)

Grade	3
Distance	14km
Height gain	974m
Height loss	1205m
Time	6½hrs
Location	Southwest of Mürren

The Sefinenfurke is one of the classic non-glacial passes of the Bernese Oberland, its crossing being seen as one of the highlights of the Alpine Pass Route. From Mürren to Griesalp is an arduous stretch, but it's also a very scenic one, and given good weather conditions the Sefinenfurke makes a magnificent perch from which to view some of the giants of the Alps. After a long but acceptably graduated approach over pastureland, the final climb to the pass is steep and tiring, while the initial descent on the western side is severe enough to warrant the use of fixed cables and reinforced steps to deal with a slope of black gritty scree. At the end of the walk Griesalp is a tiny hamlet at the head of the Kiental, with overnight accommodation (beds and dormitories), and an infrequent postbus service that goes through the Kiental to Reichenbach in the Frutigtal (the lower Kandertal), where trains may be taken to either Kandersteg or Spiez.

From Mürren follow directions in Route 54 as far as **Spielbodenalp** (1793m *accommodation, refreshments*) reached after about 40–50mins. Just beyond the restaurant/inn take the right-hand path to climb a series of zig-zags up a steep spur to the Brünli viewpoint where there are two bench seats to exploit the wonderful view. The path now contours across a large area of pasture, and eventually brings you to the **Rotstock Hut** (2039m *accommodation, refreshments*) in 2–2¼hrs.

Ahead lies a large bowl of rough pasture dotted with rocks and boulders. Cross to its western side and gain height over old moraine banks with the pass clearly seen before you reach it. The way steepens, with the final approach zig-zagging up a slope of gritty black shale and scree.

The **Sefinenfurke** is reached about 4hrs after leaving Mürren. It's a very narrow pass, rocks rising on both sides, the east and west faces falling dramatically away. But views are grand. Back the way you have come the Eiger, Mönch and Jungfrau are seen side-on. Go up the rocks of the ridge to the left (south) a short way, and you can gaze on the Blüemlisalp massif to the southwest. It's a wonderfully wild scene.

Take great care on the initial descent. The slope is both extremely steep and unstable, with long sections of fixed cable and reinforced steps created on the shifting shale and grit. At the foot of the scree the path resumes across grassy hillocks on the right bank of a stream, and a little over an hour from the pass you come to the alp hut of Ober Dürrenberg (1995m). Just below this cross the stream and follow the winding path down a steep grassy hillside with fine views up to the Blüemlisalp.

Eventually the path brings you to **Bürgli** (1617m), a small dairy farm where you bear right to cross the Dürrenberg stream, and take the farm road down towards Griesalp. This leads past the hamlet of Steinenberg, shortly after which you come to Berggasthaus Golderli (1440m *accommodation, refreshments*) which has beds and dormitory accommodation (☎ 033 676 21 92 **www.golderli.ch**). The road forks here, and you take the left branch down to **Griesalp**, where accommodation may be had at Berghaus Griesalp (☎ 033 676 12 31). In the square there's a small shop and a postbus link with the lower Kiental.

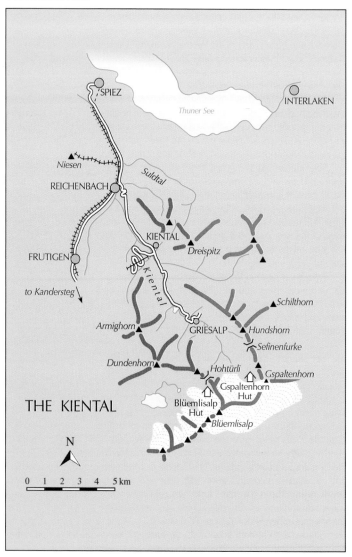

THE KIENTAL

N

0 1 2 3 4 5 km

KIENTAL

The Kiental is one of those quiet, unassuming valleys tucked away from the main tourist circuit, and as such reserves its delights for those with an independent spirit. It is a lovely back-country glen, green, open and pastoral, yet it has its dark defiles too, and at its head the wild torrents, huge walls of rock, and snowfields and glaciers of the Blüemlisalp massif. It's a valley of many faces, but each one is full of charm.

ACCESS AND INFORMATION

Location	West of the Lauterbrunnental, rising below the Blüemlisalp and flowing northwestward into the Frutigtal at Reichenbach above Spiez.
Maps	LS 254T *Interlaken*, 264T *Jungfrau*, 263T *Wildstrubel* at 1:50,000 Kümmerly + Frey *Saanenland-Simmental-Kandersteg* at 1:60,000
Bases	Reichenbach (707m), Kiental (958m), Griesalp (1408m)
Information	Verkehrsbüro Reichenbach, Bahnhofstr, CH–3713 Reichenbach (☎ 033 676 23 76 **www.reichenbach.ch**) Verkehrsbüro Kiental, CH–3723 Kiental (☎ 033 676 10 10 **vvkiental@datacomm.ch ferein@kiental.ch www.kiental.ch**)
Access	By train to Reichenbach via Spiez, then postbus as far as Griesalp.

The eastern flanks of the Blüemlisalp sweep round to form, with the help of the neighbouring Gspaltenhorn and Büttlassen, a tight amphitheatre down which flows the Gamchi Glacier. Below the glacier lies a roughly moulded terrain that is slowly being tamed by Nature's patience and artistry. On shelves above the main valley stream there are one or two summer-only dairy farms. Pine forests clothe the lower hillsides; waterfalls cascade down crags, and as the valley progresses northwestward, so little meadowlands open out, starry with flowers in spring and early summer, adorned with clusters of farms and neat Oberland chalets.

Travelling downvalley Griesalp is the first habitation of note, although a little higher Steinenberg and Golderli both have a few houses. Griesalp is tiny; a square with a few buildings round it. Below the hamlet the valley falls steeply and the road fights the gradient with some excessively tight hairpin bends between rock slabs cleft with waterfalls. Then the valley eases and there's a lake, the Tschingelsee, spread among the pastures, forest-clad slopes rising to modest craggy peaks on either side.

All this upper part of the valley is known as Gornerngrund, but just before you come to the village of Kiental, roughly two-thirds of the way along the main Kiental valley, another valley flows in from the southeast. This is Spiggengrund, a glen serviced by farm track and with footpaths that lead to a secluded patch of country with prospects for walkers of a high pass or two to cross at its head.

Kiental itself is the only true village in the valley, and then there's not very much to it. It has a pretty church overlooking both village and valley, some pleasant houses and a soft pastoral outlook. It has made few concessions to winter tourism, which is commendable, and the only mechanical aid is a chairlift rising on the west side of the valley to Ramslauenen, which can be useful to gain height for one or two high-level walks in summer.

After Kiental it's almost as though you're turning your back on the valley, for the road eases along the hillside, rounds a spur and then looks out over the broader Frutigtal, whose upper reaches fork as the Kandertal and Engstligental, respectively noted for the resorts of Kandersteg and Adelboden. And at the foot of

The Blümlisalp massif walls the Gornergrund at the upper limit of the Kiental

the road, where the Kiental joins the Frutigtal, lies the unassuming village of Reichenbach, with the pyramid peak of Niesen rising before it.

The valley, then, is missed by the majority of visitors to the Bernese Alps. It is not for the Kiental to have internationally famous resorts. There are no sumptuous hotels, no intertwining cats' cradles of cableways, their steel towers catching the sun. Instead, a modest landscape where farmers continue to graze their cattle and make hay untroubled by an overt tourist industry. But there are footpaths a-plenty; walks that will take you hour after hour in the peace of the hills; walks that give a taste of solitude with dreamy views all around. There are arduous long routes that entice over high passes to east or west, and gentle low-valley strolls to be had alongside streams or a lake. The Kiental may be little-known, but it's much loved by those who have discovered it, and it will certainly repay a few days' exploration.

MAIN BASES

REICHENBACH (707m) Not to be confused with the falls of the same name above Meiringen, Reichenbach owes its allegiance more to the Frutigtal than to the Kiental, but it sits at the mouth of the latter valley and is on the route of all traffic going into it. It's also set beside the railway from Thun or Interlaken via Spiez, so is additionally important to Kiental economy and communications. The village itself is unimposing yet attractive enough, and is backed by a slope of fine meadows liberally dotted with chalets and farmsteads. To the northeast rises the Niesen, a conical peak with a funicular going from Mülenen to the very summit for one of the finest panoramas of any mountain in the Bernese Alps. (Go either early morning or in the evening.) Reichenbach has a few shops, a bank, and accommodation at Gasthaus Bären (☎ 033 676 12 51 **baeren.reichenbach@bluewin.ch**), Hotel Bahnhof (☎ 033 676 12 13 **heinz.trachsel@bluewin.ch**), and Hotel Kreuz (☎ 033 676 11 06). There are also several apartments to rent.

KIENTAL (958m), according to Baedeker in the 1901 edition of his guide to Switzerland, is 'charmingly situated, and well adapted for a stay of some time.' Those sentiments remain true today. It's a village of only 200 or so inhabitants, and yet is still the largest community in the valley proper, sitting in the midst of an unspoilt landscape dominated by grass and tree and with the snows of the Blüemlisalp seen to the south. The modern church is most attractive, and it makes a photogenic foreground with the big mountains framed beyond. A short distance up-stream the valley is fed by the Spiggebach coming from its own glen above to the left, mostly hidden from the village by a dense covering of forest. Accommodation in Kiental is limited to four hotels: Hotel Bären (☎ 033 676 11 21 **baerenkiental@bluewin.ch**), Hotel Chalet (☎ 033 676 16 46 **chalet-**

Oberland chalet near Griesalp

peeters@datacomm.ch), Hotel Kientalerhof (☎ 033 676 26 76 **info@kien-talerhof.ch**), and the Hotel Alpenruh (☎ 033 676 11 35), but in addition there are some 300 beds in holiday apartments. In the main street a few shops provide the basic necessities. A chairlift swings up the western hillsides to Ramslauenen for winter skiing and summer walking. A large car park is found on the southern outskirts of the village, and a toll is levied on all who wish to drive beyond it. A postbus service operates six times a day to Griesalp.

176

GRIESALP (1407m) makes a fine, out-of-the-way base for a walking or mountaineering holiday. It is only a tiny hamlet with limited facilities, including accommodation (beds and dorm places) available at Berghaus Griesalp (☎ 033 676 12 31). More accommodation may be found a short way upvalley at Gorneren – see Other Bases below. From the square footpaths branch off to a variety of high mountain destinations, to remote passes, mountain huts, lonely alps and waterfalls. The postbus terminates here and car parking is forbidden except for bona fide hotel guests.

OTHER BASES
Elsewhere, either in the valley or high above it, there are several little inns or farms with *matratzenlagers* providing accommodation of one sort or another. To the northeast of Kiental village a few metres below the **RENGG PASS**, and just below the summit of Wätterlatte, there's a hut with dormitory places for about 30, located midway on a route to the Suldtal; it has fine views north to the Thunersee, and south to the snow-capped mountains. On the western hillside above Kiental, where the chairlift terminates, **BERGHAUS RAMSLAUENEN** has dormitory places (☎ 033 676 22 26). Above Griesalp the **NATURFREUNDHAUS GORNEREN** has room for 60 in its dormitories (☎ 033 676 11 40 **gorneren@naturfreunde.ch www.naturfreundehaeuser.ch**), while **BERGGASTHAUS GOLDERLI** also has beds and dormitory accommodation (☎ 033 676 21 92 **mail@golderli.ch www.golderli.ch**). More dormitory accommodation is available at Oberi Bundalp on the way to the Hohtürli, where the **BERGGASTHOF ENZIAN** (Berghaus Bundalp) is open from June to mid-October (☎ 033 676 11 92 **a-r.steiner@freesurf.ch www.bundalp.ch**).

MOUNTAIN HUTS
BLÜEMLISALP HUT (2834m) Situated just above the Hohtürli pass, with a near view of glaciers, this hut is owned by the Blüemlisalp (Thun) Section of the SAC. With 138 places, it is permanently manned from the end of June to mid-October, when a full meals service is provided. For reservations ☎ 033 676 14 37 **h.u.mani@bluewin.ch www.mypage.bluewin.ch/bluemlisalphuette**.

GSPALTENHORN HUT (2455m) Reached in 3hrs or so from Griesalp, this hut is owned by the Bern Section of the SAC and has spaces for 75. Tucked below Büttlassen and Gspaltenhorn, there's a resident guardian from late-June to early September, when meals are provided. For reservations ☎ 033 676 16 29.

ROUTE 60

Reichenbach (707m) –
Engelgiess (990m) – Kiental (958m)

Grade	1
Distance	5km (one way)
Height gain	390m
Height loss	149m
Time	1hr 40mins
Location	South of Reichenbach

This easy but pleasant stroll makes a gradual introduction to the Kiental. It wanders between sloping pastures, passes a number of handsome chalets and enjoys bright views.

From Reichenbach walk up the Kiental road to the nearby village of Scharnachtal, which you reach in about 20mins. As you enter the village, with houses on the left, the road crosses a stream. Leave the road here and walk up the left-hand side of the stream, over a lane that crosses the path, and ahead on a track making a rising traverse of hillside towards Engelgiess. As you wander along this some lovely views are to be had; neat cropped meadows and big snow-bound mountains rising in the distance, the Frutigtal sliding below between the hills and Niesen marking the northern end of a long ruffled ridge.

From **Engelgiess** (reached in a little under an hour) continue to rise a little over pastures, pass through some woods and then join a lane that winds downhill towards the buildings marked on the map as Rufene. But at the final hairpin of this lane break away left to follow a track which cuts round the hillside and brings you to the northern end of **Kiental** (*accommodation, refreshments*). To return to Reichenbach take the postbus.

ROUTE 61

Reichenbach (707m) –
Gehrihorn (2130m)

Grade	3
Distance	8km (one way)
Height gain	1423m
Time	4½–5hrs
Location	South of Reichenbach

The entrance to the Kiental is guarded on the northeast by the 2007m Wätterlatte, and the southwest by the Gehrihorn; modest mountains both, but superb viewpoints. This ascent of the Gehrihorn is straightforward and worth giving a day for.

First head south along the Frutigtal to the village of Kien, then up the hillside behind it to Aris (826m), a small hamlet overlooking the valley. From here the route heads directly up the hillside spur heading south again towards woodland (signed to Brandweiden and Ober Geerene). By a combination of track and footpath the way leads on to Chüeweid (1475m – also known as Kuehweide), about 2hrs or so from Reichenbach.

Ober Geerene lies almost 300m above Chüeweid, but there's nothing difficult about the route to it, although you have the option of going to left or right from Chüeweid to Bachwald. **Ober Geerene** (1766m *accommodation, refreshments*) is reached about 3½hrs after leaving Reichenbach and from it there are some very fine views. A Bergweg leads on from here, climbing steeply up to the northern ridge by which the **Gehrihorn** summit is gained; the panorama is magnificent.

Descend by the same path, allowing 3hrs. Alternatively, take the descending path from the summit, but instead of breaking away westward from the ridge towards Ober Geerene, continue down the arête and then veer right (eastward) on a clear path that leads to the chairlift station at Ramslauenen. From there go down to Kiental for the postbus back to **Reichenbach.**

ROUTE 62

Kiental (Ramslauenen; 1409m) –
Chüeweid (1475m) –
Aris (862m) – Kiental (958m)

Grade	2–3
Distance	11km
Height gain	640m
Height loss	1090m
Time	4hrs
Location	Southwest of Kiental

A variation of Route 61 above, this walk is a little less demanding than its predecessor, since most of the way is either downhill or along a steady contour. It makes good use of the chairlift from Kiental to Ramslauenen, crosses the northern shoulder of the Gehrihorn and descends to the hamlet of Aris. From there a return is made to the Kiental proper by way of an easy lane and a forest track. Refreshments are available at Ober Geerene, above Chüeweid.

From the top of the chairlift take the uphill path heading west towards the Gehrihorn. Climbing steeply in places, you gain the shoulder of the mountain and go up the ridge a short way. Veer right when the path forks, and descend towards the clutch of buildings of **Ober Geerene**

(1769m *accommodation, refreshments*). Now continue down on the trail marked **Chüeweid** (or Kühweide), and from there all the way to **Aris** (862m), a hamlet near the foot of the slope on the left bank of the Kiene river. A narrow road passes through Aris. On coming to this road turn right and walk along it (and the track that continues from its end), through forest and alongside the river all the way back to **Kiental**.

ROUTE 63

Kiental (958m) –

Aris (862m) – Frutigen (780m)

Grade	1
Distance	9km (one way)
Height loss	178m
Time	2½hrs
Location	Northwest of Kiental

This is a valley walk, not unduly demanding yet with an undeniable charm. It follows a track or narrow road all the way and makes for a very pleasant morning's outing.

At the southern (upvalley) end of Kiental village take the street which leads down to cross the river, then immediately bear right on a track that runs parallel with it. Through meadows and woods this track eases its way along the lower slopes of hillside for about 4km or so before coming to the little hamlet of **Aris** in just over an hour from Kiental. Approaching Aris views open out with the broader Frutigtal cutting at right angles ahead and the cone of Niesen rising abruptly to the northwest.

Leave the road at the first hairpin bend and contour round the hillside on a track heading southwest to Schwandi, a scattering of chalets and farms where another minor road is joined for the final approach to **Frutigen**. (To return to Kiental take the train from Frutigen to Reichenbach, and either follow Route 60 or ride the postbus from there to Kiental.)

ROUTE 64

Kiental (958m) – Kilchfluh Pass (2456m) – Grütschalp (1486m)

Grade	3
Distance	21km
Height gain	1498m
Height loss	970m
Time	7½hrs
Location	Southeast of Kiental

A long and arduous route, maybe, but this is a very rewarding one for those who enjoy wild country with a sense of remoteness. On this cross-country trek there are scattered farms, soft pastures and wild corries. The valleys of Spiggengrund to the west of the pass, and the Soustal to the east, complement one another, yet the ultimate destination for walkers tackling this route must surely be Lauterbrunnen below Grütschalp, and the Lauterbrunnental is in stark contrast to that of the Kiental. Taken on its own, this makes a challenging day out. But when combined with Routes 34 (Grütschalp–Mürren) and 59 (Mürren–Griesalp), a superb 2–3 day circuit can be achieved.

Walk south through Kiental and bear left where the road forks on the outskirts of the village, soon to leave the road in favour of a path that slopes above it ahead to the left.

This takes you through forest, and climbs above water-falls cascading through a narrow cleft which drains the Spiggengrund valley. Once in this side glen the footpath brings you onto a farm track that crosses to the southern (true left) bank of the Spiggebach and leads deeper into the valley. It's a wildly romantic glen, and as you progress through it, so the tight amphitheatre of mountains at its head appears wild, yet attractive. The pass is detected from a long way off; a saddle in the long ridge that links Schwalmere to Kilchfluh and the Schilthorn.

Passing several farm buildings, between rough pastures and through patches of forest, make steady progress towards the head of the valley. After about 3hrs the track swings left to cross the stream again, and soon after gives way to a Bergweg path at the huts of Glütschnessli (1638m). Now the trail climbs round to the hut of Barenfeld, on to Hohkien (2027m; 3hrs 45mins), then climbs northward for about 500m before veering south on a slight descent towards the **Kilchfluh Pass**. There will invariably be snow patches on the way to it, even in the middle of summer, so take care. The saddle is reached about 5hrs from Kiental, and a new valley system with long views spreads out before you.

The descent into the Soustal goes down over snow and scree, making for the left-hand side of the Sousbach stream. Once down on pastures follow the stream to the alp hamlet of Oberberg (1997m) about 1hr below the pass, where you cross to the right bank. Continue in the same direction until joining another path just beyond the building of Souslager (1680m). Now follow the signed trail veering to the right through forest almost all the way to **Grütschalp** (about 50mins from Souslager). From here either take the funicular down to Lauterbrunnen, or the train along to Mürren.

For details of accommodation etc in Lauterbrunnen or Mürren, please see the previous section headed Lauterbrunnental.

ROUTE 65

Griesalp (1407m) – Golderli (1440m) – Tschingelsee (1150m) – Pochtenfall – Griesalp (1407m)

Grade	1–2
Distance	5km
Height gain	290m
Height loss	290m
Time	2½–3hrs
Location	North and northwest of Griesalp

Although there are some short steepish ascents and descents, this circular walk is mostly undemanding, but with long valley views, a lake and a waterfall, it's quite popular.

From Griesalp wander upvalley along the continuing road to **Golderli** (there are obvious footpath alternatives which are steeper than the road). On reaching Berggasthof Golderli (*accommodation, refreshments*) on your right, turn left and follow a clear track heading northwest along the hillside. Passing a few scattered buildings, and with charming views along the valley which stretches far ahead, the track ends and a footpath continues. When it forks, take the left-hand option to descend in zig-zags to join the main valley road just north of the **Tschingelsee**. Here you bear left and wander along the road to a point at the far end of the lake where another footpath breaks away left to climb above the valley past the Pochtenfall. It then veers right and returns to **Griesalp**.

ROUTE 66

Griesalp (1407m) – Hohtürli (2778m) –
Blüemlisalp Hut (2834m)

Grade	3
Distance	6km (one way)
Height gain	1427m
Time	4½–5hrs
Location	Southeast and south of Griesalp

Hohtürli is a lofty, wind-scoured saddle on the north-projecting ridge of the Blüemlisalp massif, from which a sensational view shows nearby glaciers, wave-like ridges and the misty hint of the Kandertal deep below and seemingly far away to the west. Above the saddle stands the Blüemlisalp Hut, a comfortable refuge from which a good many climbs are made possible. As the destination and high-point of a walk it makes an obvious goal. Be warned, though, the way to it is rough and arduous in places.

Oberi Bundalp on the way to the Hohtürli

At the remote Oberi Bundalp beds and dormitory accommodation can be had at **Berggasthof Enzian** (☎ 033 676 11 92).

Behind Berghaus Griesalp lies a dark stretch of forest. Near the building a signpost marks the start of the route, where you take a path rising through woodland to reach a farm road. Bear left. Although it would be possible to remain on the road as far as Oberi Bund, it's better to take footpath shortcuts. The first of these comes shortly before the road makes a sharp bend. A path breaks left of the road and heads through forest, across pasture and over streams, before rejoining the road in the Bunderalp pasture near **Untere Bundalp** (1690m). Leave the road once more and go up the continuing grass path to gain an upper shelf of pasture, where you come onto the farm road again shortly before reaching **Oberi Bundalp** (1840m) in 1½hrs from Griesalp. ◄

Continue along the road for a few mins, then take a signed path that rises over rough pastureland to a steep slope of black shale, grit and old moraine deposits. The badly eroded path is surprisingly severe, but you gain height quickly, and at last emerge onto a grey rock ridge. Now make a rising traverse before tucking against the left-hand side of the ridge. The way improves, but steepens again as you mount towards the pass, courtesy of ladders, fixed cables and a long succession of timber steps overhung by crags. Then up the final zig-zags to emerge on the **Hohtürli** after about 4hrs 15mins. The **Blüemlisalp Hut** is seen above to the left, and it will take about 15mins to gain it by a clear and obvious path.

BLÜEMLISALP HUT

The Blüemlisalp Hut is a very well equipped and popular with both mountain walkers and climbers, and is visited by trekkers on the Alpine Pass Route. Owned by the Thun-based Blüemlisalp Section of the SAC it can sleep 138 in its dormitories (20 in the winter room), and has a resident guardian from late-June to mid-October, when a full meals service is provided. For reservations (☎033 676 14 37 h.u.mani@bluewin.ch www.mypage.bluewin.ch/ bluemlisalphuette.

To return to Griesalp allow about 2½hrs, but take special care on the initial descent, and again when tackling the steep slope of grit. Snow is often lying late into summer and at such times the way down can be rendered difficult and potentially dangerous.

The Blümlisalp Hut at 2834 metres

ROUTE 67

Griesalp (1407m) –
Hohtürli (2778m) – Kandersteg (1176m)

Grade	3
Distance	15km
Height gain	1371m
Height loss	1602m
Time	7½hrs
Location	Southeast and southwest of Greisalp

Crossing the Hohtürli is one of the great walks of the Bernese Alps. It's a famous route, used by generations of mountain folk as well as by mountaineers and walkers crossing from the Kiental to the Kandertal and vice-versa. It is also the highest crossing on the Alpine Pass Route and one that features in a variety of traverses and circuits. But although the crossing is tackled by a good many each summer, it remains an arduous undertaking.

Take Route 66 from Griesalp to the **Hohtürli** (4¼hrs), and descend on the western side by way of a clearly marked path that initially makes the most of well-graded zig-zags over broad slopes of scree. The way continues below the screes along a rocky balcony in view of fast-receding glaciers. A descent from this balcony leads onto the crest of a moraine wall, at the end of which you descend to the right into a rough bowl of pasture dotted with boulders and with a stream winding through. In 5½–6hrs you come to the huts of Ober Bergli (1973m) where it's sometimes possible to get refreshments. Shortly after this you look down into the great basin of the Öeschinensee.

A veritable stairway of a path descends to the lake, passing the lower alp of Unter Bergli (1767m) where the trail veers right, crosses a stream and continues along the northern side of the lake, but some way above it. On coming towards the western end of the **Öeschinensee** the path slopes down, passes through trees and comes to a

High pastureland above Oberi Bundalp in the upper reaches of the Kiental

collection of hotels and restaurants (1593m *accommodation, refreshments*). ▶

A service road continues ahead from here. It's very steep in places, but there are footpath shortcuts, and about an hour from the lake you will arrive in **Kandersteg** (*accommodation, refreshments*). For details of accommodation and other facilities, please refer to the following chapter, Kandertal.

Other routes from the Kiental

* One cross-country route worth considering from Kiental village heads roughly northward over the Rengg Pass and down to the **SULDTAL** (4hrs, Grade 3), with an option then of continuing north to **LEISSIGEN** on the shores of the Thunersee, or upvalley and across the **RENGGLIPASS** to **SAXETEN** and **WILDERSWIL.**

* A more demanding 5hr route from Kiental to **SULD** goes through the glen of Spiggengrund to cross the pass of **LATREJEFELD** (1993m). This is another Grade 3 walk. But also by way of Spiggengrund the ascent of the **SCHILTHORN** (2960m) is made possible. This is a fairly arduous route, Grade 3, which joins Route 56 at the Roter Härd saddle.

* The **PANORAMAWEG KIENTAL–THUNERSEE** is a walk with its own leaflet available from the Kiental tourist office. This 5½hrs route makes an interesting and scenic traverse of the northern hillsides high above the Frutigtal. On good clear paths and way-marked throughout, this is a highly recommended tour.

* Another walk promoted with its own leaflets is the so-called **NORDRAMP**, a high-level path originally created in 1961 but upgraded and improved since then. This 5½–6hr route links the Kiental with **KANDERSTEG**. It begins at the chairlift station of Ramslauenen, crosses the shoulder of the Gehrihorn to Chüeweid (Kuhweid) and makes a southward traverse above the Frutigtal and Kandertal all the way to Kandersteg.

At the western end of the much-loved Öeschinensee, and overlooking the beautiful lake, accommodation (beds and dorm places) may be found at the Hotel Öeschinensee (☎ 033 675 11 19 **www.oeschinensee.ch**), and Berghaus am Öeschinensee (☎ 033 675 11 66). About 20mins from the hotels there's a chairlift link with Kandersteg.

189

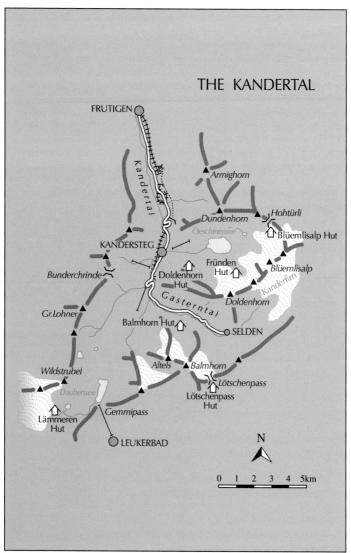

THE KANDERTAL

FRUTIGEN

Kandertal

▲ *Armighorn*

▲ *Dundenhorn*   ▲ *Hohtürli*

Oeschinensee

⬆ Blüemlisalp Hut

KANDERSTEG

Fründen
Hut ⬆   *Blüemlisalp*

Kanderfirn

Bunderchrinde

Doldenhorn
Hut ⬆

Gasterntal   ▲ *Doldenhorn*

▲ *Gr.Lohner*

Balmhorn Hut ⬆   ➤ SELDEN

▲

Wildstrubel   ▲ *Altels*   ▲ *Balmhorn*

▲   ⬆ *Lötschpass*

Daubensee   Lötschenpass
Hut

⬆   *Gemmipass*
Lämmeren
Hut

◯ LEUKERBAD

N

0 1 2 3 4 5km

KANDERTAL

After the Lütschental and Lauterbrunnental, the Kandertal is the best-known of all Oberland valleys, Kandersteg at its head being a prime location for walking and mountaineering holidays. The lower, pastoral valley of the river Kander is known as the Frutigtal; a gentle land of trim chalets set in meadows of green. But as you travel south through it, so a more austere and challenging set of landscapes beckon. Big snow peaks and stark rock walls block the valley and soar in an uncompromising gesture, setting a contrast to the lower pastures and flower-filled meadows.

ACCESS AND INFORMATION

Location	South of Spiez on the Thunersee, the Kandertal is the upper section of the Frutigtal. The valley actually rises as the Gasterntal between the main watershed ridge of the Bernese Alps and western peaks of the Blüemlisalp massif.
Maps	LS 254T *Jungfrau* and 263T *Wildstrubel* at 1:50,000
	Kümmerly + Frey *Saanenland-Simmental-Kandersteg* at 1:60,000
	See also *Wanderkarte Kandersteg* at 1:25,000 available locally
Bases	Kandersteg (1176m), Selden/Gasterntal (1552m)
Information	Kandersteg Tourismus, CH–3718 Kandersteg (☎ 033 675 80 80 info@kandersteg.ch www.kandersteg.ch)
Access	By train to Kandersteg via Thun and Spiez. Selden in the Gasterntal is served by minibus from Kandersteg railway station.

At Frutigen the valley is joined by two distinct branches. From the southeast the Engstligental has Adelboden at its head; to the south it's the upper valley of the Kander – the Kandertal – with Kandersteg a further 12km away, both valley and resort known for more than a century for their mountaineering potential and, much longer, as a base from which to cross the mountains into the sun-trap of the Rhône Valley.

The Kandertal is separated from the Engstligental by a long ridge which terminates at its northern end on the 2341m Elsighorn. The southern end of this ridge, however, having been redirected by the partial intrusion of the pastoral Ueschinental, becomes confused beyond the Steghorn (3146m) – an outlier of the Wildstrubel massif – where other spurs and ridges run off to a tangle of rock, snow and ice above the historic Gemmipass.

Opposite this ridge, and walling the east side of the valley, a long line of modest summits rises steadily from the mouth of the Kiental to the Dündenhorn (2862m), which is linked to the Blüemlisalp massif across the saddle of the Hohtürli. The Dündenhorn and Blüemlisalp have scoured between them a deep bowl of an amphitheatre in which lies the Oeschinensee; Kandersteg is found below it where the Oeschibach flows into the Kander.

South of Kandersteg the valley appears to be blocked by a massive wall of cascade-draped rock. Above it, and easily gained by cableway, lies the surprisingly gentle upper glen that leads to the Gemmipass and the Valais. But to the east of this apparent valley-blocking wall lies a second delightful glen, also hidden by yet another set of rocky walls, and with a mini-gorge at its entrance down which the young Kander pours its way in a fury of rush and roar. This gorge is the Klus, the glen it leads to being the Gasterntal, one of the loveliest and least changed of all valleys in the Bernese Alps.

Born among the snow and ice of the Kanderfirn, a broad glacial sheet only hinted at from the valley itself, the Gasterntal is a gem. Wandering into the valley, below Altels and Balmhorn to the south and Doldenhorn to the north, one sees undisciplined streams flooding through the edge of woods and across low-lying pasture. Then as you progress deeper, feathery waterfalls spray from the cliffs, meadows lavish with flowers in early summer open out, and the pinewoods fall back to reveal the mountains at its head.

With its side glens and upper shelves of alpine meadowland, the Kandertal has plenty to offer the visiting mountain walker or climber. The mountains are big and with a distinct grace of form, their flanks abrupt and challenging. Yet they have their softer aspects too that attract rather than defy. Routes abound for walkers and climbers of all degrees of seriousness. There are short valley strolls, medium-grade outings that visit lonely alps, waterfalls and lakes, and strenuous routes that go up to lofty mountain huts or across high passes and icefields. There is something, indeed, for everyone here.

MAIN BASES
KANDERSTEG (1176m) stretches along the valley floor in a ribbon development of chalets, hotels and shops. Thanks to the railway which pierces the 15km Lötschberg Tunnel through the mountains south of the resort, the village is

Traditional Oberland house in Kandersteg

known (briefly) to many more than those who actually stay there. Not far from the railway station, the heart of Kandersteg is where you'll find a variety of shops and banks, hotels and restaurants, the post office and tourist information office. There's a range of accommodation, from ungraded pensions to the five-star Royal Park Hotel. Among the lower-priced hotels there's the National, with 13 beds and 62 dorm places (☎ 033 675 10 85 **hotelnatikander@ datacomm.ch**); Hotel Erika which also has beds and dorm accommodation (☎ 033 675 11 37 **www.hotel-erika.ch**); and the cosy 20-bed Hotel Zur Post by the church (☎ 033 675 12 58 **info@hotel-zur-post.ch www.hotel-zur-post.ch**). Kandersteg has one public campsite, terraced on the lower hillside to the east of the village by the chairlift that serves the Öeschinensee. Camping Rendez-vous is open throughout the year; it also has 28 dormitory places above the restaurant (☎ 033 675 13 54 **rest-rendez-vous@bluewin.ch**). Elsewhere there are no fewer than 1000 beds in holiday apartments and chalets. In summer Kandersteg is a walkers' paradise with more than 300km of trails, some of which are accessible from a variety of cableways. As well as a chairlift to the Öeschinensee, there's cablecar access to Allmenalp (popular with paragliding enthusiasts) above the village to the west, and the Sunnbüel cablecar for easy walking in the high valley that leads to the Gemmipass. Kandersteg has a paragliding school, swimming pool and various other sports facilities. It is also home to an International Scout Centre.

SELDEN (1550m) in the Gasterntal has no shops, banks or other facilities beyond two rustic mountain inns. For those who wish to spend a few days or weeks in the unspoilt peace and beauty of the mountains, the Gasterntal makes an ideal base. The narrow valley road is unpaved and banned to private vehicles (except permit holders), but a minibus provides a taxi service from Kandersteg railway station as far as Selden. The valley is a veritable flower garden in spring and early summer, and a joy to explore. Both Selden's inns have bedrooms and dormitory accommodation; Hotel Steinbock (☎ 033 675 11 62 **steinb.kuenzi@bluewin.ch**), and Hotel Gasterntal-Selden (☎ 033 675 11 63 **hotelgasterntal@bluewin.ch**). Further upvalley, Berggasthaus Heimritz also has dormitory places (☎ 033 675 14 34), as does Berghaus Gfällalp (☎ 033 675 11 61), set almost 300m above Selden on the route to the Lötschenpass. (There's also a 40-place *matratzenlager* in a hut at the pass itself – see below.) Downvalley, not far from the valley's entrance, Hotel Waldhaus is set in a crescent of woods. Open June to October, this offers standard bedrooms as well as dormitory accommodation (☎ 033 675 12 73).

OTHER BASES
In the **SUNNBÜEL/GEMMI REGION**, Berghotel Schwarenbach, one of the oldest of Swiss hotels, has 25 beds and 120 dorm places (☎ 033 675 12 72 **info@schwarenbach.ch** **www.schwarenbach.ch**), while at the Gemmipass, 5mins from the lift station, the modern Hotel Wildstrubel also has beds and dormitory places and claims magnificent views from every room (☎ 027 470 12 01 **info@gemmi.ch www.gemmi.ch**). Overlooking the **ÖESCHINENSEE** beds and dormitory places may be had at both the Hotel Öeschinensee (☎ 033 675 11 19 **info@oeschinensee.ch www.oeschinensee.ch**) and Berghaus am Öeschinensee (☎ 033 675 11 66 **berghausoeschinensee@bluewin.ch**).

MOUNTAIN HUTS
BLÜEMLISALP HUT (2834m) Built above the Hohtürli with close views of the Blüemlisalp Glacier, this popular hut is owned by the Thun-based Blüemlisalp Section of the SAC. With 138 dormitory places and a resident guardian from late-June to mid-October, a full meals service is provided. (☎ 033 676 14 37 **h.u.mani@bluewin.ch www.mypage.bluewin.ch/bluemlisalphuette**). It is reached by a very steep path from Kandersteg in 5–5½hrs.

FRÜNDEN HUT (2562m) This hut sits at the foot of the Fründen Glacier on a lip of rock high above the Öeschinensee. One of the largest huts in the region, it has 90 dormitory places, is owned by the Kandersteg-based Altels Section of the SAC and with a resident guardian from late May until early October, has meals and drinks available. It is gained by a steep path of about 4hrs from Kandersteg. For reservations ☎ 033 675 14 33 **f.loretan@bluewin.ch**.

DOLDENHORN HUT (1915m) Overlooking Kandersteg from a grassy alp on the northwest flank of the peak after which it is named, this hut has 43 dormitory places and a resident guardian at weekends from April to October, and throughout July and August; meals provided. It can be reached in just 2½hrs from Kandersteg. For reservations ☎ 033 675 16 60 **www.doldenhornhuette.ch**.

WINTEREGG HUT (1890m) This 36-place hut is open throughout the year and easily accessible in just 10mins from the Sunnbüel cableway. It is owned by the Biel Section of the SAC. For reservations ☎ 079 417 85 24 **r.zulauf@bluewin.ch www.sac-biel.ch**.

LÄMMEREN HUT (2501m) Reached in about 6hrs from Kandersteg (or 3½–4hrs from Sunnbüel), this hut is situated high under the southeastern glacier bowl of the Wildstrubel, and is approached for much of the way along the Gemmipass route. It can sleep 96 and has a resident guardian in the winter season (Christmas/New Year to mid-May) and from late June to mid-October; a full meals service is offered. Owned by the Angenstein (Basle) Section of the SAC; for reservations ☎ 033 470 25 15 **waeflercb@bluewin.ch www.strubel.ch/ laemmerenhuette**.

BALMHORN HUT (1956m) Due north of the Balmhorn and reached by a steeply twisting path from the Gasterntal, this small hut has just 26 places and a guardian from mid-July to mid-August, and weekends from late May to the end of September, when meals are provided (☎ 033 675 13 40 **www.luethistef.ch/ sac-altels/balmhornhuette.htm**).

LÖTSCHENPASS HUT (2690m) Built on the actual Lötschen Pass between the Gasterntal and Lötschental, this 40-place, privately-owned hut has a fine view of the Bietschhorn. It may be reached from Selden in about 4hrs. Guarded from February to the end of October (not May), meals are provided. For reservations ☎ 027 939 19 81 **info@loetschenpass.ch www.loetschenpass.ch**.

MUTTHORN HUT (2901m) This hut is useful for mountaineers and walkers with glacier experience who set out to cross the Petersgrat to the Lötschental, and is best reached from Selden in the Gasterntal in about 4½hrs. It has 100 dormitory places and a resident guardian from late-June to the beginning of September, when meals are provided. For reservations ☎ 033 853 13 44 **rolu@freesurf.ch www. solothurn.ch/sac**. It is owned by the Weissenstein (Solothurn) Section of the SAC.

The Öeschinensee above Kandersteg, starting point for a number of walks

ROUTE 68

Kandersteg (Öeschinen chairlift; 1682m) –
Öeschinensee (1593m)

Grade	1
Distance	2.5km (one way)
Height loss	89m
Time	20–30mins
Location	East of Kandersteg

The Öeschinensee is depicted on so many posters around Kandersteg that you almost know what to expect before you actually see it for yourself. But the reality is still worth capturing. This very easy stroll makes good use of a late afternoon when the weather may have been bad and at last there's promise in the sky. Or perhaps you've been travelling to the area and have just arrived and are in need of a little exercise with views to enjoy. Not least, it offers an easy way to reach the lake where you might consider spending the day with a picnic, simply lazing on the edge of pinewoods by the water and gazing at the huge peaks rising from it.

The chairlift (Sesselbahn Öeschinensee) is signed from the village street and is found on the eastern side of the valley next to the campsite. It is operational from 7.30am until 6.30pm during high summer weeks. From the upper station a signpost sets you in the right direction, walking eastwards along a broad, well-trodden track through meadows with the Blüemlisalp peaks seen in all their splendour ahead. The track soon veers to the right, but you should ignore this and continue ahead on a lesser trail gently contouring between patches of woodland. Ignore a second path which veers away leftwards (a sign directs this route to Ober Bergli and the Blüemlisalp Hut) and soon after you will come to the buildings of **Läger**

The oval-shaped **Öeschinensee** is one of the most beautiful mountain lakes in Switzerland, and is almost completely ringed by an amphitheatre of lofty peaks. →

← The Blüemlisalp-
Doldenhorn group
rises abruptly from
the lake's south and
southeast shores,
while the
Dundenhorn's crags
fall steeply to the
north shore.
Pinewoods edge the
water in places, with
intimate little 'bays'
elsewhere.

(1659m). Take the narrow footpath ahead. This takes you down through the woods to the lakeside. Turn right and wander along the shoreline trail that leads to the hotels and restaurants at the western end of the **Öeschinensee**, or go left on a rising path that climbs above the northern shore as far as you wish to go. (It is not possible to make a complete circuit of the lake, but there are plenty of idyllic places to enjoy a picnic.) Either wander back to the chairlift station for a ride down to Kandersteg, or follow the service road that leads from the hotels all the way to the village. If you decide to walk all the way, allow at least an hour for the descent. The road is extremely steep in places, but there are also footpath alternatives. ◄

ROUTE 69

*Kandersteg (1176m) – Hohtürli (2778m) –
Blüemlisalp Hut (2834m)*

Grade	3
Distance	10km (one way)
Height gain	1658m
Time	5–5½hrs
Location	East of Kandersteg

This walk is in part a reverse of Route 67. The way to the hut is, in fact, a rather easier option when tackled from Kandersteg than from Griesalp, but it remains a strenuous day out anyway, and is no less a visual delight. First there are dainty waterfalls cascading down the great slabs of the Doldenhorn as you wander up to the Öeschinensee; then the lake itself – always a joy to gaze on. Above the lake there are rough boulder-strewn pastures with glaciers hanging from the Blüemlisalp massif, and the path climbs below them, on crests of old moraine before finally tackling a long slope of gritty scree. Once at the hut an amazing scene of high alpine splendour is an adequate reward for the time and energy required to get there.

Either take the chairlift route to the Öeschinensee (Route 68), thus reducing the time required for the walk by about 50mins, or follow the service road through the Öeschinental to the east of Kandersteg, rising steeply alongside pinewoods to reach the lake in about 1hr 15mins (*accommodation, refreshments*). (Should you decide to take the chairlift there is an alternative path which leaves the main trail just before Läger. It skirts high above the northern side of the Öeschinensee and joins the lake shore path at Ober Bergli.)

Wander along the lakeside path which bears left just after the hotels, and keep with it as it begins to rise along a shelf above the northern shore. For a while it hugs steep cliffs, then through shrubs and trees on the way to the alp buildings of **Unter Bergli** (1767m). From the upper buildings the continuing path climbs steeply on a stairway to emerge on a lip above the Öeschinensee's deep bowl. Soon after, you arrive at **Ober Bergli** (1973m; 2hrs 45mins) set in a rough landscape of boulders. Refreshments can sometimes be bought here.

The way wanders along the right-hand side of a stream, then crosses it and begins to rise once more towards moraine walls left by the retreating glaciers. High above these, glaciers can be seen draped down the face of various Blüemlisalp summits. Now you go along a moraine crest, climb to a rocky shelf and come to an upper region of wide scree slopes. The hut can be seen perched on the ridge above. Ascend the screes by a switchback trail to gain the saddle of **Hohtürli** about 5hrs after setting out from Kandersteg. Wander up the final slope to the **Blüemlisalp Hut**, where you will have earned both rest and refreshment. ▶

From its elevated position, the **Blüemlisalp Hut** provides wonderful close views of the various peaks that make up the Blüemlisalp massif, and of its glaciers. Comfortable and well-appointed, it has 138 dormitory places, and a full meals service when the guardian is in residence: from late June to mid-October. To reserve places, ☎ 033 676 14 37.

ROUTE 70

Kandersteg (1176m) –
Öeschinensee (1593m) –
Fründen Hut (2562m)

Grade	3
Distance	9km (one way)
Height gain	1386m
Time	4hrs
Location	East of Kandersteg

The Fründen Hut is perched on the top of a rocky bluff below the north-west flanks of the 3369m Fründenhorn, almost 1000m above the Öeschinensee, and its outlook is tremendous. This route, though very steep in places, is not difficult, but with so much height to gain from Kandersteg it will be evident that the ascent can be somewhat tiring. However, the way is always interesting.

Take either the chairlift route to the **Öeschinensee** (Route 68), or follow the service road referred to in Route 69. The path to the hut is signed from the hotel/restaurants at the western end of the lake. Cross the little flood plain below the buildings and follow the path as it meanders southeastward among trees and shrubs. After about 200m it starts to rise, quite gently at first, then growing steeper. It's a clearly marked trail, well-protected with fixed cables where exposed or liable to be greasy when wet. It crosses two fast-flowing streams on plank footbridges, and makes steady progress up the mountainside. The terrain becomes more rough and barren the higher you go, the gradient steepening considerably here and there. Zigzags become more prolific; then you swing eastwards (left) and climb the final few metres of rocky tower, and suddenly emerge before the **Fründen Hut**. (Allow 2–2½hrs for the return to Kandersteg by the same path.)

FRÜNDEN HUT

The **Fründen Hut's** spectacular location deserves to be enjoyed at leisure, and if you can spare a night there, it will be worth it. Only 10mins' walk from the hut you can gaze on a veritable maze of séracs and crevasses, and enjoy a wonderful high mountain vista. The hut can sleep 90 in its dormitories, and has a guardian in residence from late May till mid-October. For reservations ☎ 033 675 14 33.

ROUTE 71

Kandersteg (1176m) –
Doldenhorn Hut (1915m)

Grade	2–3
Distance	4.5km (one way)
Height gain	739m
Time	2½hrs
Location	Southeast of Kandersteg

As the Doldenhorn refuge is the most easily accessible to visitors staying in Kandersteg, this approach makes a popular outing. It is not very arduous, but it does have some steep sections.

Walk eastward along the road that leaves the main village street in the direction of the Öeschinensee, but when it swings left to cross the Öeschinenbach, remain on the right-hand side of the stream on a minor road heading into the Öeschinen glen, and after about 30mins a path (signed to the hut) breaks away to the right and climbs a series of steep zig-zags in order to overcome a rock barrier. Once over this the trail swings to the right, crosses a stream and traverses through woods. A second stream is crossed by footbridge to a path junction. Here you take the left branch and climb alongside the stream. This path becomes steeper and then resorts to more zig-zags before the gradient eases, bears left and rises in a northeasterly direction to gain the **Doldenhorn Hut** which sits on a very pleasant alp overlooking the Öeschinen glen.

ROUTE 72

Kandersteg (Selden; 1550m) –
Kanderfirn (2411m)

Grade	2–3
Distance	4.5km (one way)
Height gain	861m
Time	2–2½hrs
Location	Southeast of Kandersteg

From flower meadows to the edge of a glacier at the head of the Gasterntal, this fine walk passes through several intermediate mountain zones. There are long views downvalley, close views of an icefall, the possibility of seeing marmots and chamois and, in midsummer, a blaze of alpenroses to brighten the day even further. It is one of the noted walks of the Gasterntal, and one that I always find totally satisfying. Taken on its own, using Selden as your base, it will require only half a day, there and back. But if you are staying in Kandersteg a full day will be required. Perhaps the best way of tackling it, if you are fit, is to make use of the minibus at the start of the day, then return on foot all the way from the Kanderfirn to Kandersteg – see Route 73 for a description of the route from Selden to Kandersteg.

Take the morning minibus from Kandersteg *bahnhof* (station) to **Selden** (*accommodation, refreshments*), then wander upvalley on the continuing track beyond the two mountain inns as far as the alp farm and **Berggasthaus Heimritz** (1632m *accommodation, refreshments*). The track finishes here and a footpath continues on the left-hand side of the river. It climbs initially through a somewhat desolate region, then enters a higher part of the Gasterntal where lovely natural rock gardens adorn the way; shrubberies of dwarf pine and juniper, and starry flowers among the rocks and tiny 'lawns'. The path then crosses to the opposite side of the Kander, joins another path where you bear left, and goes through more flowery stretches before beginning to climb increasingly rocky slopes. This is marmot country.

The trail leads onto a moraine wall and rises towards ice cliffs of the Alpetli Glacier (the lower part of the Kanderfirn). As you gain height so these ice cliffs gleam almost blue in the sunlight. The way is now less sombre as it enters a belt of alpenrose. Gazing back the way you have come there are grand views of the valley with the Balmhorn rising above it. With the aid of zig-zags the

The undeveloped Gasterntal is one of the finest valleys in the Bernese Alps

203

path then overcomes a final barrier of rocks and reaches the edge of the **Kanderfirn** glacier.

To vary the descent to Selden return downvalley on the left bank of the stream until you draw level with the Heimritz building where a footbridge takes you across to the right bank. (Allow about 1½hrs to Selden.)

ROUTE 73

Kandersteg (Selden: 1550m) –
Kandersteg (1176m)

Grade	1
Distance	10km (one way)
Height loss	374m
Time	2½hrs
Location	South and southeast of Kandersteg

Should you spend time in the Gasterntal (and all visitors to this corner of the Bernese Alps should), the walk down to Kandersteg is much more rewarding than the ride by minibus. The valley displays many of its charms; its swirling streams, waterfalls, flower meadows, woodlands and big rock walls. And then there's the Klus (or Chluse) gorge that virtually hides the glen from the main Kandertal; here the path keeps company with the furious river that leaps and crashes over rocks and boulders. And finally you enter Kandersteg among attractive Oberland houses.

Follow the service road downvalley between meadows below Selden, but in 15mins take a path on the left signed to Waldhaus, Eggeschwand and Kandersteg. Descending wooded slopes come to a crossing track and continue ahead, still descending, and eventually come to a bridge (25mins from Selden). Cross to the left bank of the Kander river and follow a broad path or track heading downstream, mostly flanked by trees. However you can still see the great walls of rock that hem the valley in, and some of the cascades pouring down them.

In 45mins come to another bridge and return to the right bank in a lovely open section. Here a path deserts the track, and cutting left the way becomes a charming riverside walk among impressive scenery. Ten mins after crossing the bridge recross to the left bank once more. Shortly after this come to a large open meadow. The path curves left, then at a crossing track you turn right. Passing a sign for the Balmhorn Hut, remain on the track to reach an old dairy farm, and just beyond it, **Hotel Waldhaus** (*accommodation, refreshments*), about 1hr 15mins from Selden.

Pass round the left-hand side of the hotel on a path which takes you into woodland and down the right bank of the Schwarzbach, the stream that drains the high valley leading to the Gemmipass. On reaching a wide track cross a footbridge on the left, after which you enter the Klus gorge. A few minutes later the way is barred by a rock wall, so you recross to the right bank and wander down the road. This soon takes you over the river again to its left bank and through a short tunnel. Immediately on emerging from this, cut back to the right on a path that descends steps and resumes alongside the wild river.

Coming out of the gorge you go onto the road once more, turn right, cross a bridge and follow the road down to the Sunnbüel cableway station. Walk through the car park and along the road once more. Just before reaching a railway bridge, turn left onto a minor service road that leads to the International Scout Centre. Beyond this keep ahead on a riverside path that later becomes a narrow tarmac road leading to **Kandersteg**.

ROUTE 74

*Kandersteg (Selden; 1550m) – Mutthorn
Hut (2901m) – Petersgrat (3126m) –
Fafleralp/Lötschental (1788m)*

Grade	3
Distance	10km
Height gain	1576m
Height loss	1338m
Time	2 days
Location	Southeast of Kandersteg

This is one of the classic walks of the Alps. Despite journeying the length of a glacier and making the traverse of a high snow- and ice-capped ridge, it is a walk and not a climb. But it's a tough one that requires a degree of competence and glacier experience. No-one should consider tackling it without the provision of ice-axe, crampons and rope, and understand their correct usage. Given these provisos, this route could be a highlight of any mountain walker's holiday.

The Petersgrat is a remnant of a vast ice cap that once covered much of the Bernese Alps. Today it divides the Gasterntal from the Lötschental – the latter valley, although included in the Bernese Alps, in fact falls within the jurisdiction of canton Valais. To gain the Petersgrat requires the ascent of the Kanderfirn, while its descent to the Lötschental on the southern side initially involves a steeply-angled ice slope, then an extremely steep and wild glen which eventually gives out to the open splendour of the Lötschental. At all stages of the walk the scenery is glorious. A night is spent in the Mutthorn Hut which gives an opportunity to capture the magic of both evening and early morning in the high mountains.

Take the minibus taxi from Kandersteg station as far as **Selden** in the Gasterntal, then follow directions given under Route 72 as far as the glacier. The path continues alongside the glacier, and when it ends you climb a series of grit-strewn rock terraces onto the icefield. The Kanderfirn rises at a very gentle gradient and should present no major crevasse difficulties. Head straight up the glacier, keeping to the right-hand side. Above to the right a higher level of glacier holds modest ice cliffs; to the left the bare cliffs of the Blüemlisalp massif are adorned with only small glacial remnants.

On reaching the head of the glacier the low crags of the flat-topped Mutthorn stand to the right of the Tschingelpass, with a second glacial saddle between the Mutthorn and Tschingelhorn. The hut is located just over this saddle, tucked against the eastern (right-hand) base of the Mutthorn's low cliffs. So reach the **Mutthorn Hut**, about 2½hrs from the edge of the Kanderfirn (4½hrs from Selden). ▶

On leaving the hut in the morning head almost due south towards the Petersgrat, aiming for the right-hand end of the Tschingelhorn's southwest ridge, where the ice folds easily little more than 200m above the height of the hut. There are a few crevasses, but they should be

The **Mutthorn Hut** sits amid an icy world, dominated by the double-peaked Tschingelhorn which looks impressive and aloof, and glows in the evening light. With 100 dormitory places and a resident guardian from late June to early September, meals are provided. To reserve a place ☎ 033 853 13 44.

The Petersgrat is a remnant of a great ice-sheet that once covered much of the Bernese Alps

detected without problem, and once on the **Petersgrat** you'll find the view is magical as you look directly across the unseen Lötschental to the Bietschhorn, while on the far side of the Rhône Valley almost the complete length of the Pennine Alps is on show, from the Dom to Mont Blanc – but without Monte Rosa or the Matterhorn, both of which are hidden by other peaks.

Below the Petersgrat the head of two valleys offer themselves for possible descent. To the left is the Inners Tal, but almost directly below is the Uisters Tal (also known as the Äusseres Faflertal). This second glen is the one to choose. Descend the steep snow and ice slope towards the left-hand side of the head of the glen, and leave the ice in favour of rocks when you can safely do so. Cairns will be seen leading down from the upper glacial slabs. They lead over modest rock bands, down slopes of scree and old snow tongues until at last you reach a proper path well to the left of the stream flowing into the glen. This path is very steep in its initial stages, but eases lower down. As you progress towards the main Lötschental, views ahead become increasingly impressive.

Once you reach the mouth of the Uisters Tal bear left on a crossing path and follow this down to **Fafleralp** (*accommodation, refreshments*) from where you can catch a postbus downvalley to Goppenstein, and from there take a train through the Lötschberg Tunnel back to Kandersteg.

ROUTE 75

Kandersteg (Selden; 1550m) –
Lötschenpass (2690m) –
Ferden/Lötschental (1375m)

Grade	3
Distance	10km
Height gain	1140m
Height loss	1315m
Time	6–6½hrs
Location	Southeast of Kandersteg

In common with Route 74, this walk makes a crossing of the high dividing ridge between the Gasterntal and Lötschental, and is another classic of its kind; the Lötschenpass (between Balmhorn and Hockenhorn) being the oldest glacier pass in the Bernese Alps, it is very popular as a walking excursion from both north and south sides. As with the Petersgrat crossing there is a glacier to contend with, but with respectful care it should give few problems. Accommodation and refreshments are available at various stages along the way, and return to Kandersteg is made by train from Goppenstein through the Lötschberg Tunnel.

Take the minibus taxi from Kandersteg station to **Selden**. Opposite Hotel Steinbock a signed path heads between trees to the river, which you cross on a wooden suspension bridge. The path then follows up the right-hand (western) side of the Leilibach stream, and becomes rather steep, but with views between the trees and shrubbery to a series of waterfalls tipping over rocks and boulders. After gaining almost 300m of altitude the path brings you to the little **Berghaus Gfällalp** (1847m *accommodation, refreshments*) reached in about 1hr from Selden.

Above Gfällalp on the way to the Lötschenpass

The **Lötschenpass Hut** stands on the site of a one-time army barracks, with a fine view of the Bietschhorn across the unseen depths of the Lötschental. With places for 40, and meals provision, the hut has a resident warden for most of the year from February to October (not May). For reservations ☎ 027 939 19 81.

The clearly marked trail continues, making steady progress up the hillside heading roughly southwest, but with the Leilibach now some way to the left. Crossing a brief shelf of pastureland, the path then resumes its zig-zag ascent, and about 1½hrs above Gfällalp you come to the edge of the Lötschen Glacier. The route across is usually marked with poles, and the last time I crossed (in 2004) there were no crevasses to be seen on the way. On the east side the path climbs a series of rock terraces, and about 1hr after leaving the glacier you gain the **Lötschenpass** with the privately-owned hut set right on the pass itself. Accommodation and refreshments are available here. ◄

East of the hut two routes are waymarked. One (the left branch) goes to Lauchernalp; the right-hand option leads to Kummenalp. Take the right-hand route. At first this is taken at a gentle angle; it goes down to a small tarn or two, after which the gradient steepens. Under normal summer conditions there should be no route-finding difficulties, and in 1hr 15mins from the pass you come to the hamlet of **Kummenalp** (2083m *accommodation, refreshments*) at the mouth of the hanging valley you've been descending. The signed trail drops steeply below and to the left of Gasthaus Kummenalp, crosses a stream, heads through forest and arrives in the bed of the Lötschental at the neat village of **Ferden** (*accommodation, refreshments*) which has a postbus link with Goppenstein for the train back to Kandersteg through the Lötschberg Tunnel.

THE LÖTSCHENTAL

The Lötschental is a real gem of a valley, and well worth spending time in. There are some delightful villages, big mountains walling it, and plenty of opportunities for walks of all grades. For further details and descriptions of some of the best routes the valley has to offer, consult Walking in the Valais, also published by Cicerone Press.

ROUTE 76

Kandersteg (1176m) –
Gasterntal – Balmhorn Hut (1956m)

Grade	3
Distance	7km (one way)
Height gain	780m
Time	3½hrs
Location	Southeast of Kandersteg

Another steep walk to an SAC hut. As its name suggests, the Balmhorn Hut is perched below the glaciers that adorn the northern flanks of the Balmhorn mountain. It overlooks the lower reaches of the Gasterntal, through which it is approached, and enjoys a privileged view from the stalls, as it were, of a wild glacial amphitheatre formed by the converging ridges of the twin peaks that so dominate the southern limits of the Kandertal: Altels and Balmhorn. For much of the way the route is straightforward, if rather steep, narrow and exposed in places. There are sections of fixed cable, others with rough ladders to help overcome certain natural obstacles. And shortly before reaching the hut there is a short (10mins) section where the path crosses directly below the ice cliffs of the Balmhorn glacier. As is the nature of such ice cliffs, every now and then some break away to create small avalanches and possible stonefall, and the objective danger inherent in this is something of which all who tackle this walk should be aware. A notice warning of this danger is positioned on the path as you approach the line of fire.

Walk up the road out of Kandersteg to Eggeschwand, valley station of the Sunnbüel cableway. Continue along the road as it winds up into the Klus gorge at the entrance to the Gasterntal, then break away on a signed footpath to **Hotel Waldhaus** (*accommodation, refreshments*). Continue upvalley in front of the hotel on a farm track for another 600m or so. As you cross a large open meadowland look for a noticeboard and a finely carved sign showing two marmots indicating the start of the path to the Balmhorn Hut. The path branches to the right and heads among trees. On coming to the foot of the cliffs the steep ascent begins. There are no alternative routes, so simply follow the trail as it makes its way directly up the mountainside. As mentioned above, there are places where fixed cables aid the way; others with sections of rough ladder. Caution is advised for there's nearly always a degree of exposure as the path clings precariously to the cliff face.

Eventually the trail leads into a mid-height glacial cirque where the hut can be seen on the far side. High above the glacier's ice cliffs hang ominously. From the danger sign as far as the hut you should step warily and move fast across moraine, streams and debris. Then, with a sense of relief, come to the **Balmhorn Hut** on its grassy promontory.

Note: At the time of writing a new path from the Balmhorn Hut to the Lötschenpass is being promoted. Not having an opportunity to check this personally, I pass

Owned by the Altels (Frutigen) Section of the SAC, the **Balmhorn Hut** has 26 dormitory places, and a resident guardian from mid-July to mid-August, and weekends from May to the end of September. For reservations ☎ 033 675 13 40.

The Balmhorn Hut is approached through the Gasterntal

on the comments of correspondent Kenneth Penny who warns that this route descends a series of gullies partly equipped with fixed ropes. He says the descent is 'unbelievably loose' and cannot be recommended. It's possible, of course, that with further use, conditions may improve – but for now, be warned!

ROUTE 77

Kandersteg (1176m) – Sunnbüel (1936m) – Gemmipass (2314m)

Grade	2
Distance	15km (one way)
Height gain	1138m (378m with cablecar)
Time	5–5½hrs (2–2½hrs with cablecar)
Location	Southwest of Kandersteg

The Gemmi is an ancient crossing between the cantons of Bern and Valais, and over the centuries it has been traversed by countless thousands of farmers, traders, pilgrims and tourists. In the early 18th century a remarkable staircase of a path was created up the almost perpendicular wall from Leukerbad to the pass; a route that was tackled by mule as well as by men, though accidents were not unknown, as may be guessed by anyone who studies the route today. Nowadays there's cableway access from Leukerbad to the pass, while the route from Kandersteg is similarly eased by mechanical means. Yet despite this taming of the Gemmi and the approach to it, nothing can detract from the sheer splendour of the panorama that greets those who arrive there. From the pass one gazes south to the great chain of the Pennine Alps including Monte Rosa, the Mischabelhörner, Matterhorn, Dent Blanche, Weisshorn and Bouquetins and many, many more. A fabulous view it is, and one that gives a considerable lift to this walk. The valley that leads to the pass from the upper station of the Eggeschwand–Sunnbüel →

← cablecar is a noted flower garden, spoilt only by high tension power lines and their pylons. Mountains and glaciers wall it, and shortly before reaching the Gemmi you pass alongside the grey limestone-bordered Daubensee. The Wildstrubel rises to the west, Altels and Balmhorn to the east.

Leaving Kandersteg wander upvalley as far as **Eggeschwand** where the cablecar swings up to Sunnbüel. There are two footpath routes for those who prefer to walk all the way; both entail very steep sections as outlined below.

Option 1: Continue along the road beyond the cablecar station until it makes a hairpin bend to the left to enter the Gasterntal. The footpath to Sunnbüel begins at this bend and works its way among trees and shrubbery, climbing very steeply and in 3hrs from Kandersteg arrives at the upper cablecar station.

Option 2: From the car park by the Eggeschwand–Sunnbüel cableway station walk through the Klus gorge into the Gasterntal as far as Hotel Waldhaus (see Route 76 for details). At the Waldhaus take the path heading off to the right. It takes you up the left-hand side of a narrow cleft on a series of tight zig-zags, the path made safe in places by fixed cable. It works its way ever higher among woods and emerges at last in the upper valley of the Schwarzbach just south of the Sunnbüel cablecar station and restaurant. Continue upvalley along a broad clear path.

For those who choose to ride the cablecar, the way from the upper station is straightforward and signed. Continue upvalley on a well-trodden track. At the alp pasture of Spittelmatte (1875m; 15mins) you cross an area devastated in September 1895 by the collapse of part of the western glacier draped down the Altels (seen above to the left) which killed six herdsmen and their cattle. Beyond this the way crosses a stony region and comes to **Berghotel Schwarenbach** (2060m *accommodation, refreshments*), about 4hrs from Kandersteg (a little over 1hr from Sunnbüel). Between Spittelmatte and

Schwarenbach you cross the cantonal boundary from Bern to the Valais.

Leaving Schwarenbach you steadily gain height over rocky ground, come to the shallow Daubensee, sometimes semi-frozen in early summer, skirt along its eastern (left-hand) shore, and then rise beyond it for about 10mins to reach **Hotel Wildstrubel** (*accommodation, refreshments*) and the Gemmipass with its magnificent views and abundance of wild flowers in the early summer.

Allow 4hrs to return to Kandersteg by the same route. Should your plan be to continue as far as Leukerbad, however, the way is obvious, if rather dizzy with its staggering number of zig-zags. The descent will take about 1³⁄₄–2hrs from the pass. Or, alternatively, you could take the cableway.

ROUTE 78

Kandersteg (1176m) – Sunnbüel (1936m) – Lämmeren Hut (2501m)

Grade	3
Distance	18km (one way)
Height gain	1325m
Time	6hrs (3¹⁄₂–4hrs via Sunnbüel cablecar)
Location	Southwest of Kandersteg

For those who fancy a night spent in the wilds of the Gemmipass region, the Lämmeren Hut offers one option. It's set in grey limestone country to the west of the Gemmipass, under the Lämmerenhorn which is itself embraced by the crescent of snow, ice and rock of the Wildstrubel. The hut, owned by the Angenstein Section of the SAC, can sleep 96 in its dormitories.

Follow directions for Route 77 as far as the Daubensee. Take the path along the western (right-hand) side of the lake, go through the Lämmerendalu ravine beyond it and then bear right round a spur, following the stream to the Lämmerenalp (2296m) where there's a tarn off to the right. The trail heads away from the tarn to make the final ascent to the hut. This is achieved by way of tight zig-zags to gain the shelf below the Lämmerenhorn where the hut rests.

Other routes in the Sunnbüel-Gemmipass region

Study of the map reveals numerous walking options in the valley stretching from the Sunnbüel cableway and the Gemmipass, as well as routes that cross the west-walling ridge. The following is merely a sample of possibilities.

- From the cableway middle station (Stock; 1825m) a trail goes up onto the **Üeschinegrat** by skirting the 2284m Gällihorn. It follows the ridge southwestward, then descends to **Berghotel Schwarenbach** (4hrs), and returns to Sunnbüel or Stock through the valley. A fine circuit of about 5–5½hrs.

- From a base at **Berghotel Schwarenbach** an easy circuit of the **Daubensee** would suit those who want an undemanding yet scenic half-day walk.

- It would be possible to walk from Sunnbüel to **Berghotel Schwarenbach**, then make a steep 300m climb northwestward to cross the **Schwarzgrätli** (2383m) – at the southern end of the Üschinegrat mentioned above. Here you descend in tight zig-zags into the pastoral **Üschenental** and descend through this all the way back to Kandersteg. A superb full-day's hike, Grade 3.

- One of the classic routes worth tackling here is a crossing of the **Rote Chumme** and **Engstligengrat** to reach the wonderful **Engstligenalp** south of Adelboden. This crossing begins at the northwestern end of the Daubensee and is fairly demanding; allow 4½–5hrs to reach the Engstligenalp where accommodation is available (see the following chapter, Engstligental, for details).

ROUTE 79

*Kandersteg (Allmenalp; 1732m) – Usser
Üschene (1595m) – Kandersteg (1176m)*

Grade	1–2
Distance	8km
Height loss	556m
Time	2½hrs
Location	Southwest of Kandersteg

On the western hillside above Kandersteg a shallow scoop of pasture below the Bunderspitz (2546m) is occupied by the little Allmenalp farm where visitors can often watch cheese being made. The farm also doubles as a restaurant, and on the terrace one may sit in the sunshine with a lovely view across the valley towards the Öeschinensee and the Blüemlisalp peaks, while a nearby slope has been adopted as the launching site for a paragliding school. A small, eight-person cablecar serves the Allmenalp region between May and October, and gives inspiration for several worthwhile walks. This is just one of them, an easy walk, it follows a broad track for much of the way, and has constant fine views to indulge in, especially to the twin peaks of Altels and Balmhorn guarding the entrance to the Gasterntal.

The valley station of the Allmenalp cableway is located a little southwest of Kandersteg *bahnhof*. The cabin takes only five minutes to gain the upper hillside where initially all paths head in one direction; uphill. After a few paces take the first path branching left. It leads directly to the chalet-farm of **Allmenalp** (Undere Allme; *refreshments*) and continues, climbing a short section, then becomes a broad track with magnificent views of the mountains heading the Kandertal. The track contours comfortably along the mountainside. Passing a few alp buildings where a narrow path drops steeply to

In the lower reaches of the Üschenental

Kandersteg, remain with the track as it curves into the mouth of the Üschenental.

The track, now a farm road, winds into the valley, passing several farms, then comes to a junction. Bear left and wander eastwards to leave the valley, and when you see a signpost as the road descends, break away on the footpath which short-cuts the road route. No specific descriptions of this descent are necessary; sufficient to say the trail leads through a gorge, then in forest almost all the way down, and finally brings you into a meadow near the International Scout Centre. From there an easy riverside path returns you to **Kandersteg** railway station.

ROUTE 80

Kandersteg (Allmenalp; 1732m) –
First (2549m) – Stand (2320m) –
Kandersteg (1176m)

Grade	3
Distance	10km
Height gain	817m
Height loss	1373m
Time	5½–6hrs
Location	West of Kandersteg

Two summits linked by a good path, followed by a steep descent to the valley, make this a strenuous but very rewarding day out. The summits in
question, First and Stand, may not be mountains of great stature, but they
have a certain elegance and there's nothing second-rate about the
panorama they enjoy. Standing up there on a clear day you can see Mont
Blanc far off. The Matterhorn too, and Jungfrau and Eiger. Not forgetting the
nearer-to-hand Blüemlisalp above the deep jewel of the Öeschinensee. It's
a route that demands a good clear day, and if snow is lingering on the high
ridges you should retreat unless you're equipped and experienced to cope
with any possible difficulties.

Take the Allmenalp cablecar, and from the upper station
walk uphill on a steep path that winds through rough
sloping pastures. This is a good flowery stretch, with St
Bruno's lily on show in late June/early July. The upper
farm of Obere Allme (1946m) is reached, above which
you branch right on a path heading northeast. This leads
directly to the building of Steintal (2027m) where you
swing left and climb in gradient-easing loops, then with
steeper zig-zags to gain the Allmegrat ridge just below
the summit of **First**.

The continuing route from First to Stand (seen off to the north beyond Howang) avoids a narrow arête. To do so it descends to the western side of the ridge, passes below Howang on a traverse and then by an easy trail up the southwest ridge to the summit of **Stand**.

Now descend the steep northwest ridge a short distance. The path then bears right, contours below the summit and reaches the Golitschepass (2180m) which links the Kandertal with the Engstligental. The path loses height on the eastern side by a series of zig-zags, and in about 40mins from the pass comes to Golitschealp (1833m). Veering to the right at the alp building the trail slopes round to cross a prominent stream, passes round a spur, crosses a boulder field and works its way steadily down to the valley.

ROUTE 81

*Kandersteg (1176m) – Bunderchrinde
(2385m) – Adelboden (1353m)*

Grade	3
Distance	16km
Height gain	1209m
Height loss	1032m
Time	6½–7hrs
Location	West of Kandersteg

Another classic pass crossing, the Bunderchrinde is a narrow cleft in the high wall of mountains west of the Kandertal. It actually links the ridge of the Gross Lohner with that of the Bunderspitz, and offers an interesting way for walkers to travel from the Kandertal to the Engstligental.

The route leaves Kandersteg by the railway station, follows a tarmac footpath to the left (upvalley) running parallel with the railway line, veers right beneath a bridge and crosses the Kander river. Now along a surfaced lane you pass near the Allmenalp cableway and take a footpath alongside the river as far as the International Scout Centre (*Pfadfinder Zentrum*). Just beyond the buildings a path breaks away to the right and crosses open meadows. On coming to a fork in the path, marked by a signpost midway across one of these meadows, bear right into woods.

The path climbs through the woods, then crosses a road on a short-cut. On coming to the road a second time, walk along it for 6–7mins until it makes a right-hand hairpin. Now go ahead on a waymarked path rising above a stream. It comes onto the road once more, but you leave it immediately for the continuing path which enters a narrow gorge, above which you come into the pastures of **Ausser Üschene** (1hr 15mins).

Walk ahead across the pastures, and at the far end you come to a junction of farm tracks and take the upper branch winding uphill. Shortly before coming to an alp building take a path on the left, climbing towards a line of crags. The path swings left before climbing steeply through a natural fault in the crags and bearing right above them. You then make a steady traverse high above the valley, with good views into the Gasterntal.

About 3hrs from Kandersteg you come to the huts of **Alpschele** (2094m), and have a first real view of the Bunderchrinde above. Bear left between the buildings, then make a steady rising traverse to the right before winding up to a junction of paths and a signpost on the edge of a band of scree. Slant across the scree at a comfortable gradient and you'll arrive at the rocky 2385m pass of **Bunderchrinde** about 50mins from the alp.

Descending to the west the path goes steeply down more screes, then veers towards the right-hand side of a stony corrie. The way is obvious, and it loops down without difficulty to reach a grassy bluff with a cattle byre almost sunken into it (Bunderchumi 2098m). The trail descends beyond this across rough pastures to a farm set a little above a road. Drop to the road and walk along it a short distance to the right. You will come to **Berghaus Bonderalp** (1755m *accommodation, refreshments*) where you have a choice of routes down to Adelboden – both taking 1½–2hrs. A footpath on the left offers a way down over pastures and through woods, while the continuing road twists its way with less commitment down the hillside. Both arrive in the valley to the south of **Adelboden**. You then face a last uphill walk to gain the main part of the village.

ROUTE 82

Kandersteg (1176m) –

Schedelsgrättli (2512m) –

Artelengrat – Engstligenalp (1955m)

Grade	3
Distance	13km
Height gain	1336m
Height loss	557m
Time	5–5½hrs
Location	Southwest of Kandersteg

The great grassy basin of the Engstligenalp lies at the foot of the Wildstrubel south of Adelboden, and this route crosses the mountains that separate Kandersteg's valley from that of Adelboden in order to reach it. It's a very fine walk, mostly on good paths or farm tracks, although there are sections where the way is either not evident on the ground, or is rather exposed. Good visibility is necessary to avoid route-finding difficulties. But in fair weather the diverse landscapes and long views make this a real winner.

Follow directions given for Route 81 as far as the pastures of **Ausser Üschene** (1548m; 1hr 15mins). From the sign-post you can see towards the head of the valley (the Üschenental) where the 2735m Tschingellochtighorn appears as several rocky fingers bursting from a ridge. The ridge immediately right of those 'fingers' is the Schedelsgrättli which will be crossed later.

View downvalley from the upper Üschenental

Cross the pastures ahead on a narrow grass trail which, beyond an alp building, crosses minor streams and comes onto a farm road. This road is now followed upvalley for about 40mins, passing on the way several alp buildings. A few minutes after wandering below the farm of **Inner Üschene** (shown as Uf der Egge on the map), a path slants above the road towards Ortele, Engstligengrat and Engstligenalp.

This path brings you to a low building, then climbs steeply above it, twisiting to the right of a stream. About 5mins later cross the stream and continue up the slope following vague waymarks and eventually coming onto a track a short way above a cluster of alp buildings. Turn right and walk along the track to reach a solitary building about 3mins later. Branch right along a line of waymarks to reach a clear path that rises into a high pastureland from where you have good views southeast to Altels and Balmhorn.

Enter an upper basin of pastureland and go up the slope to the right to find a continuing path climbing steeply onto a small shelf of pasture in a little over 3¼hrs. The way climbs on steeply once more to gain another shelf with a direct view up to the Tschingellochtighorn which rises above a great fan of scree. Picking a way over the last of the pastures, the path then cuts across a slope of shale to reach the **Schedelsgrättli** in 3hrs 40mins.

Bear left (south) and wander along the crest whose west side falls steeply away into the Engstligental some 1100m below. Pass along the left flank of a small domed hump, and regain the crest at a saddle marked by a signpost (2512m; 3hrs 45mins). Directly ahead rise the finger-like rocks of the Tschingellochtighorn. One route cuts below the north face of the mountain, another makes a traverse of its east flank to gain the Engstligengrat.

Branch right here to make a slightly descending traverse below the north face on a narrow but clearly-defined path across a slope of shale. (Do not attempt if snow-covered.) Across this turn a spur and pick your way over a rock tip, after which there's another slope of shale to traverse. At the end of this come onto the **Artelengrat** (4¼–4½hrs) and gain a first view into the Engstligenalp basin.

Walk down the broad ridge with splendid views to right and left. Towards the lower end of the ridge it narrows and the path cuts left to descend into the vast alp basin. At a broad crossing path turn left to complete the descent, coming to **Berghotel Engstligenalp** (*accommodation, refreshments*) and a major junction of paths. Off to the right there's a cable lift that descends to Unter dem Berg at the head of the Engstligental for a bus ride to Adelboden. Alternatively turn left and shortly after passing the Berghotel a path branches right which also descends to Unter dem Berg in 1hr.

ENGSTLIGENTAL

After the big mountains and steep-walled valleys to the east, the Engstligental appears benign, with a subtle gentility. It welcomes rather than challenges, seduces with open basins of pastureland backed by mountains of more modest appeal. This is country for walking in. It's not so much a mountaineer's landscape, other than among a few medium-grade peaks, but there are plenty of opportunities for pedestrian outings of all standards of seriousness, from easy valley strolls to longer circuits and multi-day expeditions into neighbouring valleys. And there's no shortage of accommodation.

ACCESS AND INFORMATION	
Location	West of the Kandertal, the Engstligental flows northeast from the Wildstrubel and joins the Kander at Frutigen.
Maps	LS 263T *Wildstrubel* at 1:50,000
	Kümmerly + Frey *Saanenland-Simmental-Kandertal* at 1:60,000
Base	Adelboden (1353m)
Information	Adelboden Tourismus, CH–3715 Adelboden (☎ 033 673 80 80 info@adelboden.ch www.adelboden.ch)
Access	By train to Frutigen via Thun and Spiez, then postbus to Adelboden.

On entering the Engstligental at Frutigen one of the first impressions the visitor gains is that the valley seems to become much more narrow, forested and steep-walled than that of the Frutigtal just left behind, but farther upvalley this perception changes as the aspect becomes one of open, sunny benevolence. The road takes its time to reach that upper region, though, and winds carefully above the west bank of the river with numerous streams pouring through gullies from the long ridge of peaks above. Up there, at mid-height, little alp huts and hamlets are linked by ancient paths used by generations of peasant farmers and chamois hunters, and in a few places little-known passes lead across the mountains to the Diemtigtal beyond.

On the eastern side of the valley the Elsighorn marks the northern end of a ridge that runs from the snowy Wildstrubel; this ridge divides the Engstligental

ENGSTLIGENTAL

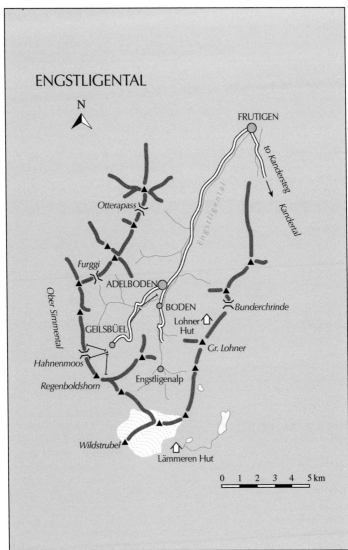

N

FRUTIGEN

to Kandersteg

Engstligental

Kanderal

Otterapass

Furggi

ADELBODEN

Ober Simmental

BODEN

Bunderchrinde

Lohner
Hut

GEILSBÜEL

Gr. Lohner

Hahnenmoos

Regenboldshorn

Engstligenalp

Wildstrubel

Lämmeren Hut

0   1   2   3   4   5 km

from the Kandertal. But as you progress through the valley, so the Wildstrubel comes into view, impressing itself upon the valley in a picturesque way.

The road climbs higher and deeper into the valley and crosses to the true left bank at Rinderwald to avoid the gorge of Pochtenkessel, only to return to the western side again after another 4km shortly before reaching Oey where it makes the final steep ascent to the sunny terrace occupied by Adelboden.

South of Adelboden the head of the valley is a large grassy bowl sub-divided into minor glens and the hidden pastoral basin of Engstligenalp which is topped by the Wildstrubel itself. Apart from the Wildstrubel's snow crown and the craggy Lohner group, most of the peaks have grass virtually to their summits. Green mountains with easy walkers' passes between them, they offer a friendly, welcoming face and make a direct contrast to the higher mountains experienced at the head of other Oberland valleys farther to the east. It's a land of pasture and forest, of stunning waterfalls and attractive hidden corners, of clear streams and flower meadows. A walker's landscape with over 300km of trails to explore.

MAIN BASE
ADELBODEN (1353m) looks across the valley to the Wildstrubel and Lohner ranges. It's a lovely view and one that encourages visitors to go exploring. Adelboden is mainly a ski resort, but summer visitors will nevertheless find plenty to enjoy, and as a base for a holiday it has a lot to offer in the way of shops, restaurants, banks, PTT and, of course, numerous hotels and pensions. Among the lower-priced options: Pension-Restaurant Ruedy-Hus (☎ 033 673 33 22 **ruedy-hus@bluewin.ch**), and Pension-Restaurant Bodehüttli (☎ 033 673 37 00 **bodehuettli@bluewin.ch**) which also has dormitory places in nearby Boden. There are some 7000 beds in holiday apartments and chalets, and two campsites. Reached by train as far as Frutigen and bus from there (15km), Adelboden is easily accessible to those without their own transport, while a minibus serves the two upper stems of the valley as far as Unter dem Berg (for Engstligenalp) and Geils (for the Hahnenmoos) to shorten the approach to some fine walking areas. There are also several cableways. Adelboden has a few old buildings in the village and surrounding areas, while the church of St Anton dates from the 15th century.

OTHER BASES
Above Adelboden to the east, on the way to the Bunderchrinde, **BERGHAUS BONDERALP** (1750m) has 26 beds, plus simple accommodation – sleeping in the hay (☎ 033 673 33 65). At the head of the valley **ENGSTLIGENALP** (1955m) below the Wildstrubel is a great place to stay for a night or so, with two accommodation choices: **BERGHOTEL ENGSTLIGENALP** (closed Weds) has 33 beds and 150 dorm places (☎ 033 673 22 61 **berghotel.engstligenalp@bluewin.ch**),

The Wildstrubel dominates the great pastoral basin of Engstligenalp

while **BERGHAUS BÄRTSCHI** nearby (closed Mon) has 18 beds and 55 dorm places (☎ 033 673 13 73 **berghaus@bluewin.ch**). At **UNTER DEM BERG** (1400m) in the head of the valley below Engstligenalp, **GASTHOF STEINBOCK** has 14 beds and 20 dormitory places (☎ 033 673 16 26 **steinbock.engstlige-nalp@bluewin.ch**). Elsewhere, on the way to the Hahnenmoos Pass dormitory accommodation may be found at **RESTAURANT GEILSBRÜGGLI** (☎ 033 673 21 71) at Geilsbüel, while at the pass itself **BERGHOTEL HAHNENMOOSPASS** has 15 beds and 52 dormitory places (☎ 033 673 21 41 **spori@hahnenmoos.ch www.hahnenmoos.ch**).

MOUNTAIN HUT

LOHNER HUT (2171m) The only SAC hut accessible from the Engstligental nestles below the western crags of the Gross Lohner east of Adelboden. Owned by the Adelboden-based Wildstrubel Section of the SAC, it has 40 places, self-cooking facilities, and a guardian only at weekends from the end of June to mid-October. For reservations ☎ 033 673 04 87.

ROUTE 83

Adelboden (1353m) –
Engstligenalp (1955m)

Grade	2
Distance	7km (one way)
Height gain	602m
Time	3hrs
Location	South of Adelboden

Engstligenalp is very much a show-piece among the upper reaches of the valley. It's a glorious high-level plateau-like basin at the foot of the Wildstrubel. Scattered about the plateau are a few farms and barns, but there's accommodation to be had too, and cablecar access from Unter dem Berg. A bus travels from Adelboden along a narrow lane through pastures as far as the Unter dem Berg roadhead, so it would be quite easy to reach Engstligenalp virtually without walking at all, but that would be to miss much.

From the main village street follow signs to the swimming pool and continue down the steep hillside slope until you can cross the river (the Allebach) by bridge to the south side. Then up to Fuhre (Uf der Fure on the map) and the neat suburb of **Boden** (1289m *accommodation, refreshments*) which you reach in about 30mins. Directly ahead the Wildstrubel, and an impressive waterfall pouring from the lip of the Engstligenalp, lure you along a gentle wooded valley following a narrow road through flowery meadows. When it draws close to the Engstligenbach, cross the stream on a bridge to its left-hand side and continue upvalley on a riverside path. This brings you onto the road again just before it reaches **Unter dem Berg**.

Turn right for a few paces, and when the road recrosses the stream cut back to the left on a path which

takes you through woodland towards the lower water-falls. After about 500m swing left, then take the right-hand path (still among woods) at a junction to climb steeply on a mule-track that goes directly beneath the

The Engstligen Falls, classified as a Swiss national monument

231

cableway. The path is very steep in places, but it's well-made and there are one or two opportunities to stray slightly to gaze on the magnificent **Engstligen Falls**, among the finest in Switzerland. The falls have been a Swiss national monument since 1948.

The path continues, making height against dark crags, the falls to one side and long views out towards Adelboden and the hills above the village. Then at last you emerge to a sudden open pastureland, a direct contrast to the confines of the last section of climb, and **Engstligenalp** is spread before you, a crescent of peaks cradling a huge level meadowland – it has no equal anywhere in the Alps. Refreshments and accommodation are both available here.

ROUTE 84

Adelboden (1353m) –
Unter dem Berg (1400m) –
Hinterberg – Engstligenalp (1955m)

Grade	2–3
Distance	9km (one way)
Height gain	602m
Time	3½hrs
Location	South of Adelboden

This walk is a variation of Route 83. While it misses the opportunity for a close view of the Engstligen Falls, the Hinterberg corrie is the haunt of marmot, chamois and ibex, and there may well be the chance to catch sight of one or more of these animals as you wander through.

The approach is the same as for Route 83, except that you follow the riverside path all the way to **Unter dem Berg** (*accommodation, refreshments*) in about 1–1½hrs from Adelboden. Almost opposite the cable-car station a path heads north in woodland, then veers right and climbs the wooded slope in zig-zags, emerging from the trees onto more open ground before swinging southeast round a spur on a very steep slope to enter the **Hinterberg** corrie. This is formed by the ridge running from the Mittaghorn to Vorder Lohner, then south to the Tschingellochtighorn. Crossing streams the trail now works round to the western end of the Artelengrat which forms the southern wall of the corrie, to be confronted by the great grassland bowl of **Engstligenalp.** An easy descent takes you into the pastureland near Berghotel Engstligenalp (*accommodation, refreshments*).

Either return to Unter dem Berg by cablecar, or follow the broad path beyond the Berghotel to find a signed path breaking to the right (northwest); this descends to Unter dem Berg in 1hr.

ROUTE 85

Adelboden (Engstligenalp; 1955m) – Ammertenpass (2443m) – Lenk (1068m)

Grade	3
Distance	15km
Height gain	488m
Height loss	1375m
Time	5½hrs
Location	Southwest of Engstligenalp

This crossing has a justifiable reputation among experienced mountain walkers, for its diverse nature, the challenging descent from the pass, and a series of spectacular views. Easily reached from Engstligenalp, the Ammertenpass is on the northwest arête (Ammertengrat) of the Wildstrubel, connecting the Grossstrubel and Ammertenspitz, and forming an effective divide between the Engstligenalp and the upper reaches of the Simmental. Though reached by an easy path, the descent is anything but easy; it's extremely steep and with several tricky places where a slip could have serious consequences. Caution is advised. But the gradient eases after a while and the rest of the way down to Lenk becomes more relaxed.

The very steep descent from the Ammertenpass into the Ammertentälli

From Berghotel Engstligenalp walk upvalley along the main gravel path towards the Wildstrubel. On coming to the southwest corner of the pastures (15mins) cross a stream and angle up the hillside ahead on a clear path. This brings you into an upper grass basin where you pass a small stone-built hut tucked against a boulder. Rising still, after about 1¼hrs you draw level with a hut marked as Schönbüel on the map. Ten minutes later gain an upper stony basin and mount a final slope of shale to reach the bare, windblown saddle of the **Ammertenpass** (2443m; 1hr 45mins). To the east you can see the Balmhorn and Altels, Blüemlisalp and Doldenhorn across intermediate ridges. In the west the Wildhorn is clearly seen, while to the south the Wildstrubel is a close neighbour, its glaciers shining in the sunlight.

Turn left and walk up the ridge which soon narrows with a steep drop to the right. About 2mins from the pass, the trail begins to descend the right-hand (south) side of the ridge, slanting down across a steep shale slope. It then zig-zags precipitously downhill heading southwest (**caution!**) with plenty of loose stones and tile-like slabs that could be lethal in snow or immediately after rain. It then leads onto an old moraine rib and continues down the wild Ammertentälli.

The first 300m of descent are the steepest, but below this the way eases across a stony area, then descends steeply once more. In about 2½hrs you come onto the Schäfberg bluff of pasture (1932m) where there are a few ruined walls. Lenk can now be seen in the distance. Descending again, the path works its way along a grassy rib, then cuts down its left-hand side in tight zig-zags above the Ammertenbach, passing a tiny timber-built hut tight against abrupt crags.

At the foot of the steep descent the trail takes you across two stems of the Ammertenbach (two footbridges), and continues among low-growing trees and shrubs before entering a strip of forest. Out of the trees come onto a track which 2mins later crosses the stream, winds downhill and soon curves through meadows to reach a junction at 1467m (3¼hrs). Stay on the track going downhill along the edge of more meadows, passing a newly-built farm. When it forks take the right branch (unsigned), still winding downhill among trees. In a few paces come to another junction marked as **Stalden** (1370m). Bear right again on the continuing track which takes you past the impressive **Simmenfalle** waterfalls in another 30mins, and continues without complication all the way to **Lenk**, reached about 1hr from the waterfalls. (Please see the Ober Simmental chapter for details of accommodation and facilities in Lenk.)

ROUTE 86

*Adelboden (Engstligenalp; 1955m) –
Ammertenpass (2443m) –
Iffigenalp (1584m)*

Grade	3
Distance	14km
Height gain	966m
Height loss	1337m
Time	5½–6hrs
Location	Southwest of Engstligenalp

This long and demanding – but very rewarding – walk is a variation of Route 85. It keeps away from the lower valleys by crossing ridge spurs in seemingly remote countryside, and ends at the Berghotel Iffigenalp at the head of one of the upper stems of the Simmental, in the midst of more splendid walking country.

Follow directions given in Route 85 across the Ammertenpass and down to where the track forks just above the **Stalden** junction at 1370m (about 3½hrs). Take

the left branch, soon to be joined by another track coming from Lenk. After crossing the Ammertenbach, the
track rises through pastures and then crosses a second
stream, the Laubbach. The track forks again. Keep ahead
and before long you'll reach **Restaurant Siebenbrunnen**
(also known as Gasthaus Rezliberg; *accommodation,
refreshments*) and the end of the track. About 5mins from
here the Siebenbrunnen waterfalls burst out of the steep
rock wall.

About 1min beyond the restaurant turn right on a
signed path which crosses a meadow, then over the
stream that comes from the waterfalls. Bear left along a
track rising among woodland, then out of the trees continue over the large open Rezliberg meadows that are
backed by soaring limestone crags. On the far side of the
meadows a sign directs a path away from the track,
climbing steeply through woodland before emerging
onto the track once more.

Turn left, but a few paces after, you'll find the continuing path on the right. Go through a gate and climb a
steep grass slope which brings you to the few chalets and
barns of **Langer** (1703m), with a magnificent view back

*Gasthaus Rezliberg,
near the Sieben-
brunnen waterfalls*

towards the Ammertenpass. Turn left on the track for a few paces to find a signpost with a memorial to a number of locals who died in an avalanche in 1999.

The continuing path goes up the slope above the sign, and about 30mins later you come onto a large, fairly level pastureland saddle where you'll find the solitary farm of **Langermatte** (1857m). Refreshments are available here, as well as 4–5 places for an overnight stay. (For reservations (mobile) ☎ 079 582 09 68).

Go along the right-hand side of the farm to a path junction. Ignore the right branch which goes up to the Oberlaubhorn viewpoint in 30mins, and keep ahead, soon coming onto a minor track which you follow briefly before descending on a path to another alp farm (Ritz). Pass to the left of the buildings, cross more pasture then descend in zig-zags to the Iffigenalp meadows. Cross the Iffigbach and come to a road. Turn left and in a few minutes you will reach a complex of buildings at the roadhead. Here stands **Berghotel Iffigenalp** (*accommodation, refreshments*) with plenty of good walks leading from it. (See the Ober Simmental chapter for a choice of routes; Iffigenalp is served by postbus from Lenk.)

ROUTE 87

Adelboden (1353m) – Hahnenmoos (1956m) – Lenk (1068m)

Grade	2
Distance	13km
Height gain	603m
Height loss	888m
Time	4½hrs
Location	Southwest of Adelboden

The Hahnemoos Pass is an ancient crossing between the valleys of Lenk (the Ober Simmental) and Engstligental. It was the site of a local festival held centuries ago; a broad grassy saddle where villagers from both valleys used to meet to take part in trade and compete in athletic contests, but as a result of an epidemic which killed hundreds of Adelboden's inhabitants, the pass was closed for a while in 1669. Nowadays it is again a popular place in winter as well as summer, thanks to its ease of access. This is by far the simplest route across the mountains to Lenk, and for much of the way it follows quiet surfaced roads among pastureland. The route to the pass is straightforward, wandering through the gentle Geilsbach (or Gilbach) valley, while views on the descent from the saddle are beautiful.

Descend from the centre of the village to the Silleren gondola lift, then walk through the car park to a path which takes you upvalley alongside the Allebach stream. At the first bridge cross to the north bank, turn left on a crossing path and follow this until it reaches a second bridge. Cross back to the south bank and resume upvalley on a raised path. About 25mins from the gondola station come to a confluence of streams where the Geilsbach joins the Allebach. Here you cross the Geilsbach, then turn left on a broad stony path, but before long cross to the left-hand side and continue upstream.

Come to a narrow service road about 40mins from the start. Turn left, then shortly after bear right along a narrow farm road. When it curves left keep ahead on a woodland path, then cross the Geilsbach once more to **Bergläger**, the Silleren gondola lift's middle station. A narrow road now takes the route upvalley for about 10mins, but when it makes a right-hand hairpin, you recross the Geilsbach by footbridge and resume on a path through woods. Beyond the woods open pastures lead directly to **Geilsbüel** (1707m; 1½hrs; *accommodation, refreshments*) where there's a gondola lift to the Hahenmoos Pass.

A minor paved road leads you past the gondola station and up the hillside towards the pass. Footpath

Welcome water stop near Büelberg on the descent from the Hahnenmoos Pass

A brief diversion from the Hahnenmoos Pass is worth considering. A path goes along the ridge to the left of the pass, and in 40mins arrives at an unnamed saddle, formerly known as the Pommernpass (2055m). Above the saddle to the south rises the 2193m **Regenboldshorn**. A 15min ascent of this minor summit (there's a path), brings you onto a splendid vantage point. Allow 1½–2hrs for a there-and-back diversion.

shortcuts can be taken, and about 40mins from Geilsbüel you come onto the busy saddle of the **Hahnenmoos Pass** (1956m) about 2½hrs from Adelboden. Accommodation and refreshments are available here at the large Berghotel Hahnenmoospass (☎ 033 673 21 41). The panorama is excellent, with the Wildstrubel dominating, but as you descend towards Lenk, new views of a lush green landscape hold your attention.

Bear right onto a track easing across the hillside in a gentle descent, and about 30mins later you come to the **Büelberg** restaurant, which has a postbus service down to Lenk. The walker's route, however, turns right alongside the restaurant, then takes a signed path which descends a grass hillside towards Lenk, now seen below. Join the road at Brandegg, but after passing a number of houses, go along a track on the right which leads to a farm. Beyond this a path takes you down the final slope to **Lenk**. (See the Ober Simmental chapter for details of accommodation and other facilities here.)

DIEMTIGTAL

The Diemtigtal is a beautiful, peaceful valley that branches unobtrusively to the south of the Simmental, and is therefore largely ignored by the majority of visitors travelling between the Thunersee and Zweisimmen and beyond. But those who do stray into it, and spend time exploring its inner recesses and remote passes, can hardly fail to respond to its charms.

ACCESS AND INFORMATION	
Location	Northwest of the Engstligental. The valley flows northeast from the Spillgerten and joins the Simmental at Oey, west of Spiez.
Maps	LS 253T *Gantrisch* and 263T *Wildstrubel* at 1:50,000
Bases	Oey (669m), Diemtigen (809m), Grimmialp (1220m)
Information	Verkehrsbüro, 3753 Oey (☎ 033 681 26 06 info@diemtigtal.ch www.diemtigtal-tourismus.ch)
Access	By train to Oey–Diemtigen from Thun via Spiez or Zweisimmen, then postbus as far as Grimmialp.

This is a distinctly pastoral valley, with neat meadows and handsome woods, with unspoilt hamlets scattered along it, and attractive peaks of medium-height at its head. Although these mountains are only of modest altitude compared with the better-known Oberland peaks, some of them have very difficult routes to their summits, while passes on either side make for interesting walks that reveal broad views along the way.

The unspoilt nature of the Diemtigtal is a tribute to its conservation-minded commune, and in 1986 it was awarded the Wakker Prize by the Swiss Heritage Foundation in recognition of the efforts made to preserve the valley's rural heritage and the fine architectural style of its buildings. The ski industry (one of the major threats to mountain landscape and the development of valleys throughout the Alps) has made little impact here, and as a consequence the walker and lover of unsullied hillsides has much to admire and enjoy.

The valley is a dead-end. Or to be precise, two dead-ends, for near its head at Grimmialp it forks; the Senggibach flows from the southwest, the Fildrich from the southeast. Both are closed off by alp-occupied cirques, while downvalley at Zwischenflüh the sub-valley of Meniggrund cuts back to the west.

Few of its summits rise above 2500m, and those that do achieve this height are located above the glen of the Fildrich: Männliflue (2652m) is the highest, the neighbouring Winterhorn (2608m) is next. There are no glaciers, nor permanent snowfields, but the lovely Spillgerte (2476m) at the head of the Senggibach (perhaps the finest and most dramatic of all the Diemtigtal peaks), has a splendid

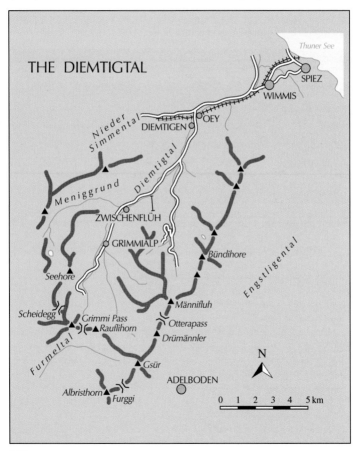

Summer in the Diemtigtal

wall of rock thrusting northward above the Grimmi pastures. Walkers on their way to the Grimmi Pass can wander in full view of this wall and admire the contrasts of bleak rock and flower-strewn hillsides. North of the Spillgerte rises Seehore (2281m) whose summit, reached from Grimmialp by a trail coming deviously from the north, commands a broad panorama, while between Spillgerte and Seehore the Fromattgrat has another impressive wall of steep crags overlooking the walkers' pass of Scheidegg.

Most of the hamlets scattered along the valley offer accommodation of some sort or another; and most have interesting walks leading from them. For those visitors without their own transport, the valley is still easily accessible, for there's a railway station at Oey-Diemtigen at its northern end (served by train from either Spiez or Zweisimmen), and a daily postbus service that meets the train and goes south as far as Grimmialp.

MAIN BASES

OEY (669m) Guarding the entrance to the valley, Oey has a few shops, PTT, bank, restaurant and a railway station. In terms of accommodation, there are four hotels with a total of about 60 beds, several apartments for holiday let, and a campsite.

DIEMTIGEN (809m) has holiday apartments, about 30 beds in three *gasthofs* and group accommodation in a Naturfreundehaus. It's an architectural gem, with an interesting priest's house, and the largest private dwelling in the Simmental area, the Grosshaus, dating from the early 19th century.

An attractive old barn door in the Diemtigtal

SCHWENDEN/GRIMMIALP (1163m) Near the roadhead, Grimmialp has a campsite, holiday apartments, four hotels and a number of *matratzenlagers*, and a restaurant. The valley postbus terminates at Hotel Spillgerten (1220m), a little above Grimmialp.

ROUTE 88

*Grimmialp (1220m) – Grimmi Pass
(2057m) – St Stephan (996m)*

Grade	2–3
Distance	13km
Height gain	837m
Height loss	1061m
Time	5–5½hrs
Location	South of Grimmialp

One of the particular pleasures of this walk is the sensation of remoteness that comes from fading footpaths and long views over a barely-habited landscape. It's rich in wild flowers early in the summer, abundant with wild fruits in season, and every metre gained is worth reliving. The Grimmi Pass (also known as Grimmifurggi) is a lush divide, a green saucer of yellow flowers dipped between the Spillgerte Rothorn and the Rauflihorn; a col that links the upper Diemtigtal with the Farmeltal and thence the Ober Simmental. As this is an 'A to B' route, transport will be required at one end or the other. If you're staying in the Diemtigtal your return will be by train from St Stephan to Oey via Zweisimmen, and then by postbus from Oey. If you have your own transport and are based outside the valley, leave your car in Oey and take a postbus to Grimmialp to begin the walk, and train from St Stephan at its conclusion. There are no opportunities for refreshment along this route, other than the chance to buy goats' cheese at an alp just below the pass!

Take the postbus as far as Hotel Spillgerten (Grimmialp), which is as far as the public road goes. Walk upvalley along the continuing (private) road for a short distance, then fork left on a track that leads through trees and meadows, initially alongside the stream, then to one or two farm buildings. *Bergweg* paint flashes direct a path

The Spillgerte wall flanks the Grimmi Pass

Rising to the left of the Grimmi Pass is the easy **Rauflihorn** (2323m). To gain its summit simply wander up the ridge – about 1hr from the pass.

uphill to another farm, where you come onto a track again. This takes you into forest, where you continue to follow this track veering south all the way up to an alp in a rough green undulating bowl with the long and lovely wall of the Spillgerte rising ahead.

The track leads to a lonely little alp building where you can sometimes buy goats' cheese. The pass you're aiming for is an obvious saddle seen above to the south, and the path (narrow and faint in places) heads directly to it over hillocks of alpenrose and, before the cattle have been brought up for summer grazing, acres of wild flowers and with streams dancing down. The **Grimmi Pass** is reached in about 3hrs from Grimmialp. ◄

The steep grass slopes on the southern side of the pass can be very greasy after rain and caution is advised in descending them. Go down to the solitary farm of Obere Bluttlig (1983m), then continue to a second farm, Untere Bluttlig (1752m) where the path forks. Take the right branch on a descending traverse that takes you through forest, in and out of gullies and over streams, and round an open shoulder of hillside at the alp of Dachbode where you come to a farm track.

Wander along the track, but do not follow it down to the valley. Instead look for a paint flash that leads you away from the track and along a footpath going south-west across meadows to pass a second isolated farm. A line of telegraph poles is the only intrusion on what is otherwise a peaceful and unspoilt pastoral scene. Follow the telegraph poles as far as another farm, now overlooking the Simmental, where you bear left and drop to a farm road. This leads all the way to St Stephan, but there are numerous short-cuts available that lead over meadows and through woods. The way is clear and well waymarked, and you eventually arrive in **St Stephan** near the railway station.

ROUTE 89

Grimmialp (1220m) – Grimmi Pass (2057m) – Rauflihorn (2323m) – Fildrich (1353m) – Grimmialp

Grade	3
Distance	14km
Height gain	1103m
Height loss	1103m
Time	7–7½hrs
Location	South of Grimmialp

An exhilarating day's wandering, this round trip links the two upper glens of the Diemtigtal via the summit of the Rauflihorn, but it should only be tackled by experienced mountain walkers. There's nothing particularly difficult about it, but caution is advised.

Follow directions as far as the **Grimmi Pass** (3hrs) as given for Route 88 above. Now wander up the left-hand grassy ridge to the top of the Rauflihorn in about 1hr. The descending path goes steeply down the northeast spur of the mountain (take care) then veers right and left to the Raufli alp (2119m) in an upper corrie. Continue down to another farm building at a junction of tracks. Bear left on a hillside traverse, then down a spur all the way to the hamlet of **Fildrich** in the valley bed. Follow the road north, and just beyond Allmi break away left to cross the stream and join a track leading along the western hillside back to **Grimmialp**.

The flower-starred Grimmi Pass at the head of the Diemtigtal

ROUTE 90

Grimmialp (1220m) –
Scheidegg (1991m) – Blankenburg (957m)

Grade	2–3
Distance	11km
Height gain	771m
Height loss	1034m
Time	5–5½hrs
Location	Southwest of Grimmialp

Like Route 88 this offering also crosses the mountains to descend into the Simmental, but this time it's the valley's upper west wall that is crossed, using the Scheidegg breach at the southern end of the Fromattgrat.

From Hotel Spillgerten at the end of the public road where the postbus terminates, continue ahead and follow sign-posts on a graded farm road leading gently up to **Alpetli**, a large new-looking alp building, altitude 1626m. There are fine views from here across the valley to the Männliflue ridge beyond which lies the Engstligental. From Alpetli a trail gradually takes you higher towards an inner hanging valley below the stark rock faces of the Fromattgrat, and to another alp building at 1794m. From here to the pass will occupy about 1–1¼hrs, and the way leads through a short corrie, a charming basin embraced by a semi-circle of mountain walls. In the centre of this basin lies a dazzling pool of water in spring and early summer, (it's usually dry by the autumn) above which are stands of old gnarled trees and bushes straddling an ancient rock slide. The alpenroses here are beautiful.

Keep to the left-hand (east) slope as you head up to the pass, for the path almost disappears. You make directly towards the broad bulwark of Hindere Spillgerte; a short ascent over bumpy pasture to the 1991m saddle of **Scheidegg**. From here the whole Spillgerte and Fromattgrat display themselves in a splendid view and make an acceptable reward for those who gain this point. To the west across the forested Betelreid Graben, with the houses of Blankenburg at its confluence with the Simmental, the view goes over low ranges between the Jaun Pass and the Saanental, and the long serrated ridge of the Salbelspitzen, Dent de Ruth and the Bern-Vaud borderlands.

From Scheidegg the descent is straightforward, but it can be extended slightly for a short detour to the right to visit the alp of Fromatt (1855m) where you enjoy an extensive view which includes the Jaun Pass, the Wildhorn and the projecting tops at the western end of the Plaine Morte on the Wildstrubel. The path goes through forest and over pasture and finally joins a road alongside the Betelreid Graben stream into the village of **Blankenburg** (1½–1¾hrs from the pass).

(Trains go from Blankenburg southward to Lenk or north to Zweisimmen and on to Oey for a return to the Diemtigtal.)

Other routes in the Diemtigtal

- From Schwenden/Grimmialp paths lead west then north to climb to a hidden upper pastureland with the tarn of **SEEBERGSEE** nestling in it. From here you can either cross the saddle of Luegle and descend to **BOLTIGEN** or **ZWEISIMMEN** in the Simmental, or make a steady descent of the pastures to **ZWISCHENFLÜH** back in the Diemtigtal, for a circular walk of considerable charm.

- Another pass crossing takes you over the **GRIMMI** (as in Route 88), but instead of wandering westward to the Simmental, branch off east to the head of the Farmeltal and over the **FURGGELI** to **ADELBODEN**. A long route, this would be a Grade 3.

- Further downvalley walks can be had from most of the hamlets. **ZWISCHENFLÜH** offers a variety of

circular routes on both sides of the valley. A 4hr circuit of the **SCHWARZENBERG** to the east is one possibility; a route round the back of the **HOHMAD** to the alp of **WIRIE** and return through the valley, is another.

The Diemtigtal is a pastoral gem of a valley

• **ENTSCHWIL**, a village to the north of the Schwarzenberg, is another hidden base from which to tackle more circular walks, a little shorter in length than those at some of the higher hamlets, while both **HORBODEN** and **DIEMTIGEN** provide a variety of half-day and full-day walks to suit. A brochure is available from the valley's tourist information office.

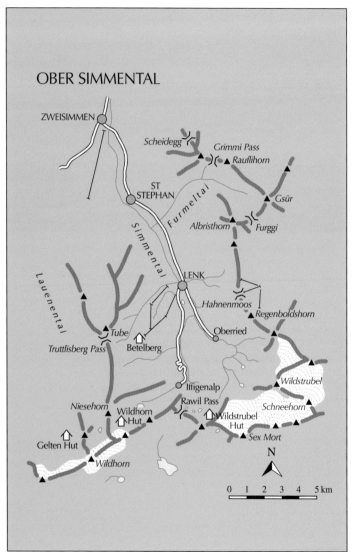

OBER SIMMENTAL

OBER SIMMENTAL

Noted for its finely decorated wooden houses and its cattle, the Simmental is an important valley of communication between the lakes of Geneva and Thun with the cross-country link between the two being completed by either Col du Pillon or the Jaun Pass. It's a great arcing bow of a valley, broad and sunny in places, dark and narrow in others where the river comes foaming through in a series of wild cataracts. Much of the valley is delightfully pastoral; most of its mountains are snow-free and wooded to a regular height, but towards its head these mountains grow in stature and promise, and there is good walking to be had on their smooth grass slopes. Above Lenk especially, where powerful waterfalls burst out of the mountain walls, trails lead to a wide variety of scenes: some wild and rocky, others green and rolling. Small tarns lie dotted among the folding hills; limestone ribs protrude here and there, and several easy summits provide uplifting panoramic views.

ACCESS AND INFORMATION

Location	Southwest of the Diemtigtal. The Ober Simmental is the upper part of the long and regionally important Simmental valley.
Map	LS 263T *Wildstrubel* at 1:50,000
Bases	Zweisimmen (941m), Lenk (1068m)
Information	Zweisimmen Tourismus, CH–3770 Zweisimmmen (☎ 033 722 11 33 **www.zweisimmen.ch/tourismus**)
	Lenk Simmental Tourismus, Rawilstrasse 3, CH–3775 Lenk (☎ 033 733 31 31 **info@lenk-simmental.ch www.lenk-simmental.ch**)
Access	By train via Thun and Spiez as far as Lenk. The postbus fills in any gaps.

The valley is arbitrarily divided into two; the Nieder Simmental being the lower region from the foot of the Jaun Pass eastwards to the Lake of Thun, the Ober Simmental covering all the valley south of Boltigen. Zweisimmen is the main town, being situated in a broad basin at the confluence of the Kleine Simme

The small lake on the outskirts of Lenk

(coming from the hills above Saanenmoser) and the main Simme which begins its life among the glaciers of the Wildstrubel above Lenk. The river itself is a favourite among kayak enthusiasts, but it has plenty of wild stretches to put it out of bounds to novices.

Above Lenk, or to be more precise above Oberried, a great knot of mountains breaks out of the Wildstrubel's Glacier de la Plaine Morte. Seen from a distance the snow and ice of this region gleams like a beckoning tiara, but from the valley pastures in the southern Simmental, only a jumble of heights and a blue line of ridge systems reveal themselves. There are hinted inner recesses that invite discovery, and grassy flanks speckled with haybarns and secluded alp farms accessible to all. To east and west the ridges quickly lose height to allow easy crossings from one valley to the next. These ridges grow broad and pastoral. Cattle graze them, flowers shimmer in the summer breeze. Footpaths meander round boggy patches or circumnavigate limestone pits and curious hummocks. And the views catch a walker's breath with pleasure.

Lenk is the highest resort. Once known mainly as a spa, it has now entered the list of mainstream alpine resorts with a growing ski industry, although it has contained both size and ambition to modest proportions. In summer it is both a walking and, to a lesser degree, a mountaineering centre with ease of access via road or rail.

Travelling north away from Lenk, away from the higher mountains, the next village you come to is Matten at the mouth of the Farmeltal, from which point there's access by foot over the Grimmi Pass to the Diemtigtal. Then comes St Stephan, spread across the floor of the valley with its leaning towards light industry.

Just before Zweisimmen, Blankenburg crouches on the eastern side of the valley. Both road and railway curve round to serve it, but the river twists away, as though reluctant to be joined by the Betelreid Gruben. Zweisimmen, by contrast with other villages in the valley, is a teeming place with crowded streets and an air of authority. From the southwest comes the Saanen road alongside the Kleine Simme, then it's a long run north, the road and railway almost ignoring Mannried and Grubenwald, tucked on the east side of the river. But Weissenbach lines the road, as does Reidenbach at the foot of the Jaun Pass. Then a kink in the valley makes a northeasterly curve, and there sits Boltigen, with the Nieder Simmental shafting darkly towards the east.

The valley as a whole has much of interest for the general tourist, while the walker will find plenty to appeal, in particular in the upper reaches of the Ober Simmental where footpaths lead into landscapes of great beauty. That is where the majority of the following walks take place.

MAIN BASES

ZWEISIMMEN (941m) is ideally situated as a holiday base for those with their own transport, since there are many neighbouring areas accessible by car, although it also has excellent public transport services. As the main village in the valley (it may be considered almost a town by comparison with others in the region), it has many fine wooden buildings characteristic of the Simmental, a museum of local crafts and a 15th-century church containing murals and a fine timber ceiling. There are several good walks to be had from here, including an ascent of the Hundsrugg for superb views to Mont Blanc, Grand Combin and some of the major Oberland peaks to the southeast. A gondola lift goes up to the Rinderberg to the south; another fine viewpoint. For accommodation there are several hotels, ranging from the ungraded to three-star, some of which have budget-priced dormitories: Gasthof Derby near the bahnhof (☎ 033 722 14 38 **gasthof_derby@bluewin.ch**); Berghotel Sparenmoos above the village in good walking country (☎ 033 722 22 34 **berghotel.sparenmoos@smile.ch**); and Berggasthaus Gobeli at the middle station of the Rinderberg gondola (☎ 033 722 12 19 **www.gobeli.ch**). There's also Berghaus Rinderberg owned by the Allschwil Ski Club; it has 44 dorm places and is open all year (☎ 061 712 56 07 **www.skiclub-allschwil.ch**). Zweisimmen has no shortage of holiday apartments, and two campsites. There are plenty of shops, restaurants, banks, a PTT, tourist information office, and a busy railway station (trains to Gstaad, Lenk or Spiez).

LENK (1068m) is an attractive little resort located among level pastures with gentle hills rising to east and west. Outliers of the Wildstrubel massif rise to the south, and the valley forks just outside the village to create a choice of walking areas to explore. Lenk has a fair selection of shops and restaurants. It has banks, a PTT and tourist information office. There are plenty of hotels and pensions – among the lower-priced are the excellent Hotel-Garni Alpina (☎ 033 733 10 57 **alpina_lenk@bluewin.ch www.lenk.ch/mini/alpina.html**), Hotel-Garni Alpenruh (☎ 033 733 10 64) and the Hotel Waldrand (☎ 033 736 82 82). Lenk has around 5000 beds in holiday apartments and chalets, and two campsites, one of which is located towards the head of the valley near the Simmenfälle. There's an open-air swimming pool, and a gondola lift to Betelberg (Leiterli) on the western hillside, from which a selection of walking trails can be accessed.

OTHER BASES
Above Lenk several mountain inns, restaurants and gondola lift stations have accommodation that could be useful to walkers. Among them **BERGHOTEL LEITERLI** (1943m) at the upper station of the Betelberg gondola has 77 dormitory places (☎ 033 733 35 16 **info@leiterli.ch www.huettenzauber-lenk.ch**), and at the roadhead, the rustic **BERGHAUS IFFIGENALP** (1584m) is reached by postbus from Lenk. Open from May to October it has 27 beds in an atmospheric 100 year-old building on the edge of splendid walking country. To the northeast of Iffigenalp, perched on an alp saddle at 1857m, the little dairy farm of **LANGERMATTE** has just four or five places in a very remote setting (mobile ☎ 079 582 09 68).

At the head of the Oberried stem of the upper valley **RESTAURANT SIEBENBRUNNEN** (also known as Gasthaus Rezliberg) has dormitory accommodation (☎ 033 733 12 86), while downvalley a short way, **HOTEL SIMMENFÄLLE** near the famous falls, has both bedrooms and dormitories (☎ 033 733 10 89 **simmenfaelle@bluewin.ch**).

MOUNTAIN HUTS
FLUESEELI HUT (2049m) This tiny hut is owned by the Flueseeliverein, a Lenk-based club. With just 12 places and no resident guardian, it is a self-catering only hut built near the lovely tarn after which it is named, on the northwest slopes of the Wildstrubel – about 3hrs walk from the Simmenfälle roadhead.

WILDSTRUBEL HUT (2791m) There are two huts with a total of 70 places, owned by the SAC; they stand on a shelf a little below the summit of the Weisshorn and have a resident guardian from February to the end of May, and late June to mid-October when meals are provided. For reservations ☎ 033 744 33 39

With almost 100 places, the Wildhorn Hut offers comfortable lodgings in a wild setting

wildstrubelhuette@bluewin.ch   www.wildstrubelhuette.ch.   From Iffigenalp the huts can be reached in about 3½hrs.

WILDHORN HUT (2303m) Standing in a somewhat bleak, stony valley south-west of Iffigenalp, the Wildhorn Hut is comfortable nonetheless. It has 94 places and a full meals service when the guardian is resident, from mid-March to early May, and from late June to the end of September (☎ 033 733 23 82 **wildhornhuette@bluewin.ch www.wildhornhuette.ch**)

ROUTE 91

Zweisimmen (941m) – Garstatt (858m) –
Weissenbach (842m) – Boltigen (818)

Grade	1
Distance	10km (one way)
Height gain	39m
Height loss	162m
Time	2–2½hrs
Location	North of Zweisimmen

This gentle valley walk gives an opportunity to visit several small Simmental villages, passing old timbered farmhouses, cutting through pastures and following the course of the river northward. Initially there are views of the ruined Mannenberg castle on the opposite bank of the river on the outskirts of Mannried.

From the centre of Zweisimmen take the minor road heading north to Obegg, which is reached in about 20mins. From here a track branches half-right ahead and cuts off towards the river, joining a service road running parallel with the main valley road. This ends and a footpath continues ahead along the hillside to Laubegg (961m). Crossing the railway you come to **Garstatt** and go over to the right bank of the river. The trail now follows the river to **Weissenbach,** most of which village is on the opposite bank, and continues to **Boltigen**. Here you cross again to the left bank to gain the village proper *(accommodation, refreshments)*. The train may be caught from here back to Zweisimmen.

Other routes from Zweisimmen

Zweisimmen makes a good base for a holiday and there are numerous possibilities for walks leading from it. The tourist information office will provide further details, but the following outline suggestions immediately come to mind. Study of the map and local brochures will provide more ideas.

- An obvious valley walk goes in the opposite direction to that given above as Route 91. This leads along the true left (west) bank of the Simme and goes to **RIED**, **SCHADAULI** and **LENK** in 3–3½hrs. (Grade 1)

- A more taxing outing crosses the river to **MANNRIED** and goes northeast up the hillside to **MEIENBERG** and on to the hidden tarn of **SEEBERGSEE** (1831m) in a little over 3½hrs. An alternative return may be made by going southwest to **STIERBERG** and down to **OBERRIED** in another 3hrs, making a good 6½hr circuit of Grade 3.

- By use of the gondola lift to **RINDERBERG** a 3½hr crossing to **GSTAAD** can be achieved. This gives an opportunity for a lovely ridge-walk along the **GANDLOUENEGRAT** (2078m), followed by a high-level traverse of the southern flanks of **HORNTUBE** and **HORNFLUE** with spectacular views much of the way. This also warrants Grade 3.

- Views from **HUNDSRUGG** (2047m) include not only the big Oberland peaks, but Mont Blanc too. A steep walk from Zweisimmen via **HEIMCHUEWEID** and **NUJEBERG**, on a combination of footpath and farm road, leads you there in 3½–4hrs. Grade 3 again.

Routes from St Stephan

- Midway between Zweisimmen and Lenk, St Stephan is on the edge of an area worth exploring on foot. A long (6½hr) walk takes you through the **FARMELTAL** and over the pass of **FURGGELI** (2336m) to **ADELBODEN**. This strenuous route will be Grade 3. But even without going as far as the pass, the valley is still worth wandering in.

- An easy valley walk along the east side of the river, linking the villages of **MATTEN**, **GUETEBRUNNE** and **LENK** makes a gentle morning's outing (2½hrs) at Grade 1.
- On the far side of the valley to the south, the viewpoint of the **FLOSCHHORN** (2079m) may be reached by path in 3½–4hrs. The route goes via **MATTEN**, then across the river and up the north spur of the mountain, passing through two or three small alps on the way.

ROUTE 92

Lenk (Büelberg; 1661m) – Hahnenmoos (1956m) – Pommernpass (2055m) – Oberried (1103m)

Grade	2–3
Distance	8km
Height gain	394m
Height loss	952m
Time	3½hrs
Location	East of Lenk

On the east side of the valley above Lenk two easy passes cross the mountains into the upper Engstligental. The Hahnenmoos was described in the opposite direction as Route 87, while the Pommernpass was also mentioned in that crossing. By linking these two passes, a fine loop trip can be achieved, which also gives an opportunity to visit the well-known Simmenfälle cascades. A bus is taken from Lenk to Hotel Büelberg, and at the end of the walk another from Oberried downvalley to Lenk.

From **Büelberg** (*refreshments*) follow the track easily up to the **Hahnenmoos Pass** (*accommodation, refreshments*). Bear right and walk along the east (left) side of the grassy ridge on a clear path that takes you to the saddle of the Pommernpass immediately below the lump of Regenboldshorn (2193m). This is reached in about

The Pommernpass, an alternative ridge crossing to that of the Hahnenmoos Pass

261

40mins from Hahnenmoos. **Note:** there are no signs indicating the Pommernpass. (A short diversion to the summit of the Regenboldshorn is recommended: there's a steep but easy footpath and it will take only 10–15mins to reach the top.)

Descend on the south side of the pass, using the left-hand of two paths. This takes you steeply down over grass slopes passing haybarns and farms, then enters forest. At a junction of paths follow signs for the Simmenfälle. Do not cross the bridge at the top of the falls, but descend a track down to the Simmenfälle restaurant (*refreshments*) at **Oberried**. From there an hourly bus service travels downvalley to Lenk.

ROUTE 93

Lenk (Iffigenalp; 1584m) –
Iffigsee (2065m)

Grade	2
Distance	4km (one way)
Height gain	481m
Time	1½–2hrs
Location	Southwest of Iffigenalp

South of Lenk the Simme is joined by the Iffigbach, a substantial tributary coming from the southwest. The valley through which this tributary flows has a narrow road leading through it from Lenk as far as the Iffigenalp. This road is two-way as far as Färiche (Pöschenried; 1210m), but from there to Iffigenalp vehicles are subjected to a timed one-way system with access restricted to 15mins every hour. It's possible to drive to Iffigenalp, but there is also a postbus service from Lenk. This walk to the Iffigsee is steep in places, but never difficult, while the lake itself is a beautiful deep well set amid wild-looking mountain scenery. It makes a justifiably popular destination.

From Berghaus Iffigenalp follow a clear track upvalley. Beyond farm buildings it leads through pastures flanked on the left by the abrupt limestone wall of the mountains, and on the right by steep green slopes with patches of forest and grey crags. The track crosses a stream and winds up the valley to cross a second stream. Leave the track as it curves right, and take a footpath up the slope ahead to reach the alp farm of **Groppi** (1741m). (**Note:** an alternative path breaks away to the right here, leading to the Hoberg ridge and the Iffighorn in 2hrs.)

Ahead can be seen a waterfall pouring over a rock slab. The Iffigsee path climbs above its right-hand side, then mounts a long grassy cone – an old moraine wall. At the top of this cone the path levels out, goes through a rocky defile and emerges above the deep blue **Iffigsee**. The shoreline at the far northwest corner is attractive and accessible, with rumpled grass slopes and a solitary building overlooking the water.

While here, a circuit of the lake is a possibility. This will take about 30mins, while the return to Iffigenalp by the same path will require about 1hr.

The lovely Iffigsee is reached by an easy walk of less than 2 hours from Iffigenalp

ROUTE 94

Lenk (Iffigenalp;1584m) –
Iffigsee (2065m) – Iffighorn (2378m)

Grade	2
Distance	6km (one way)
Height gain	794m
Time	2–2½hrs
Location	North of the Iffigsee

The Iffighorn (Iffighore on some maps) is an unassuming grass dome that rises from the shore of the Iffigsee. However, the hill's north flank is enhanced by an abrupt limestone wall that soars out of the charming Stigelberg valley, and summit views are terrific. An easy 30min ascent of the Iffighorn from the lakeside is highly recommended.

Follow Route 93 directions as far as the **Iffigsee**, but instead of descending to the water's edge, remain on the north shore path beyond the far end of the lake. When the Wildhorn Hut path breaks left, continue up the slope ahead to a second junction. Turn right here (sign for Iffighorn and Hoberg) to climb the grass-covered hillside heading north before bearing right to contour along the upper slope. When the path suddenly begins to descend to the Hoberg crest (with a splendid view of the Oberland wall in the distance), leave the path here, turn sharp left and mount the final slope to the crown of the **Iffighorn**. The Wildhorn looks impressive to the south, but it is the lovely rolling hill country spreading to the north that is especially attractive.

To return to the Iffigsee, continue west for about 5mins (caution as the ridge plunges dramatically to your right), then a red arrow painted on a rock directs you

down the slope to rejoin the path of ascent. An alternative return to Iffigenalp could be made by descending eastwards from the summit on the Hoberg trail, eventually turning hard right at a three-way junction to gain the Iffigenalp track at alp Groppi (2hrs Iffighorn to Iffigenalp).

The Iffighorn provides a wonderful vantage point from which to study the foothill country above Lenk

ROUTE 95

Lenk (Iffigenalp; 1584m) – Iffigsee (2065m) – Wildhorn Hut (2303m)

Grade	2
Distance:	6km
Height gain	719m
Time	2hrs 45mins
Location	Southwest of the Iffigsee

Perched on a rocky knoll in wild and desolate surroundings, the Wildhorn Hut makes an interesting destination for a walk or an overnight stay. In the main summer weeks refreshments are available at the hut, so it's tempting to make a round trip, arriving in time for lunch with a view of a raw mountain landscape outside. **Note:** another route to the Wildhorn Hut is given below in Route 97.

Trapped in a deep basin of scree, the little Iffigsee is visited on the way to the Wildhorn Hut

Take Route 93 as far as the **Iffigsee** and continue above the north shore until you come to a junction of trails. Ignore the left-hand path which descends to the solitary isolated building above the lake, and continue to a second junction where the left branch is signed to the hut. Taking this trail the way now angles uphill across the hillside to gain a flat basin – usually dry in the mornings, but running with snowmelt streams in the afternoon. The hut can be seen from here backed by screes and massive moraine walls. Having crossed the initial basin, the path resumes the ascent among numerous tiny plants that are slowly transforming an otherwise stony landscape into a vast rock garden. About 5mins before reaching the **Wildhorn Hut** another path breaks away to the right, and is the one to take for the Gelten Hut (see Route 96).

Owned by the Moléson (Fribourg) Section of the SAC, the comfortable **Wildhorn Hut** is used as a base for climbs on several nearby peaks. It has 94 dormitory places and a resident guardian from mid-March to early May, and late-June to the end of September (☎ 033 733 23 82 **wildhorn-huette@bluewin.ch www.wildhornhuette.ch**).

ROUTE 96

Wildhorn Hut (2303m) – Chüetungel (1786m) – Gelten Hut (2002m)

Grade	3
Distance	7km
Height gain	216m
Height loss	558m
Time	3½hrs
Location	Southwest of the Wildhorn Hut

This rewarding hut-to-hut walk experiences a rich variety of landscapes as well as some challenging terrain. Although used by trekkers on the Tour of the Wildhorn, the route is a little tricky and exposed in several places, so caution is needed throughout.

By contrast with the gaunt surroundings of the Wildhorn Hut, the Gelten Hut's setting is open and colourful, with a basin below laced with streams fed by tumultuous cascades and a backdrop comprising the glacier-hung Wildhorn-Arpelistock ridge. The **Gelten Hut** belongs to the Oldenhorn (Saanen) Section of the SAC, has 90 places and a resident guardian from mid-March to end of April, and late June to early October, when there's a full meals service on offer. For reservations ☎ 033 765 32 20 **www.gel-tenhuette.ch**.

Descend from the hut for about 3mins, then branch left when the path forks. Over the stream angle across the left flank of the valley rising at a steady gradient, and on crossing a grassy bluff you will gain a splendid view down onto the Iffigsee. The path now contours round the spur at the end of the Wildhorn glen where you cross a screeslope and come to a junction at 2360m. Continue up the slope in the direction of the Tungelpass (also known as the Dungelpass). After mounting a slope of shale and grass, you go through a saddle to the left of a low domed hill and enter a rocky landscape.

Wander along the right-hand side, mostly on grass and rock, and in 55mins come to another path junction. Keep ahead (the way is marked *Vorsicht!* – Caution), but shortly after you veer right at another junction, and make a steep descent on grass at first, then along narrow and exposed rock ledges.

At the foot of this steep descent the way tacks below a line of crags, then eases over vegetated slopes (bilberry and alpenrose). On coming to the Chüetungel pastures – a delightful region with a rock amphitheatre to the left and streams to the right – walk ahead with views across the unseen Lauenental. The group of **Chüetungel** alp buildings are reached about 2hrs from the Wildhorn Hut. Just beyond these cross a stream to yet another junction of paths.

◀ Wandering on the path rises across a grass slope to a crest with a view into the Lauenental, then brings you to a metal ladder, at the top of which steep zig-zags bring the trail to a narrow, exposed section protected by fixed cables. The path continues with very steep views into the valley several hundred metres below. Eventually the exposed trail eases into sloping pastures, passes the alp buildings of **Usseri Gelten** (the magnificent Geltenschuss waterfall below), climbs over ribs of rock and more grass bluffs, then descends directly to the **Gelten Hut**. (For other routes to and from the Gelten Hut, please refer to the Lauenental chapter.)

ROUTE 97

Lenk (Leiterli; 1943m) – Tungelpass (2084m) – Wildhorn Hut (2303m) – Iffigenalp (1584m)

Grade	3
Distance	16km
Height gain	360m
Height loss	719m
Time	5½hrs
Location	Southwest of Lenk

On the hillside above and southwest of Lenk, the Betelberg gondola gives access to a network of footpaths, a wonderland of trails leading over high pastures rich in wild flowers and with gentle views in all directions. Leiterli is the top station of this lift, and one of the longest routes from it is this one to the Wildhorn Hut and down to Iffigenalp for the bus back to Lenk.

Buy a one-way ticket (*Bergfahrt*) on the gondola lift to Leiterli and take the broad signed path directly beyond the upper station (*accommodation, refreshments*). At first on the right-hand side of the ridge, in less than 15mins you cross to the left flank and a path junction. Ignore the descending path here and remain on the ridge route, soon winding among limestone pits and grassy

Gentle Ober Simmental country on show from the Tungelpass

hummocks above the pastoral valley of the Abibach. About 40mins from Leiterli reach the Gryden junction (1987m), climb the slope ahead and come onto the ridge crest of Stübleni (2058m). Bear left and descend to the 1992m **Stüblenipass**.

Continue ahead, keeping to the east (left-hand) side of the ridge, contouring round to the Äbigrat, and from there heading west of south to reach (in 1½–2hrs from Leiterli) the 2084m **Tungelpass**. Keep ahead on the right-hand side of a fence and work your way in steep zig-zags up to a path junction in a stony landscape at about 2317m.

Veer left, still rising before the path slopes down towards the Iffigsee, but you should branch right (sign-post) on a stony route that curves round a shoulder of the Niesenhorn and traverses steep grass slopes above the hanging valley containing the **Wildhorn Hut**. Caution should be exercised on the last stretch of this path before dropping into the valley below the hut. The hut is reached after 3hrs 45mins from Leiterli. (Please see Route 95 for hut details.)

Descend the scree-ridden valley below the hut to pass above the western side of the **Iffigsee**, then take the right fork at a junction. This path takes you above the lake's north shore and continues easily all the way down to **Iffigenalp** *(accommodation, refreshments)*. A postbus goes to Lenk from the car park below the hotel.

ROUTE 98

Lenk (Leiterli; 1943m) –
Tungelpass (2084m) –
Pöschenried (1200m) – Lenk (1068m)

Grade	2–3
Distance	15km
Height gain	141m
Height loss	1016m
Time	5–5¼hrs
Location	Southwest of Lenk

This long walk explores verdant foothill country on the upper west flank of the valley, giving ever-changing vistas and a wonderful day's exercise. For much of the way there's little habitation and you'll probably have most of the trails to yourself. As refreshment facilities are few and far between, you should carry food and drink with you.

Ride the Betelberg gondola to its top station (Leiterli; *accommodation, refreshments*) and follow directions given for Route 97 as far as the **Tungelpass** (1½–2hrs). Keep on the east side of the pass and walk ahead alongside a wall for a few paces, then descend left down a steep grass slope guided by marker posts to join a narrow path heading a little north of east. This passes through a clutter of rocks, then keeping to the right-hand side of the Stigelberg valley below the abrupt slab face of the

271

Iffighorn, it weaves a route among bilberry, alpenrose and then larchwoods.

Out of the woods turn left at an unmarked crossing path to reach the two alp buildings of **Saanenstafel** (1843m). Here you join a farm track which you then follow downhill until it forks about 10mins later. Take the lower option, and in another 10mins you'll come to a junction of tracks by a farm building. A sign here gives this as **Stigelberg** (1680m), although the map says Ufem Läger. Take the right branch which curves round the side of the building.

The track ends by another small alp farm, but a path continues ahead into a lengthy stretch of forest. Before

On the descent to Pöschenried, the Wildstrubel massif is glimpsed through the trees

long this twists steeply downhill with occasional views of the Wildstrubel glimpsed between the trees. When at last you emerge from the trees to cross a sloping meadow, the lovely Iffigfälle cascades come into view. On reaching a narrow road turn left and a few paces later come to a bridge spanning the Chimpach. Immediately before this turn right on a continuing path (direction Pöschenried and Lenk) to drop steeply through more forest and eventually arrive at another road. Turn left and cross a bridge to the Wirtschaft Alpenrösli (*refreshments*) and a bus stop for the Lenk–Iffigenalp route. This is **Pöschenried** (1200m).

Turn right through a small gate, cross the Iffigbach and turn left to follow the river downstream, at first through woodland, then along the edge of meadows. With more fine views of the Wildstrubel, reach the bed of the valley at the confluence of the two upper stems of the Simmental, to join a service road from the Oberried (Simmenfälle) stem. Cross a bridge on the left, then turn right at a T-junction of narrow roads. Moments later take the left fork – a narrow service road that cuts between flat meadows with Lenk seen ahead. When you reach the reedy Lenksee lake, follow whichever bank takes your fancy and continue from there into the heart of **Lenk**.

ROUTE 99

Lenk (Leiterli; 1943m) – Trüttlisberg Pass (2038m) – Lauenen (1241m)

Grade	2
Distance	9km
Height gain	95m
Height loss	797m
Time	3hrs
Location	Southwest of Lenk

A fine, easy walk over the ridge of mountains dividing the Ober Simmental from the Lauenental, this is a delight of far views and flowers. The Betelberg gondola lift begins the day with a ride to the top station at Leiterli. From here to the pass the trail follows an almost horizontal course along a ridge, first on one side, then on the other, with lovely views into the craggy combes of the Wildhorn and Wildstrubel. (For those who choose to disregard the cableway and prefer to walk all the way from Lenk to Lauenen, see Route 100 below.)

Leaving the gondola lift, take the broad path used at the start of Route 97, and follow this as far as the **Gryden** junction (1987m), reached in about 40mins. The continuing route crosses the Stüblenipass and also goes to Lauenen but, for the Trüttlisberg Pass, branch right here on a good path which cuts below the block of Stübleni above spiny limestone ribs overlooking the head of the Wallbach valley. Mount easily to the rocky ridge which proves to be an exciting tight-rope path among a mass of mini-craters, passes a small shelter hut and descends left to join the path from the **Trüttlisberg Pass**.

The descent route is straightforward. The trail takes you over steep pastures to reach the farm buildings of

The Betelberg gondola lift leads to some fine walking country

Vordere Trüttlisberg (1818m). From here the path becomes a farm track leading to a metalled road. You can either follow this road all the way down to Lauenen, or take the signed footpath which cuts left after a short distance. This gives a pleasant descent through pastures and small patches of woodland, passing attractive chalets before entering **Lauenen** beside the post office. (For details of accommodation and other facilities, please refer to the Lauenental chapter.)

ROUTE 100

Lenk (1068m) – Trüttlisberg Pass (2038m)
– Lauenen (1241m)

Grade	2–3
Distance	14km
Height gain	970m
Height loss	797m
Time	5–5½hrs
Location	West and southwest of Lenk

From Lenk to Lauenen over the Trüttlisberg Pass is a walk of almost constant pasture or forest. It's limestone country bright with flowers, and near the pass there are curious hillocks and hollows from which huge panoramas gaze off to the main crest of the Bernese Alps in the south. Though reasonably long, it is not a difficult route, and is only given a partial Grade 3 on account of the distance involved. The Trüttlisberg crossing forms part of the Alpine Pass Route.

From Lenk tourist office walk up the main street to Hotel Kreuz and turn right alongside it. After about 400m go left into Rütitstrasse and walk along this narrow road

The path to the Trüttlisberg Pass enjoys a broad panorama

parallel with the Wallbach stream. When it curves to the left leave the road in favour of a broad path or track which enters woodland.

The way climbs steeply alongside the stream, then you ascend a series of ladders and stone steps with waterfalls to one side. About an hour after setting out, leave the trees near **Berghaus Wallegg** (1325m *refreshments*), turn right and walk up the right-hand side of a sloping meadow for about 100m, then take a track into the woods once more. Contouring for a while, you then gain a little height and cross the Wallbach again, shortly after which you come out of the woods and reach a farm track. Turn left.

A few paces after crossing a streambed, take a path on the right to climb a rough hillside. This can be very muddy, especially after rain, and it takes you past several isolated farms, the last of which is **Ober Lochberg** (1910m; 3hrs). Just beyond this farm the way forks. Take the left branch over a stream, and then continue up towards the saddle passing a small hut on the way. The **Trüttlisberg Pass** is reached about 3½hrs from Lenk, and is marked by a signpost at a path junction.

Over the pass bear left and follow a slightly rising path to another junction where you begin the descent to Lauenen. This is straightforward, and is described in Route 99 above.

ROUTE 101

Lenk (1068m) – Trüttlisberg Pass (2038m)
– Turbachal – Gstaad (1050m)

Grade	3
Distance	24km
Height gain	970m
Height loss	988m
Time	7½ hrs
Location	West and southwest of Lenk

A long day's walking but an utterly delightful one, the route leads through a glorious pastoral countryside. First, the way to the Trüttlisberg Pass wanders through flower meadows with long views. Then it traverses round to a second easy pass before dropping into the lush green Turbachtal that takes you all the way down to Gstaad. Parts of this walk may be a little boggy, and around one or two farms it's not unusual to find a quagmire of churned mud after rain. But mostly the paths are well-drained and easy to follow.

Follow Route 100 as far as the **Trüttlisberg Pass**, but instead of crossing over towards Lauenen, bear right and, rising a little, cut round the left-hand side of a minor peak named Tube (2107m) and make for an obvious saddle between it and the steeper Lauenehore seen ahead. Once at this saddle (1986m), a narrow path descends to the right towards a lone farm building and continues on the west side of the sweeping corrie, boggy in places but with plenty of flowers. As you lose height so the path takes you past cattle byres and hay barns, over side streams and eventually leads to a bridge to aid the crossing to the right bank of the main Turbach stream. A farm track leads on and eventually becomes a surfaced road that goes all the way down to Gstaad.

However, there is an alternative (signed) footpath route after a while. This crosses back to the left bank of the stream and gains height initially as it traverses the steep hillside; an interesting path, climbing and falling through forest, over pastures, crossing curious stiles and passing occasional haybarns. The path is not universally clear, but a route is practicable – with care. You will finally come to a surfaced road that leads directly to **Gstaad**. (Please refer to the Lauenental chapter for details of accommodation and facilities in Gstaad.)

Other routes from Lenk

- There's no shortage of walks heading out of Lenk. Some are gentle valley strolls: upvalley to **OBER-RIED** and the **SIMMENFÄLLE**, for example (Grade 1), or to **PÖSCHENRIED** and the **IFFIGFÄLLE**.
- The unmanned **FLUESEELI HUT** (3hrs from the Simmenfälle roadhead) makes a challenging Grade 3 destination, with prospects of continuing from there on a 4hr ascent to the **WILDSTRUBEL HUT** at 2791m.
- The **WILDSTRUBEL HUT** is more often approached from Iffigenalp by a steeply climbing path in about 3½hrs (Grade 3).
- To the west of the Wildstrubel Hut lies the 2429m **RAWILPASS** with a continuing route to **LAC DE TSEUZIER** and eventual descent to the Rhône Valley at **SION**; a long Grade 3 crossing from Iffigenalp.

LAUENENTAL

The Lauenental is a short, green and beautiful valley. As you travel into it from Gstaad, so the Wildhorn massif beckons from the south with a ridge of snow and ice to complement the neat, shorn hillsides and trim patches of forest that lead to it. And it is this contrast of formidable grandeur and tended gentility that helps to invest the whole area with an atmosphere of welcome.

ACCESS AND INFORMATION

Location	West of the Ober Simmental, the Lauenental flows north from the base of the Wildhorn to Gstaad where it connects with the Saane and Turbach valleys.
Map:	LS 263T *Wildstrubel* at 1:50,000
Bases	Gstaad (1050m), Lauenen (1241m)
Information	Gstaad Saanenland Tourismus, CH–3780 Gstaad (☎ 033 748 81 81 gst@gstaad.ch www.gstaad.ch) Verkehrsbüro, CH–3782 Lauenen (☎ 033 765 91 81)
Access	By train from Montreux or Bern to Gstaad, and postbus to Lauenen.

There's only one village in the valley, and a modest one at that. Gathered among meadows on the east bank of the Louwibach, Lauenen has a number of attractive houses set in a shallow scoop of pasture, like a hammock slung between the mountains and, like a hammock, it gives an air of comfort and calm relaxation. South of the village the Lauenental has its marshy regions where streams flow from the hillsides to seep among trees and damp meadows; at the roadhead there's a charming lake, the Lauenensee, one of the loveliest in the region with its reed- and grass-fringed edges casting a deep green tint across the shallows.

Above the lake, above a forest-clad rise, a superb little glen (a nature reserve) is flush with flowers and highlighted by a great water spout – the Geltenschuss. Rise above that and you'll find a hidden basin fed by numerous streams and cascades pouring from glaciers draped across a ridge linking the Wildhorn (3248m) and Arpelistock (3035m). It's a magical place, full of beauty, and with a mountain hut nearby.

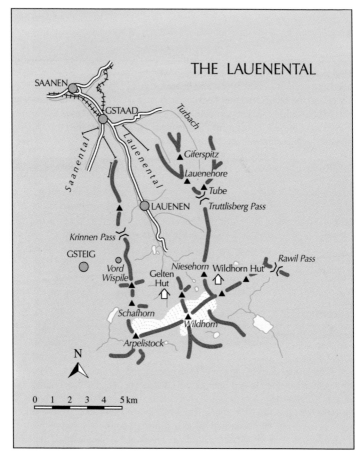

THE LAUENENTAL

SAANEN

GSTAAD

Turbach

Saanental

Lauenental

▲ Giferspitz

▲ Lauenehore

LAUENEN

▲ Tube

Truttlisberg Pass

Krinnen Pass

GSTEIG

Vord
Wispile

Niesehorn

Gelten
Hut

Wildhorn Hut

Rawil Pass

▲

⌂

Schafhorn

▲

⌂

▲

▲

Wildhorn

▲

Arpelistock

N

0   1   2   3   4   5 km

On either side of Lauenen, to east and west, the hills grow to broad and easy ridges. On the eastern hillside one or two alp hamlets have been set among rumpled terraces open to the sun, while above them the crest of the ridge eases to high pasture. On the west, the ridge is a little lower (it doesn't touch 2000m until Chlys Hüri, the last rocky eminence projecting from the Arpelistock) and for much of its length forest reaches right to the top. On both sides there are gentle passes: to the east the Trüttlisberg, Stübleni and Tungel provide ways over the mountains to Lenk. The Turli and Turnelsattel lead to Gstaad via the Turbachtal, while to the west the Krinnen (or Chrine) gives easy access to Gsteig at the foot of Les Diablerets.

Moving north, away from Lauenen and downstream towards sophisticated Gstaad, the valley narrows slightly. On its western side the crest remains largely forested, while above to the east the mountains have grown somewhat, rising above the tree-line and offering ridge-walks of open splendour. But ridges on both sides of the valley have attractive routes along them; the Höhi Wispile which divides the valleys of Lauenen and Gsteig being a particular favourite.

On the very edge of Gstaad the Louwibach stream that started out as the Geltenbach and Tungelbach among glaciers in the south, flows into the Turbach to become the Saane, the river whose name is adopted by a whole region: Saanenland.

MAIN BASES

GSTAAD (1050m) is the St Moritz of the Bernese Oberland, a small resort with a pretence of sophistication, where personalities of sport and screen gather when the snow falls and the mountains are transformed into minor ski playgrounds. In the summer it's famed as the venue for the Swiss Open Tennis Championships, and of cultural extravaganzas such as the Yehudi Menuhin Festival held in the Mauritius Church in nearby Saanen. But Gstaad also has access to a wide choice of mountain areas, and with a variety of cableways in close proximity, walkers are

Lauenen farmhouse

able to reach various high points from which to begin their outings. As a holiday base, it is very much a fashionable resort focussing on one long main street lined with an assortment of shops and restaurants. There are banks, PTT, a tourist information office and good public transport with postbus services to Lauenen in the south and Gsteig and Col du Pillon in the southwest; and railway links with towns as far apart as Montreux and Thun by way of the MOB (*Montreux-Oberland Bahn*). The nearest campsite is 1km north of town, and there's no shortage of hotels or holiday apartments. As might be expected, Gstaad has some luxurious hotels for visitors with deep pockets (no less than three are five-star rated), and most accommodation is on the expensive side, but there's a youth hostel in nearby Saanen (☎ 033 744 13 43 **www.youthhostel.ch**).

LAUENEN (1241m) is very different to Gstaad. It's a small, pretty village with an unpretentious street and a number of lovely old timbered buildings characteristic of the region, one of which (dated 1765) is a gem of local craftsmanship. The 16th-century church provides a central focal point, while from almost every corner one gazes south to the Wildhorn. Along the street are two general stores, a PTT, bank and tourist information office. There are only three hotels: the three-star Hotel Alpenland (☎ 033 765 34 34 **hotel@alpenland.ch www.alpenland.ch**) on the southern edge of the village; Hotel Geltenhorn (☎ 033 765 30 22), and the lovely 100 year-old Hotel Wildhorn (☎ 033 765 30 12 **hotel@wildhorn.ch www.wildhorn.ch**) in the heart of the village near the PTT. In addition there are plenty of holiday apartments, and low-price dormitory accommodation in the old schoolhouse (Fereinlager Gemeinde ☎ 033 765 32 73) and the Fereinlager Grünbühl (☎ 033 765 30 45).

MOUNTAIN HUT
GELTEN HUT (2002m) This commands a wonderful situation above the Geltenschuss waterfalls. It not only has the high mountains as a backdrop, but a fine view along the Lauenental. The approach walk from Lauenen takes about 3½hrs. With dormitory places for 90, and a resident guardian providing a full meals service from mid-March to the end of April, and late-June to early October, the Gelten Hut is owned by the Oldenhorn (Saanen) Section of the SAC. For reservations ☎ 033 765 32 20 **www.geltenhuette.ch**.

ROUTE 102

Gstaad (1050m) – Turbachtal –
Turli (1986m) – Lauenen (1241m)

Grade	3
Distance	16km
Height gain	936m
Height loss	745m
Time	5½hrs
Location	East and southeast of Gstaad

One of the many pleasant aspects of this walk is the joy of being drawn deeper into the peaceful Turbachtal. The route leads all the way through it, from its entrance on the edge of bustling Gstaad, to the grassy saddle at its very head between the Lauenehore and Tube. The Turbachtal really is a charming glen, and this exploration offers an ideal day out. Return to Gstaad may be made by postbus from Lauenen.

Set out from the heart of Gstaad on the road signed to Lauenen. When it forks to cross the river, leave the Lauenen road and remain on the left branch which takes you into the Turbachtal. Again the road forks, with the right branch crossing the river to Bisse; but once more keep on the left of the Turbach, heading deeper into the valley. At a sharp left-hand hairpin, leave the road and continue straight ahead on a farm track which continues for a considerable distance, steadily gaining height with the stream for company. After about 2½hrs come to a bridge at **Steineberg** (1560m) and cross to the true left bank (west side). Passing a farm (Marchli; 1647m) a footpath continues, rising towards the head of the valley where an obvious saddle is seen to the south. The way becomes a little boggy in places and the path is faint at

283

times. Make towards an alp building just below the saddle, and then beyond it to gain the pass of **Turli** (1986m) after about 4–4¼hrs.

Lauenen lies almost directly below to the west. The descent path takes you past the alp of Hindere Trüttlisberg, over pasture and through patches of forest on an easy yet delightful descent, and in a little over an hour from the pass you arrive in the centre of **Lauenen**.

ROUTE 103

Lauenen (1241m) – Lauenensee (1381m)

Grade	1
Distance	4km (one way)
Height gain	159m
Time	1–1¼hrs
Location	South of Lauenen

For a gentle introduction to the seductive nature of the Lauenental no walk could be better designed than this one. It's short and easy, yet what it offers is a series of views showing the pastoral beauty of the region. It winds among meadows, passes attractive chalets and old farms, gazes on the high mountains that block the valley, and comes down to the tranquil shores of the Lauenensee tarn. There's a restaurant at the far end and you can sit on a grassy knoll outside with a cool drink in your hand and plan your next excursion into the mountains that rise temptingly to the south.

From Lauenen walk along the road heading upvalley. On the southern edge of the village by Hotel Alpenland the road forks. Take the right branch, rising past several fine chalets set in steep meadows. The paved road becomes a hard track, and you continue along it, now heading through forest and out again to pass more farm buildings

and chalets. There are lovely views to the mountains ahead. Then the track begins to lose height and you suddenly have a view overlooking the **Lauenensee** between a screen of trees. Wander down and along its left-hand (east) shoreline to find Restaurant Lauenensee (*refreshments*) at the far end. It's possible to take a postbus back to Lauenen. Alternatively, make a circuit of the lake and then return by the outward route.

The Wildhorn massif blocks the head of the Lauenental

ROUTE 104

Lauenen (1241m) – Geltenschuss – Gelten Hut (2002m)

Grade	2–3
Distance	7km
Height gain	761m
Time	3½hrs
Location	South of Lauenen

This is one of the most pleasant hut approach walks in the book. It's not at all difficult or dangerous. There are no screes, no rock slabs to scale by use of ladders or fixed ropes. Instead there's a well-graded path all the way, and it leads unerringly into a magnificent series of varied and multi-coloured landscapes. Part of the route goes through a nature reserve. Through meadows lush with flowers and up past a pair of huge cascading waterfalls while above rise the big snow and ice drapes of the Wildhorn massif, circling round as in an embrace. Then at last you come over a steep grassy knoll and find the Gelten Hut perched in a commanding position with a secret bowl of pasture between it and the glaciers. It's a great place to spend a night.

The **Gelten Hut** looks up to the snow-bound Wildhorn-Geltenhorn-Arpelistock massif, and the waterfalls that spray into the secretive basin that lies between hut and mountain. With places for 90 and a guardian in summer residence to provide meals and refreshments, the hut makes a fine overnight stay. For reservations ☎ 033 765 32 20.

Follow directions for Route 103 as far as the Lauenensee. At the southern end of the lake take a track among trees, then break away left on a signed path which climbs steeply through forest and finally emerges to a delightful open pasturage with the cascades of the Geltenschuss pouring down ahead. A cornflower-blue stream hurries through the meadows and a wooden bridge takes you over to the west side. This is **Feissenberg** (1600m), a nature reserve rich in alpine flowers.

The path heads through this lovely pastureland aiming towards the waterfalls, then bears right to climb the southwest slope in long switchbacks, crosses a stream and, climbing still, ducks behind a waterfall. Alpenroses clamber over the hillside and there are superb views to enjoy. The path veers to the right and wanders alongside the Geltenbach. The stream here has bored great holes and swirls in the limestone. Once more you cross the stream to the left-hand side and climb a little farther, now over a large grassy bluff speckled with flowers, and come to the **Gelten Hut** with its glorious views. ◄

To return to Lauenen by the same path will take 2½hrs. The way can be varied, though, by heading to the right at the southern end of the Lauenensee and taking a footpath and track back to the village. For an even better return, however, follow directions for Route 105 below. Added to the ascent route, this will give a very fine full day's circuit. As such it is certainly one of the classic walks in the Alps; but note that the grade is slightly higher than the approach route and there are some exposed sections to tackle.

A walk of little more than an hour brings you to the charming Lauenensee

ROUTE 105

Gelten Hut (2002m) – Chüetungel
(1786m) – Lauenen (1241m)

Grade	3
Distance	9km
Height loss	761m
Time	2½–3hrs
Location	North of the Gelten Hut

As an alternative return route to Lauenen, this takes a lot of beating. But it will not suit anyone who suffers vertigo. Should you be nervous about steep drops and ladders, reverse Route 104.

On the northeast side of the hut a steep grass-covered knoll has a narrow path snaking up to its crown. Clamber up this and follow the ridge heading north. The path is narrow in places but not difficult. There are grandstand views overlooking the Lauenental stretching ahead. Having gained the grassy ridge, the path then crosses and descends its northern side, and makes a hillside traverse to pass the alp buildings of **Usseri Gelten**. Continue round the exposed slopes of the Follhore (fixed cable protection) where the trail descends steeply, using a metal ladder in one place, and comes to the pastureland of **Chüetungel** (1786m) whose buildings stand on the far side of a stream (about 1hr from the hut).

At the stream there's a junction of paths and a sign-post giving directions. Cross by footbridge and bear left on a narrow path. (**Note**: This follows the most potentially dangerous and exposed section of the circuit. Anyone nervous about taking it should follow the alternative signed route down to Lauenen.) After wandering across rough

Cattle graze the steep hillside high above the Lauenental

pastures, the way then goes tightly against rocky crags with a steep and exposed drop to your left. For several minutes the exposure (and a very narrow section of trail) continues, but there are fixed cables in the worst places.

Eventually the path eases and goes through forest, then over pastures again, passing solitary alp huts and farms on a marked *Bergweg* path that eventually brings you down into the valley and onto a narrow road south of **Lauenen**. Wander along the road into the village.

ROUTE 106

Lauenen (1241m) –
Krinnen Pass (1659m) – Gsteig (1184m)

Grade	1
Distance	8km
Height gain	418m
Height loss	475m
Time	2½–3hrs
Location	Southwest of Lauenen

The Krinnen (or Chrine) Pass is an easy wooded col at the southern end of the Höhi Wispile ridge, and it makes a convenient crossing to Gsteig, the most westerly village in our coverage of the Bernese Alps.

About 400m south of Lauenen centre, on the road to the Lauenensee, a signpost on the right directs the start of the route to the pass. A narrow path descends to a footbridge over a stream, then rises to a farm road. Wander up this, passing several houses, and, on coming to the uppermost farm, you will find a sign directing the way left up a sloping meadow towards two barns. Go along the left-hand side of these and up the continuing slope towards trees. Eventually come to **Sattel** (1400m) near the top of a ski lift where you then follow a track over a stream. A path now climbs on through woodland – very boggy in places – and in a little under 1½hrs from Lauenen you arrive at the little gap in the wooded ridge known as the **Krinnen Pass**. Ahead the massif of Les Diablerets is revealed.

On the western side go down a meadow to a farm whose track leads to a narrow road. Follow this downhill through a minor valley, using obvious shortcuts across meadows and through woodland. About 30mins after leaving the pass a sign directs the path to the left, where you then descend beside a stream before rejoining the road which takes you into **Gsteig**. (See the Saanental chapter for Gsteig details.)

ROUTE 107

Lauenen (1241m) –
Höhi Wispile – Gstaad (1050m)

Grade	2
Distance	12km (one way)
Height gain	666m
Height loss	857m
Time	4–4½hrs
Location	Southwest and west of Lauenen

An easy and popular ridge-walk with long views north over a corrugated landscape, this makes a fine day out. There is the possibility of shortening it by descending by cableway, thus saving about 1½hrs of walking time if needed.

Take Route 106 as far as the **Krinnen Pass** (1½hrs) and descend the meadow beyond as far as the farm. Now bear right, rising among trees, and when you emerge on an open ridge bear right once more to gain the crest of Höhi Wispile. Head to the left and take the path northwards. Follow this for about an hour to **Wispile** (1911m *refreshments*) where you can take the cableway if required. The path continues down to **Underi Bodme** and the middle station of the cableway. A combination of service road, track and footpath leads all the way down to **Gstaad**. (Take the postbus from Gstaad back to Lauenen.)

291

Other routes from Lauenen

Numerous variations of walks, or combinations of routes, will extend the range of possibilities for a holiday based in Lauenen. The following is a very brief selection, but the map provides lots of inspiration.

- A crossing of the 1992m **STÜBLENIPASS** to **LEITERLI** and **LENK** makes a very rewarding day. Or you could create a fine circuit by linking the **STÜBLENI** and **TRÜTTLISBERG PASSES**, finishing with a descent to Lauenen.

- A hut-to-hut route reversing Route 96 takes you from the **GELTEN HUT** to the **WILDHORN HUT** across some beautiful but challenging country.

- On the west side of the valley go up to the **KRINNEN PASS**, but instead of crossing over to Gsteig, bear left and follow the ridge to **HINDERI** or **WALLISER WISPILE** (superb views), then backtrack down the ridge a little to find an alternative path descending to the **LAUENENSEE**.

SAANENTAL

Walking in and around the Saanental is as rich and varied an experience as in most other areas visited within these pages. Some of the passes are surprisingly arduous to reach, their modest altitude distorting their true value. Certainly there are many surprises in store for those whose days have been largely spent in the heart of the Oberland and who suspect this western region of being rather tame by comparison. Those with an eye for the subtle shades and textures of the Alps, for the variations in form and substance and for the soft brilliance of mountain light will find many rewards here.

ACCESS AND INFORMATION

Location	Immediately west of the Lauenental, and from Col du Pillon to Gstaad.
Maps	LS 262T *Rochers de Naye* and 263T *Wildstrubel* at 1:50,000
Bases	Gsteig (1184m), Gstaad(1050m)
Information	Tourismusbüro, CH–3785 Gsteig (☎ 033 755 81 81 gsteig@gstaad.ch)
	Gstaad Saanenland Tourismus, CH–3780 Gstaad (☎ 033 748 81 84 gst@gstaad.ch www.gstaad.ch)
Access	By train from Montreux or Bern to Gstaad, then postbus to Gsteig

The massif of Les Diablerets contains the most westerly summits of the Bernese Alps. It is a great hulk of limestone with several peaks over 3000m whose shrinking glaciers hang on the north and east slopes, while elsewhere the landscape is abundantly green.

Les Diablerets is a watershed in several respects. Firstly, in the true sense, its streams flow south into the Rhône Valley, and also west by a devious route to join the Rhône farther down near the Lake of Geneva. But other streams drain from it too, to the east side of the Col du Pillon where they become the Saane and flow awkwardly through central Switzerland to join the Aare, which in turn feeds the Rhine. While the Rhône eventually spills into the Mediterranean, the Rhine empties into the North Sea.

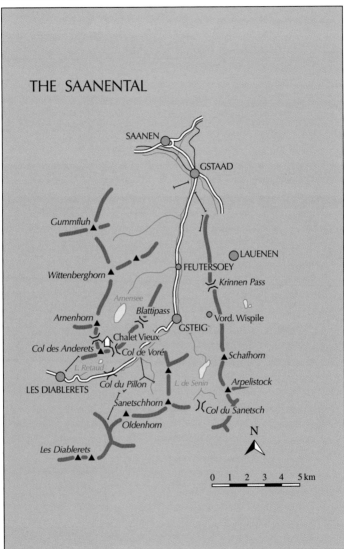

THE SAANENTAL

SAANEN

GSTAAD

Gummfluh

LAUENEN

Wittenberghorn

FEUTERSOEY

Krinnen Pass

Arnensee

Blattipass

Vord. Wispile

Arnenhorn

GSTEIG

Chalet Vieux

Col des Anderets

Col de Voré

Schafhorn

L. Retaud

Arpelistock

LES DIABLERETS

Col du Pillon

L. de Senin

Col du Sanetsch

Sanetschhorn

Oldenhorn

N

Les Diablerets

0 1 2 3 4 5 km

Les Diablerets also marks the border, not only between the cantons of Bern and Vaud, but of Valais as well. In addition it signals the linguistic divide. East of the Col du Pillon, for example, all the Bernese Alps is German-speaking territory; to the west all villages and towns use French as their main language.

Below Les Diablerets the trim little village of Gsteig straddles the Col du Pillon road, and in the marshy meadows just outside it the Ruschbach and Saane streams converge. All is broad and gentle here: neatly shorn meadows sweep up to forest-clad hillsides. Set among the meadows are characteristic timber farm-houses, their roofs shallow-pitched, their eaves overhanging, their windows and balconies ablaze with petunias and geraniums. The valley flows gently northward with no great drop in altitude. Minor streams join the Saane from the eastern slopes, while two side valleys, the Tscharzistal and Meielstal, enter from the west. In the first of these lies the attractive Arnensee, at the head of the second rises the majestic slab of the Gummfluh (2458m). As you approach Gstaad some of the slopes have been laced with cableways, mainly used by winter skiers, but also useful for summer walkers.

If the lower hills are green and wooded, those at the head of the valley, form-ing a semi-circular basin, rise with a sense of drama. Oldenhorn and Sex Rouge, Mont Brun, the Schluchhorn and Mittaghorn come directly from Les Diablerets, while the conspicuous Spitzhorn sends its ridges south to the Schafhorn and Arpilhorn – the latter to act as a southeast bastion above the Col du Sanetsch, a traditional way from the Saanental to the Rhône Valley in Canton Valais.

MAIN BASES

GSTAAD (1050m) is dealt with under the previous section, the Lauenental, which should be consulted for details of facilities, accommodation etc.

GSTEIG (1184m) is a tiny village with character. It has a photogenic heart, with the flower-adorned Hotel Bären beside the road, the slender-spired church imme-diately behind it and the Mittaghorn, Schluchhorn and Les Diablerets as a backdrop. The Col du Pillon road begins its twisting ascent at this point, and a short distance along it is the only campsite in the valley. Camping Heiti (☎ 033 755 11 97) is open from the end of May to the end of September. Gsteig has lim-ited shopping facilities, although as far as food for self-catering/backpacking is concerned, the general store is very good. There are just three hotels: the 18th-century Hotel Bären (☎ 033 755 10 33 **hotel@baerengsteig.ch www.baerengsteig.ch**); Hotel Viktoria (☎ 033 755 10 34 **viktoria@bluewin.ch**); and Hotel Sanetsch (☎ 033 755 11 77). There are also several chalets and holiday apartments in Gsteig and neighbouring Feutersoey. Dormitory accommodation may be had at Lager Zeig and Lager Schule (both con-

Gsteig

tacts via the tourist office ☎ 033 755 81 81 **gsteig@gstaad.ch**). At the Arnensee restaurant 40 dorm places are also available (☎ 033 755 14 36) from mid-May to the end of October. The valley is served by postbus which travels between Gstaad and the village of Les Diablerets on the far side of the Col du Pillon.

ROUTE 108

Gsteig (1184m) – Krinnen Pass (1659m) –
Hinderi Wispile (1868m) – Gsteig

Grade	2–3
Distance	11km
Height gain/loss	684m
Time	4½hrs
Location	Northeast of Gsteig

This is a truly delightful walk, full of contrasts and with magnificent views. In places the path may be a little thin on the ground, in others the views are shrouded by trees, but taken as a whole it makes a glorious day out. Choose a bright day of sunshine and wander slowly in order to absorb all the good things this corner of the Alps has on offer. There are no possibilities for refreshment along the way, so take a packed lunch and a drink and make a day of it.

The walk begins opposite Hotel Bären where a signpost gives directions to a number of destinations. Walk along a side street heading northeast; within a minute or two you will have passed several chalets and continue ahead through open meadows along the road, but before long a sign directs you onto a footpath aiming straight ahead up a sloping meadow. Through meadow and forest for much of the way, the waymarked path leads up to the **Krinnen Pass** (using a narrow winding road in places). The pass is reached in a little over 1½hrs from Gsteig.

The Krinnen Pass has grass slopes on its western side, forest on the east. There are very fine views from here back towards Les Diablerets. Go through a fence and turn right to follow a narrow footpath among trees rising steadily along the ridge. Views are shielded for a while,

The alp of Hinderi Wispile has the great massif of Les Diablerets as a neighbour

but suddenly you come to a brief opening with a viewpoint overlooking the Lauenental to the left.

Continue up the ridge, finally leaving forest behind and crossing above meadows dense with alpine flowers early in the season. The path leads on and brings you directly to the alp hamlet of **Hinderi Wispile** with a magnificent panorama. There are two ways now to Gsteig; one continues up the ridge to Walliser Wispile, then cuts down to the alp of Vordere Wispile and rejoins our route. The other path (our route) swings off to the west.

Keeping to the left of a little pool pass a farm on your right and find the continuing path. It is likely to be confused by cattle tracks, but persist and you will find it. It skirts to the left of a deep limestone pit and occasional waymarks lead southwestward sometimes through small boggy areas. Continue through a rather run-down alp (1854m) and steadily descend beyond it across rough pasturelands, to come to a clear farm track that goes to the busy alp of **Vordere Wispile** (1756m).

The track winds all the way down to Gsteig, and as you set off along it you will notice various alternative shortcut footpaths to take. On arriving at the alp of Burg, follow signs for Burgfälle and Gsteig. This path takes you down a tight wooded gorge with a series of waterfalls cascading into it. The trail itself is a delight, at times almost a catwalk of little bridges and balconies. Then through lovely woods and along a lane back to **Gsteig**.

ROUTE 109

Gsteig (1184m) – Blattipass (1900m) –
Col du Pillon (1546m)

Grade	3
Distance	11km
Height gain	921m
Height loss	559m
Time	4hrs
Location	West of Gsteig

Blattipass is not marked on the 1:50,000 map. It's not a pass at all really, just one part of an easy green ridge separating the Tscharzistal from the upper Saanental. But from it there is a surprisingly expansive view that includes many of the big Oberland summits stretching as far as the eye can see. The path to it is much steeper than appears at first glance. It leads through rampant vegetation with wild fruits in season tempting to all who struggle by. On the far side of the pass one looks down on the gleaming Arnensee, then the trail takes you round to a second pass, that of Voré (1917m) with a grand prospect of Les Diablerets directly ahead. Lastly, there is an interesting descent to the Lac Retaud and through forest to Col du Pillon for the postbus back to Gsteig.

From the centre of Gsteig wander along the road towards Feutersoey and Gstaad, until just before Hotel Viktoria where you turn left on a minor road to pass several houses and farms. After about 7mins turn right on another narrow road which soon becomes a track. A few metres before reaching a barn, take a path on the left which climbs a steep meadow bordered by trees. Above this the way goes through a jungle of wild raspberries, a grove of fir trees and up yet another meadow to the **Schöpfi** (1502m) farm.

THE BERNESE ALPS

Col de Voré marks the cantonal boundaries of Bern and Vaud

A vague grass path now veers left, rising through steep pastures guided by marker posts, to reach the farms and barns of **Vordere Walig** (1716m; 1½hrs). The route continues uphill a short distance to join an upper track that contours round to the solitary alp of **Topfelsberg** (1814m). Leading south the track ends, and is replaced by a narrow path which climbs in long twistings to gain the panoramic **Blattipass**, about 2–2½hrs from Gsteig.

Descend leftward on the western side of the ridge, passing Ober Stuedeli in another 10mins, and continuing to the farm of **Seeberg** (1712m) which overlooks the Arnensee. There's a signed path junction here. The way now climbs among alpenrose, juniper and bilberry in the direction of Voré. At the head of the slope go through a grassy col and enter a shallow pastureland basin. Pass a tarn on your right to gain **Col de Voré** (1910m) about 3½hrs from Gsteig. Lined by a drystone wall, the col marks the borders of Cantons Bern and Vaud.

Take the path on the south side descending steeply at first, and veering right to reach a farm track. Turn right along it and very shortly you will reach the lovely **Lac Retaud** *(refreshments)*. The track brings you to a road where you bear left, but then you soon break away on a footpath descending through forest to **Col du Pillon** *(refreshments)*. From here you can catch a postbus down to Gsteig.

ROUTE 110

Gsteig (1184m) – Blattipass (1900m) – Arnensee (1542m) – Feutersoey (1130m)

Grade	3
Distance	13km
Height gain	716m
Height loss	770m
Time	4½hrs
Location	West of Gsteig

This walk consists of two very distinct sections. The first entails a long and strenuous climb to the Blattipass, while the second is virtually all downhill, over shrub-bright hillsides, past several alp farms and alongside a lake. From the lake down to Feutersoey you will no doubt share the Tscharzistal with plenty of other walkers, while the uphill stretch will be much quieter.

Follow route descriptions as far as the farm of **Seeberg** given in Route 109 above. This is reached in almost 3hrs from Gsteig. At the junction of paths take the trail leading down to the southern end of the Arnensee and walk along its left-hand (western) shore. There is a dam at the northern end *(accommodation, refreshments)* and a road that leads from it down to Feutersoey. Either follow the road, or cross to the east side and take a footpath which makes a rising hillside traverse to gain Hinter Walig

(1723m), and on to Feutersoey. A third option is to continue through the valley as far as Linders Vorschess (1392m), 30mins from the lake, and there branch away half-right on a direct footpath to **Feutersoey**. (To return to Gsteig either take the postbus or walk 3km along the road.)

ROUTE 111

Col du Pillon (1546m) –
Lac Retaud (1685m) – Col du Pillon

Grade	1–2
Distance	4km
Height gain	139m
Height loss	139m
Time	1hr
Location	North of Col du Pillon

A fine, short and easy walk, ideal if you've only half a day left before heading for home and wish to make the most of it. Lac Retaud is an idyllic little tarn set in a terrace of hillside with views across to Les Diablerets. It's accessible to motorists, but it's better by far to walk there. This route is a circular one, beginning and ending at the car park on the col.

Immediately behind the cablecar station for Les Diablerets a track leads into woods. Walk along this and leave it at a *Wanderweg* footpath sign. A path now climbs steeply among trees and over rough pastures, then brings you onto a road by the **Lac Retaud** restaurant *(refreshments)*. Bear right and over a short rise you will come to the tarn (25mins from the col). There are fine views from the north shore looking across the water to Les Diablerets.

Turn right and follow a broad farm track along the hillside passing farm buildings. After 100m you come to a solitary building where a path forks left to Voré, Arnensee and Feutersoey. Ignore this and continue along the track. It soon swings right and leads to an isolated farm. Pass to the right of the building, follow the right-hand fence, and you will come to a continuing path sloping down towards trees. This takes you through forest (boggy in places), crosses two or three streams and eventually rejoins the original upward path. Bear left and a few minutes later you arrive at **Col du Pillon**.

Lac Retaud, a tranquil tarn easily reached from Col du Pillon (Routes 109, 111, 112)

ROUTE 112

Col du Pillon (1546m) – Col de Voré (1910m) – Seeberg (1712m) – Feutersoey (1130m)

Grade	2–3
Distance	14km
Height gain	364m
Height loss	770m
Time	4hrs
Location	North of Col du Pillon

This is one of the finest walks in the region, covering much lovely green countryside, visiting Lac Retaud and looking down on the larger Arnensee.

Follow Route 111 to the path junction beyond **Lac Retaud**. Leave the farm track here and branch away on the footpath slanting up the hillside. It makes steady height to reach the drystone wall marking the cantonal boundary at **Col de Voré** (1hr from Col du Pillon). Cross over and descend the clear path to the right of a tarn seen in the pastures below. Crossing the pastures go through a minor col and descend slopes carpeted with alpenrose, juniper, larch and rowan, with views ahead to the Arnensee. The path leads to the farm buildings of **Seeberg** and a junction of trails. Bear right on the path which leads to the Blattipass, but only take this as far as the alp of **Ober Stuedeli**. Instead of climbing to the pass, continue round the hillside, in and out of trees, to **Hinter Walig** and **Scheeweid** (1720m). From here the path begins its descent to **Feutersoey**.

MULTI-DAY TOURS

By far the majority of routes contained in this guide will be used as day walks beginning and ending at a recommended valley base. But it will be evident that numerous possibilities exist for linking given routes into multi-day journeys, circuits of mountain massifs, and the traverse of individual valleys or a number of valleys by crossing walkers' passes. There are experienced and energetic mountain trekkers for whom this type of travel is the very essence of alpine wandering; working through a challenging landscape day after day, either backpacking or travelling light, staying in mountain huts or cheap inns and *matratzenlagers* overnight. Such travel demands a high degree of fitness, an understanding of mountain terrain, a sure knowledge of map and compass work, and a certain amount of luck with regard to the weather – as a prolonged spell of storm can result in several days of frustration if marooned in an isolated hut or small tent. For this class of wanderer the following suggested tours are recommended.

Walkers on the trail to Stieregg above Grindelwald are seduced by the great wall of the Fiescherwand

ROUTE 113

Oberland Passes

Grade	3
Maps	LS 5004 Berner Oberland and 5009 Gstaad-Adelboden at 1:50,000
Length	7–8 days
Accommodation	Mountain inns, hotels and *matratzenlagers*
Start	Meiringen (Haslital)
Finish	Gsteig (Saanental)
Location	East to west across the north flank of the Bernese Alps

This superb trek forms the central (and in some ways, the most spectacular) part of the classic Alpine Pass Route (Sargans to Montreux). Every day there are high passes to cross, the highest being the Hohtürli (2778m) above Kandersteg. Every day there are magnificent mountain views of glaciers, huge walls of rock, soft and gentle alpine meadows. It links most of the major resorts of the Bernese Alps and looks on all the main peaks for which the area is justly famed. In short, it is one of the finest long walks it is possible to make in the Alps.

1. Meiringen–Grosse Scheidegg–Grindelwald (Route 8)
2. Grindelwald–Kleine Scheidegg–Wengen–Lauterbrunnen (Routes 29, and 37 in reverse)
3. Lauterbrunnen–Sefinenfurke–Griesalp (Routes 33, 34, 59)
4. Griesalp–Hohtürli–Kandersteg (Route 67)
5. Kandersteg–Bunderchrinde–Adelboden (Route 81)

6   Adelboden–Hahnenmoos–Lenk (Route 87)
7   Lenk–Trüttlisberg Pass–Lauenen–Krinnen
    Pass–Gsteig (Routes 100, 106)
For a full description of the complete Alpine Pass Route
from Sargans to Montreux (326km, 16 passes and more
than 18,000m of height gain) see the guidebook, *Alpine
Pass Route* (Cicerone Press, 2004).

*Backed by Les
Diablerets, Gsteig
marks the end of the
Oberland Passes trek*

ROUTE 114

Tour of the Jungfrau Region

Grade	3
Map	LS 254T Interlaken and 264T Jungfrau at 1:50,000
Length	8–9 days
Accommodation	Mountain inns, hotels, huts and matratzenlagers
Start	Schynige Platte (Wilderswil)
Finish	Wilderswil
Location	The Lütschental and Lauterbrunnental

This is a tremendous tour. Scenically dramatic, challenging and extremely rewarding to complete, it explores the very best of the Grindelwald–Lauterbrunnen district. Begin by taking the funicular to Schynige Platte (an alternative would be to walk from Wilderswil – about 4½hrs) and wander the classic route to the Faulhorn, First and Grosse Scheidegg. Then over Kleine Scheidegg to the Lauterbrunnental. From Stechelberg at the roadhead the way goes via Obersteinberg to the Rotstock Hut, then either makes a traverse of the Schilthorn or cuts through pastures to the Blumental above Mürren. The penultimate stage leads to the Soustal and Lobhorn Hut, and finally from there over the mountains to Saxeten before descending to Wilderswil.

1 Wilderswil (Schynige Platte) –Grosse Scheidegg
   (Routes 9, and 13 in reverse)
2 Grosse Scheidegg–Hotel Wetterhorn–Stieregg
   (Routes 19, 20)
3 Stieregg–Alpiglen–Kleine Scheidegg (Routes 22, 24)
4 Kleine Scheidegg–Trümmelbach–Stechelberg–
   Obersteinberg (Routes 42, 44)

5   Obersteinberg–Sefinental–Rotstock Hut
    (Routes 48, 50)
6   Rotstock Hut–Schilthorn–Blumental
    (Routes 56, and 55 in reverse)
    or Rotstock Hut–Blumental (Route 53 in reverse)
7   Blumental–Soustal–Lobhorn Hut
    (Routes 58, and 32 in reverse
8   Lobhorn Hut–Saxeten–Wilderswil (Routes 31, 10)

On a trail near Schiltalp the Wetterhorn, Eiger and Mönch can be seen across the Lauterbrunnental

ROUTE 115

Tour of the Wildhorn

Grade	3
Maps	LS 263T *Wildstrubel* and 273T *Montana* at 1:50,000
Length	5 days
Accommodation	Mountain huts, inns and an auberge
Start	Iffigenalp (Lenk)
Finish	Iffigenalp (Lenk)
Location	North and south of the Bernese Alps watershed

As its name suggests, the Tour of the Wildhorn makes a circuit of the Wildhorn massif which stands towards the western end of the Bernese Alps chain. The route is promoted locally with a useful brochure giving accommodation details and a stage-by-stage timed itinerary. Some of the stages are quite demanding, and a few sections of path are sufficiently exposed to cause problems for anyone suffering vertigo. But it's a splendid circuit, ever-varied and scenically rewarding. The highest point reached is Col des Audannes at 2850m. As a circuit it could, of course, be tackled either clockwise or anti-clockwise. The outline given below suggests an anti-clockwise route. At the start and end of the tour, Iffigenalp is served by postbus from Lenk.

1   Iffigenalp–Wildhorn Hut (Route 95)
2   Wildhorn Hut–Gelten Hut (Route 96)
3   Gelten Hut–Hindere Wispile–Barrage du Sanetsch (not described)
4   Barrage du Sanetsch-Col du Sanetsch–Col des Audannes–Cabane des Audannes (not described)
5   Cabane des Audannes–Col des Eaux Froides–Rawilpass-Iffigenalp (not described)

APPENDIX A

USEFUL ADDRESSES

TOURIST INFORMATION
NB Details of offices in specific resorts are given at the head of each valley section

Switzerland Travel Centre Ltd, 1st Floor, 30 Bedford Street, London WC2E 9ED
☎ (Freephone) 00800 100 200 30
stc@stlondon.com www.switzerlandtravelcentre.co.uk

Swiss National Tourist Office, 222 Sepulveda Boulevard, El Segundo, Los Angeles
CA 90245 ☎ 310 335 5985

Swiss National Tourist Office, 150 North Michigan Avenue, Chicago, Il 60601
☎ 312 630 5840

926 The East Mall, Etobipoke, Toronto, Ontario M9B 6K1 ☎ 416 695 20 90

608 Fifth Avenue, New York, NY 10020 ☎ 212 757 5944

Destination Berner Oberland, Höheweg 37, CH3800 Interlaken, Switzerland
☎ 033 828 37 47 info@berneroberland.ch www.berneroberland.ch

MAP SUPPLIERS
Cordee, 3a De Montfort Street, Leicester LE1 7HD ☎ 0116 254 3579
sales@cordee.co.uk www.cordee.co.uk

The Map Shop, 15 High Street, Upton-upon-Severn, Worcs WR8 0HJ ☎ 0684 593146
themapshop@btinternet.com www.themapshop.co.uk

Edward Stanford Ltd, 12–14 Long Acre, London WC2E 9LP ☎ 0207 836 1321
sales@stanfords.co.uk www.stanfords.co.uk

Rand McNally Map Store, 10 East 53rd Street, New York NY

SPECIALIST MOUNTAIN ACTIVITIES INSURERS
BMC Travel & Activity Insurance, (BMC members only), 177–179 Burton Road
Manchester M20 7ZA ☎ 0870 010 4878
insure@thebmc.co.uk www.thebmc.co.uk

Austrian Alpine Club, 12a North Street, Wareham, Dorset BH20 4AG ☎ 01929 556 870
manager@aacuk.org.uk www.aacuk.org.uk
(AAC membership carries accident and mountain rescue insurance, plus reciprocal rights
reductions in SAC huts.)

Snowcard Insurance Services, Lower Boddington, Daventry, Northants NN11 6BR
☎ 01327 262 805
orders@snowcard.co.uk www.snowcard.co.uk

Harrison Beaumont Ltd, 2 Des Roches Square, Witney, Oxon OX8 6BE
☎ 01993 700 200

APPENDIX B

GLOSSARY

German	English	German	English
Abhang	slope	Gaststube	common room
Alp	alp, high pasture	Gefärlich	dangerous
Alpenblume	alpine flower	Gemse	chamois
Alpenverein	alpine club	Geröllhalde	scree
Alphütte	mountain hut	Gipfel	summit, peak
Auskunft	information	Gletscher	glacier
Aussichtspunkt	viewpoint	Gletscherspalte	crevasse
Bach	stream	Gondelbahn	gondola lift
Bäckerei	bakery	Grat	ridge
Bahnhof	railway station	Grüetzi	greetings
Berg	mountain	Haltestelle	bus stop
Bergführer	mountain guide	Heilbad	spa, hot springs
Berggasthaus	mountain inn	Hirsch	red deer
Bergpass	pass	Hoch	high
Bergschrund	crevasse between	Höhe	height
	a glacier and the	Höhenweg	high route
	rock wall	Horn	horn, peak
Bergsteiger	mountaineer	Hügel	hill
Bergwanderer	mountain walker	Hütte	mountain hut
Bergweg	mountain path	Jugendherberge	youth hostel
Blatt	map sheet	Kamm	crest or ridge
Brücke	bridge	Kapelle	chapel
Dorf	village	Karte	map
Drahtseilbahn	cablecar	Kirche	church
Ebene	plain	Klamm	gorge
Feldweg	meadowland	Klumme	combe or small
	path		valley
Fels	rock wall or slope	Landschaft	landscape
Ferienwohnung	holiday apartment	Lawine	avalanche
Fussweg	footpath	Lebensmittel	grocery
Garni	hotel with	Leicht	easy
	breakfast only	Links	left
Gasthaus or gasthof	inn, guest house	Matratzenlager	dormitory

German	English	German	English
Moräne	moraine	Sesselbahn	chairlift
Murmeltier	marmot	Stausee	reservoir
Nebel	fog, low cloud, mist	Steigeisen	crampons
		Steinmann	cairn
Nord	north	Steinschlag	falling rock
Ober	upper	Stunde(n)	hour(s)
Ost	east	Sud	south
Pass	pass	Tal	valley
Pension	simple hotel	Tobel	wooded ravine
Pfad	path	Touristenlager	dormitory
Pickel	ice axe	Über	via or over
Quelle	spring	Unfall	accident
Rechts	right	Unterkunft	accommodation
Reh	roe deer	Verkehrsbüro/	
Rucksack	rucksack	Verkehrsverein	tourist office
Sattel	saddle, pass	Wald	forest
Schlafraum	bedroom	Wanderweg	footpath
Schloss	castle	Wasser	water
Schlucht	gorge	Weide	pasture
Schnee	snow	West	west
See	lake, tarn	Wildbach	torrent
Seeli	small tarn	Zeltplatz	campsite
Seil	rope	Zimmer	bedroom
Seilbahn	cablecar	- frei	vacancies

APPENDIX C

BIBLIOGRAPHY

GENERAL TOURIST GUIDES

Blue Guide: Switzerland by Ian Robertson (A&C Black, London. W. W. Norton, New York) – regularly updated, with near-comprehensive coverage.

The Rough Guide to Switzerland by Matthew Teller (Rough Guides, London. 2nd edition 2003) – perhaps the best general guide to Switzerland available at present.

Switzerland by Damien Simonis, Sarah Johnstone, Lorne Jackson (Lonely Planet, Melbourne. 4th edition 2003) – good coverage of the most important places.

The Green Guide: Switzerland (Michelin Travel Publications, Watford. 2001) – presented in gazetteer form with a wide range of illustrations.

Off The Beaten Track – Switzerland (Moorland Publishing Co, Ashbourne. Published 1989)

MOUNTAINS AND MOUNTAINEERING

Countless volumes devoted to the Alps pack the bookshelves. Those containing references of particular interest to visitors to the Bernese Alps are listed below. The list is of necessity only a small selection, but there should be plenty of reading contained within it to provide a good background introduction and to whet the appetite for a forthcoming visit.

Wanderings Among the High Alps by Alfred Wills (Blackwell, London. Latest edition published 1939) – Wills' ascent of the Wetterhorn signaled the start of the Golden Age of Mountaineering.

The Playground of Europe by Leslie Stephen (Blackwell, London. Latest edition published 1936) – *Playground* ranks as one of the finest of all mountaineering books. Leslie Stephen was an eminent Victorian pioneer, some of whose adventures are recorded in this book. He made a number of first ascents in the Bernese Alps.

On High Hills by Geoffrey Winthrop Young (Methuen, London. Latest edition published 1947) – This book includes ascents in the Bernese Alps prior to 1914.

The White Spider by Heinrich Harrer (Granada, London. Latest edition published 1983) – Harrer was part of the rope that made the first ascent of the Eiger's North Face in 1938. This book recounts the history of attempts on the face up to and including that first ascent.

The Eiger by Dougal Haston (Cassell, London. 1974) – Haston took part in the epic first direct ascent of the North Face in winter. This book records the history of 'modern' routes on the face.

The Mountains of Switzerland by Herbert Maeder (George Allen & Unwin, London. 1968) – Large format book with splendid illustrations, mostly in black and white.

Alps 4000 by Martin Moran (David & Charles, Devon. 1994) – The account of Moran's and Simon Jenkins's epic journey across all the 4000m summits of the Alps in one summer's activity.

The High Mountains of the Alps by Helmut Dumler & Willi Burkhardt (Diadem, London. 1993) – A beautifully illustrated volume describing the 4000m peaks of the Alps.

The Mountains of Europe by Kev Reynolds (Oxford Illustrated Press, Sparkford. 1990) – All the major mountain ranges of continental Europe described, including, of course, the Bernese Alps.

Bernese Oberland: selected climbs by Les Swindin (Alpine Club, London. 2003) – The latest AC guide to all the major routes, including climbs on the Salbitschijen.

WALKING

The Alps by R. L. G. Irving (Batsford, London. 1939) – Not strictly a 'walking' book, but it contains much of interest that will help fire enthusiasm for an active holiday in the Alps. As with several others in this list, *The Alps* has long been out of print, but should be available on order from public libraries.

Rambles in the Alps by Hugh Merrick (Country Life, London. 1951) – A large-format book which devotes considerable space to eulogising the Bernese Oberland as a walking area.

Backpacking in the Alps and Pyrenees by Showell Styles (Gollancz, London. 1976) – Contains an account of a backpacking journey across part of the Bernese Alps by some of the routes described in this guidebook.

Alpine Pass Route by Kev Reynolds (Cicerone Press, Milnthorpe. 2nd edition 2004) – A guidebook to this classic long-distance route which traverses the Bernese Alps on its journey from Sargans to Montreux.

Classic Walks in the Alps by Kev Reynolds (Oxford Illustrated Press, Sparkford. 1991) – Large format volume which contains a number of routes in the Bernese Alps.

Walking in the Alps by Kev Reynolds (Cicerone Press, Milnthorpe. 1998) – Describes walking prospects of 19 districts, from the Maritime Alps to the Julians of Slovenia. Includes the Bernese Alps.

100 Hut Walks in the Alps by Kev Reynolds (Cicerone Press, Milnthorpe. 2000) – Includes several huts in the region covered by the present book.

Alpine Points of View by Kev Reynolds (Cicerone Press, Milnthorpe. 2004) – 100 full-page colour photographs that show the diverse nature of the Alpine chain; the Bernese Alps is well represented.

MOUNTAIN FLOWERS

The Alpine Flowers of Britain and Europe by Christopher Grey-Wilson and Marjorie Blamey (Collins, London. 1979) – A very useful pocket identification handbook.

Mountain Flowers by Anthony Huxley (Blandford Press, London. 1967) – Another fine book to help identify species found in the areas covered by the present book. Illustrations are by Daphne Barry and Mary Grierson.

Mountain Flower Holidays in Europe by Lionel Bacon (Alpine Garden Society, Woking. 1979) – This book tells you what to find and where. Although there are some good illustrations, it is best used in conjunction with one of the above-mentioned identification guides. Includes a section on the Bernese Alps.

APPENDIX D

ROUTE INDEX

Lauterbrunnental

Kiental

Kandertal

68	Kandersteg (Chairlift)-Öeschinensee	1	30mins	197
69	Kandersteg-Blüemlisalp Hut	3	5-5½hrs	198
70	Kandersteg-Fründen Hut	3	4hrs	200
71	Kandersteg-Doldenhorn Hut	2-3	2½hrs	201
72	Kandersteg (Selden)-Kanderfirn	2-3	2-2½hrs	202
73	Kandersteg (Selden)-Kandersteg	1	2½hrs	204
74	Kandersteg (Selden)-Mutthorn Hut-Petersgrat-Fafleralp	3	2days	206
75	Kandersteg (Selden)-Lötschenpass-Ferden	3	6-6½hrs	209
76	Kandersteg-Gasterntal-Balmhorn Hut	3	3½hrs	211
77	Kandersteg-Sunnbüel-Gemmipass	2	5-5½hrs	213
78	Kandersteg-Sunnbüel-Lämmeren Hut	3	6hrs	215
79	Kandersteg (Allmenalp)-Usser Üschene-Kandersteg	1-2	2½hrs	217
80	Kandersteg (Allmenalp)-First-Stand-Kandersteg	3	5½-6hrs	219
81	Kandersteg-Bunderchrinde-Adelboden	3	6½-7hrs	220
82	Kandersteg-Schedelsgrättli-Engstligenalp	3	5-5½hrs	222

Engstligental

83	Adelboden-Engstligenalp	2	3hrs	230
84	Adelboden-Hinterberg-Engstligenalp	2-3	3½hrs	232
85	Adelboden (Engstligenalp)-Ammertenpass-Lenk	3	5½hrs	233
86	Adelboden (Engstligenalp)-Ammertenpass-Iffigenalp	3	5½-6hrs	236
87	Adelboden-Hahnenmoos-Lenk	2	4½hrs	238

Diemtigtal

88	Grimmialp-Grimmi Pass-St Stephan	2-3	5-5½hrs	245
89	Grimmialp-Rauflihorn-Fildrich-Grimmialp	3	7-7½hrs	247
90	Grimmialp-Scheidegg-Blankenburg	2-3	5-5½hrs	249

Ober Simmental

91	Zweisimmen-Garstatt-Weissenbach-Boltigen	1	2-2½hrs	258
92	Lenk (Büelberg)-Pommernpass-Oberried	2-3	3½ hrs	260
93	Lenk (Iffigenalp)-Iffigsee	2	1½-2hrs	262
94	Lenk (Iffigenalp)-Iffighorn	2	2-2½hrs	264
95	Lenk (Iffigenalp)-Wildhorn Hut	2-3	2hrs 45mins	265
96	Wildhorn Hut-Chüetungel-Gelten Hut	3	3½hrs	267
97	Lenk (Leiterli)-Wildhorn Hut-Iffigenalp	3	5½hrs	269
98	Lenk (Leiterli)-Tungelpass-Pöschenried-Lenk	2-3	5-5¼hrs	271
99	Lenk (Leiterli)-Trüttlisberg Pass-Lauenen	2	3hrs	273
100	Lenk-Trüttlisberg Pass-Lauenen	2-3	5-5½hrs	275
101	Lenk-Trüttlisberg Pass-Turbachtal-Gstaad	3	7½hrs	277

Lauenental

Saanental

Multi-Day Tours

Cicerone's mission is to inform and inspire by providing the best guides to exploring the world

Since its foundation over 30 years ago, Cicerone has specialised in publishing guidebooks and has built a reputation for quality and reliability. It now publishes nearly 300 guides to the major destinations for outdoor enthusiasts, including Europe, UK and the rest of the world.

Written by leading and committed specialists, Cicerone guides are recognised as the most authoritative. They are full of information, maps and illustrations so that the user can plan and complete a successful and safe trip or expedition – be it a long face climb, a walk over Lakeland fells, an alpine traverse, a Himalayan trek or a ramble in the countryside.

With a thorough introduction to assist planning, clear diagrams, maps and colour photographs to illustrate the terrain and route, and accurate and detailed text, Cicerone guides are designed for ease of use and access to the information.

If the facts on the ground change, or there is any aspect of a guide that you think we can improve, we are always delighted to hear from you.

Cicerone Press
2 Police Square Milnthorpe Cumbria LA7 7PY
Tel:01539 562 069   Fax:01539 563 417
e-mail:info@cicerone.co.uk   web:www.cicerone.co.uk

CICERONE